ACROSS INDIA

OR

LIVE BOYS IN THE FAR EAST

ACROSS INDIA

OR

LIVE BOYS IN THE FAR EAST

OLIVER OPTIC

GYAN

Published by

Gyan Publishing House
5, Ansari Road
Daryaganj, New Delhi-110002
Phone: 011-47034999, 9811692060
E-mail: books@gyanbooks.com

Distribution Network
gyanbooks.com
India, USA, Canada, UK, Australia

ISBN: 978-93-7014-443-9 (PB)

First Published, 1895

2nd Impression 2025

Printed at: Gyan Press, Delhi.

ACROSS INDIA OR LIVE BOYS IN THE FAR EAST
Arthur OLIVER OPTIC

"He was dressed in the most magnificent robes of India.'
— Page 234.

All-Over-the-World Library — Third Series

ACROSS INDIA

OR

LIVE BOYS IN THE FAR EAST

BY

OLIVER OPTIC,

AUTHOR OF "A MISSING MILLION" "A MILLIONAIRE AT SIXTEEN" "A YOUNG KNIGHT-ERRANT" "STRANGE SIGHTS ABROAD" "AMERICAN BOYS AFLOAT" "THE YOUNG NAVIGATORS" "UP AND DOWN THE NILE" "ASIATIC BREEZES" AND UPWARDS OF ONE HUNDRED OTHER VOLUMES

BOSTON:

LOTHROP, LEE & SHEPARD CO.

To

MY LONG-TRIED FRIEND OF MORE THAN FORTY YEARS,
WITH WHOM IN ALL THAT TIME,
I HAVE NOT HAD A BICKER OR A SHADOW OF UNPLEASANTNESS
THOUGH HE HAS BEEN MY SENIOR PUBLISHER FOR MORE
THAN AN ENTIRE GENERATION, AND TO WHOM
I HAVE NOT DEDICATED A BOOK
FOR THIRTY YEARS

WILLIAM LEE

This Volume

IS RESPECTFULLY AND CORDIALLY INSCRIBED BY HIS
FAITHFUL AND EVER GRATEFUL FRIEND

WILLIAM T. ADAMS

PREFACE

"ACROSS INDIA" is the first volume of the third series of the "All-Over-the-World Library," in which the voyage of the Guardian-Mother is continued from Aden, where some important changes were made in the current of events, including the disposal of the little steamer Maud, which figured to a considerable extent in the later volumes of the library, though they also comprehended the addition of another and larger consort to the ship, in which the distinguished Pacha, as a reformed and entirely reconstructed person, sails in company with the voyagers.

A few days out from the port of departure, a stirring event, a catastrophe of the sea, adds three very important personages to the cabin passengers of the Guardian-Mother, and affords two of the "live boys" an opportunity to distinguish themselves in a work of humanity requiring courage and skill. These additions to the company prove to be a very fortunate acquisition to the party; for they are entirely familiar with everything in and relating to India. They are titled individuals, two of the trio, who have not only travelled all over the peninsula, but have very influential relations with the officers of the government, and the native princes, rajahs, kings, maharajahs, and nobles.

The commander, the professor, the surgeon, the young millionaire, and others who have hitherto given the "talks" and lectures for the instruction of the young people, and incidentally of the older ones also, find themselves almost entirely relieved from duty in this direction by those whom the ship's company have saved from inevitable death in the stormy billows of the Arabian Sea. The gratitude of the two titled members of the trio, and their earnest appreciation of the educational object of the long voyage, induce them to make themselves very useful on board.

They do not confine themselves to the duty presented to them in "Conference Hall;" but they are profuse, and even extravagant, in their hospitality, becoming the hosts of the entire party, and treating them like princes in the principal cities of India, in all of which they are quite at home. One of the Hindu maharajahs proves to be an old friend of both of them, and the party reside a week at his court; and the time is given up to the study of manners and customs, as well as to hunting and the sports of the country.

Felix McGavonty, with Kilkenny blood in his veins, is firm in his belief that he ought not to be afraid of snakes, and does for India a little of what St. Patrick did completely for Ireland. The other "live boys," though not so much inclined as the Milesian to battle with the cobra-de-capello, have some experience in shooting tigers, leopards, deer, pythons, crocodiles, and other game, though not enough to wholly satisfy their natural enterprise.

The tour of the party is made by railroad in India, from Bombay, taking in Lahore, Delhi, Agra, Cawnpoor, Lucknow, Benares, Calcutta, and by the Guardian-Mother to Madras and Ceylon. On the way and in the cities the titled conductors continue their "talks" and lectures about the places visited, with as much of history as time would permit, including an epitome of those great events in India, the Mutiny of the Sepoys, the "Black Hole," and other events of the past. The speakers were assisted by elaborate maps, which the reader can find in his atlas. Statistics are given to some extent for purposes of comparison. Brief notices of the lives of such men as Bishop Heber, Sir Colin Campbell, Henry Havelock, and others are introduced.

The party did not claim to have seen all there was of India; simply to have obtained "specimen bricks" of the principal cities, with a fair idea of the manners and customs of the people.

WILLIAM. T. ADAMS.

CONTENTS

LIST OF ILLUSTRATIONS

ACROSS INDIA

CHAPTER I

ABOUT FINDING THE LONGITUDE

"WELL, Captain Scott, what is the run to-day?" asked Louis Belgrave, the owner of the steam-yacht Guardian-Mother, which had at this date made her way by a somewhat devious course half way round the world, and was in the act of making the other half.

The young magnate was eighteen years old, and was walking on the promenade deck of the steamer with a beautiful young lady of sixteen when he asked for information in regard to the run, or the distance made by the ship during the last sea-day.

"Before I answer your question, my dear Louis, I must protest against being any longer addressed as captain, for I am not now entitled to that honorable appellation," replied the young man addressed by the owner.

"Once a captain always a captain," replied Louis. "One who has been a member of Congress is still an 'Honorable,' though his term of office expired twenty or forty years ago. The worthy commander of the Guardian-Mother was always called Captain Ringgold in Von Blonk Park and New York, though he had not been in command of a ship for ten years," argued Louis.

"That's right; but the circumstances are a little different in my case. In the first place, I am only eighteen years old, and my brief command was a very small one, as the world goes. It hardly entitles me to be called captain after I have ceased to be in command. In charge of the little Maud I was the happiest young fellow on the Eastern Continent; but I am just as happy now, for this morning I was formally appointed third officer of the Guardian-Mother, at the wages paid to Captain Sharp when he had the same position."

"I congratulate you, Mr. Scott," said Louis, grasping the hand of the new officer, though he had been duly consulted in regard to the appointment the day before.

"Permit me to congratulate you also, Mr. Scott," added Miss Blanche, as she extended to him her delicate little hand.

"Thank you, Miss Woolridge," replied the new third officer, raising the uniform cap he had already donned, and bowing as gracefully as a dancing-master. "Thank you with all my heart, Louis. I won't deny that I was considerably broken up when the Maud was sold; but now I am glad of it, for it has given me a position that I like better."

"Now, Mr. Scott, what is the run for to-day?" asked Louis, renewing his first question.

"I don't know," replied the third officer with a mischievous smile.

"You don't know!" exclaimed Louis.

"I do not, Louis."

"I thought all the officers, including the commander, took the observation, and worked up the reckoning for the longitude. We got eight bells nearly an hour ago, and the bulletin must have been posted by this time."

"It was posted some time ago. All the officers work up the reckoning; and I did so with the others. The commander and I agreed to a second."

"What do you mean by saying you do not know the run?" demanded Louis.

"I do know the run; but that was not what you asked me," answered Scott with the same mischievous smile.

"What did I ask you?"

"The first time you asked me all right, and I should have answered you if I had not felt obliged to switch off and inform you and Miss Woolridge of my new appointment. The second time you put it you changed the question."

"I changed it?" queried Louis.

"You remember that when Mrs. Blossom asked Flix where under the sun he had been, he replied that he had not been anywhere, as it happened to be in the evening, when the sun was not overhead."

"A quibble!" exclaimed Louis, laughing.

"Granted; but one which was intended to test your information in regard to a nautical problem. You asked me the second time for the run of to-day for the last twenty-four hours."

"And that was what I asked you the first time," answered Louis.

"I beg your pardon, but you asked me simply for the run to-day."

"Isn't that the same thing?"

"Will you please to tell me how many hours there are in a sea-day?" asked Scott, becoming more serious.

"That depends," answered Louis, laughing. "You have me on the run."

"You will find that the bulletin signed by the first officer gives the run as 330 miles; but the answer to your second question is 337 miles, about," added the third officer. "Just here the day is only twenty-three hours and forty minutes long as we are running; and the faster we go the shorter the day," continued the speaker, who was ciphering all the time on a card.

"I don't see how that can be," interposed Miss Blanche, with one of her prettiest smiles.

"There is the lunch-bell; but I shall be very happy to explain the matter more fully later in the day, Miss Woolridge, unless you prefer that Louis should do it," suggested Scott.

"I doubt if I could do it, and I should be glad to

listen to the explanation," replied Louis, as they descended to the main cabin; for the new third officer was permitted to retain his place at the table as well as his state-room.

The commander had suggested that there was likely to be some change of cabin arrangements; for it was not in accordance with his ideas of right that the third officer should be admitted to the table, while the first and second were excluded; and Louis was very desirous that his friend Scott should remain in the cabin. The repasts on board the steamer were social occasions, and the party often sat quite an hour at the table, as at the present luncheon. But as soon as the company left their places, Louis and Miss Blanche followed the third officer to the promenade deck, to hear the desired explanation of sea-time.

"Of course you know how the longitude of the ship is obtained, Miss Woolridge?" the young officer began.

"Papa explained it to me once, but I could not understand it," replied the fair maiden.

"Then we will explain that first. One of the great circles extending through the poles is called the prime meridian; and any one may be selected, though that of Greenwich has been almost universally adopted. This place is near London. From this prime meridian longitude is calculated, which means that any given locality is so many degrees east or west of it. Sandy Hook is in longitude 74°, or it is that number of degrees west of Greenwich. Aden is in 45° east longitude."

"Then you find how many miles it is by multiplying the number of degrees by 69," suggested Miss Blanche.

"You have forgotten about knots, or sea-miles," said Louis.

"So I have! I should have said multiply by 60," added the young lady.

"That would not do it any better," replied Scott. "Degrees of latitude are always the same for all practical purposes; but degrees of longitude are as —

> 'Variable as the shade
> By the light quivering aspen made,'"

continued the third officer, who was about to say "as a woman's mind;" but he concluded that it was not quite respectful to the lovely being before him.

"What a poetical sea-monster you are, Mr. Scott!" exclaimed Miss Blanche with a silvery laugh.

"I won't do so any more," Scott protested, and then continued his explanation. "Degrees of longitude vary from nothing at the poles, up to 69.07 statute, or 60 geographical or sea-miles, at the equator. We are now in about 15° north latitude; and a degree of longitude is 66.65 statute miles, or 57.9855 sea-miles, near enough to call it 58. By the way, Louis, multiply the number of statute miles by .87, and it gives you the sea-miles. Divide the knots by the same decimal, and it gives the statute miles."

"I will try to remember that decimal as you have done," replied Louis. "Now, Mr. Scott, don't open Bowditch's Navigator to us, or talk about 'projection,' 'logarithms,' 'Gunter,' and 'inspection;' for I am not capable of understanding them, for my trigonometry has gone to the weeping willows."

"Talk to us in English, Mr. Scott," laughed Miss Blanche.

"Let us go up to Conference Hall, where there is a table," said the third officer, as he produced a book he had brought up from his state-room. He led the way to the promenade, where he spread out a chart in the "Orient Guide," which had twenty-six diagrams of a clock, one at the foot of every fifteen degrees of longitude. At this point the commander came upon the promenade.

"Formerly the figures on a timepiece in Italy, and perhaps elsewhere, went up to twenty-four, instead of repeating the numbers up to twelve; and these diagrams are constructed on that plan," continued Scott.

"An attempt has been made to re-establish this method in our own country. I learned once from a folder that a certain steamer would leave Detroit at half-past twenty-two; meaning half-past ten. But the plan was soon abandoned," interposed the captain.

"Aden, from which we sailed the other day, is in longitude 45° east. Every degree by meridians is equal to four minutes of clock-time. Multiply the longitude by four, and the result in minutes is the difference of time between Greenwich and Aden, 180 minutes, or three hours. When it is noon at Greenwich, it is three o'clock at Aden, as you see in the diagram before you."

"Three o'clock in the morning, Mr. Scott?" queried the commander.

"In the afternoon, I should have added. Going east the time is faster, and *vice versa*," continued the young officer. "At our present speed our clocks must be put about twenty minutes ahead, for a third of an hour has gone to Davy Jones's locker."

"I understand all that perfectly," said Miss Blanche with an air of triumph.

"You will be a sea-monster before you get home. The sirens were beautiful, and sang very sweetly," added Scott jocosely.

"They were wicked, and I don't want to be one. But I do not quite understand how you found out what time it was at noon to-day," added the young lady.

"For every degree of longitude sailed there is four minutes' difference of clock-time," Scott proceeded. "You know that a chronometer is a timepiece so nicely constructed and cared for, that it practically keeps perfect time. Meridians are imaginary great circles, and we are always on one of them. With our sextants we find when the centre of the sun is on the celestial meridian corresponding to the terrestrial one; and at that instant it is noon where we are. Then we know what time it is. We compare the time thus obtained with that indicated by the chronometer, and find a difference of four hours."

"I see it all!" exclaimed the fair maiden, as triumphantly as though she had herself reasoned out the problem. "Four hours make 240 minutes, and four minutes to a degree gives 60° as the longitude.

"Quite correct, Miss Woolridge," added Scott approvingly.

"If I could only take the sun, I could work up the longitude myself," the little beauty declared.

"You have already taken the son," replied Scott; but he meant the son of Mrs. Belgrave, and he checked himself before he had "put his foot in it;" for Louis would have resented such a remark.

"I have seen them do it, but I never took the sun myself," protested the maiden.

The sea had suddenly begun to make itself felt a few hours before, and a flood of spray was cast over the promenade, which caused the party to evacuate it, and move farther aft. It was the time of year for the north-east monsoons to prevail, and the commander had declared that the voyage would probably be smooth and pleasant all the way to Bombay. It did not look much like it when the ship began to roll quite violently.

CHAPTER II

THE WRECK IN THE ARABIAN SEA

It was a sharp squall that suddenly struck the Guardian-Mother, heeling her over so that everything movable on her decks or below went over to the lee side, and sending no small quantity of salt water over her pilot-house. It had begun to be what the ladies called rough some hours before; and with them Captain Ringgold's reputation as a prophet was in peril, for he had predicted a smooth sea all the way to Bombay.

The Blanche, the steam-yacht of General Noury, which was only a trifle larger than the Guardian-Mother, rolled even more. She was following the latter, and seemed to be of about equal speed, though no trial had been made between them. Miss Blanche and Louis had retreated to a dryer place than the promenade when the shower of spray broke over the pilot-house upon them, leaving the commander and Mr. Scott there.

Captain Ringgold frowned as he looked out on the uneasy waves, for the squall appeared to be a surprise to him; but it proved to be more than a white squall, which may come out of a clear sky, while with a black one the sky is wholly or partly covered with dark clouds. It continued to blow very fresh, and the commotion in the elements amounted to nothing less than a smart gale.

"This is uncommon in the region of the north-east monsoons," said the commander, who was planking the promenade deck with Scott. "During January and February the wind is set down as moderate in these waters. I have made two runs from Cape of Good Hope to Bombay, and we had quiet seas from the latitude of Cape Comorin to our destination both times; and I expected the same thing at this season of the year on this voyage."

The captain was evidently vexed and annoyed at the failure of his prediction, though squalls were liable to occur in any locality; but the present rough weather had begun to look like a gale which might continue for several days. The north-east monsoons were what he had a right to expect; but the gale came up from the south south-west. The commander appeared to be so much disturbed, that the young officer did not venture to say anything for the next half-hour, though he continued to walk at his side.

At the end of this time the commander descended to his cabin, inviting Scott to go with him. On the great table was spread out the large chart of the Indian Ocean. From Aden to Bombay he had drawn a red line, indicating the course, east by north a quarter north, which was the course on which the steamer was sailing.

"Have you the blue book that comes with this

chart, Captain Ringgold?" asked Scott, rather timidly, as though he had something on his mind which he did not care to present too abruptly; for the commander was about the biggest man on earth to him.

"This chart is an old one, as you may see by the looks of it and the courses marked on it from the Cape of Good Hope," replied the captain, looking at the young officer, to fathom his meaning. "I put all my charts on board of the Guardian-Mother when we sailed for Bermuda the first time. If I ever had the blue book of which you speak, I haven't it now; and I forget all about it."

"I bought that chart at Aden the first day we were there, when I expected to navigate the Maud to Bombay; and with it came the blue book, which treats mainly of winds, weather, and currents," added Scott. "I studied it with reference to this voyage, and I found a paragraph which interested me. I will go to my state-room for the book, if you will permit me to read about ten lines from it to you."

The captain did not object, and Scott soon returned to the commander's cabin with the book. The autocrat of the ship was plainly dissatisfied with himself at the failure of his prediction for fine weather, and perhaps he feared that the ambitious young officer intended to instruct him in regard to the situation, though Scott had conducted himself in the most modest and inoffensive manner.

"I don't wish to be intrusive, Captain Ringgold,

but I thought it was possible that you had forgotten this paragraph," said the young officer, with abundant deference in his tone and manner.

"Probably I never saw it; but read it, Mr. Scott," replied the commander.

"'The weather is generally fine, and the sky clear, with neither squall nor rain, except between Ras Seger and the island of Masira,'" Scott began to read, when the commander interrupted him, and fixed his gaze on the chart, to find the localities mentioned.

"Ras Sajer," said the captain, placing the point of his pencil on the cape whose name he read. "That must be the one you mention."

"No doubt of it, sir; and I have noticed that the spelling on the chart and in the books doesn't agree at all. The island is Massera on my chart."

"They mean the same locality. Go on, Mr. Scott," added the captain.

"'And the vicinity of the bay of Kuriyan Muriyan, where the winds and weather are more boisterous and variable than on any other part of the coast,'" continued Scott.

"Where is that bay?" asked the commander.

"It is between the two points mentioned before; but it is Kuria Muria on the chart;" and the captain had the point of his pencil on it by this time.

"We are within three hours' sail of the longitude of that bay, but a hundred and fifty miles south of it," said the commander. "The information in the book is quite correct. Is there anything more about it?"

"Yes, sir; a few lines more, and I will read them: 'Respecting Kuriyan Muriyan Bay, Captain S. B. Haines, I. N., remarks that the sudden change of winds, termed by the Arabs *Belat*, and which blow with great violence for several days, are much dreaded; but what surprised me more than these land winds were the frequent and heavy gales from the S. S. W. during February and March, blowing for six days together.'"

"This gale, for such it appears to be, instead of a mere squall, as I supposed it was at first, has come before it was due by a few days; but it proves that what you have read is entirely correct," said the commander. "My two voyages in the Arabian Sea took me twenty degrees east of this point, and therefore I had nothing but quiet water. But, Mr. Scott, you have put an old navigator into the shade, and I commend you for the care and skill with which you had prepared yourself for the voyage of the Maud to Bengal."

"I protest that it was only an accident that I happened on that paragraph!" exclaimed Scott, blushing under his browned face.

"You found what you were looking for, and that was no accident. I feel that I have added an excellent young officer to the number of my officers," added Captain Ringgold.

"I thank you, sir, with all my heart; but may

I ask one favor of you?" inquired the third officer.

"Name it, and I will grant it if possible."

"I earnestly request that you do not mention this little matter to any person on board of the ship."

The commander of the Guardian-Mother was an honest and just man, and he was disposed to give credit to any one who deserved it, even at his own expense, and he looked at the young officer in silence for some moments. Then they argued the question for a time; but the captain finally granted the new officer's request, praising him for his modesty, which was rather a newly developed virtue in his character.

The steamer continued to roll violently when Louis assisted Miss Blanche down the stairs to the main cabin. The dozen passengers who had not gone on deck after luncheon were in excellent humor, for all of them were experienced sailors by this time, and beyond the discomforts of seasickness. All of them held the commander in such high respect and regard, that not one of them mentioned the failure of his prediction of fine weather for the next five or six days. Perhaps all of them wondered, for the captain's predictions before had been almost invariably verified; but not one of them spoke of his missing it in this instance.

The gale continued the rest of the day and during the night. When the morning watch came on duty at four o'clock, Captain Ringgold was pacing the promenade deck, peering through the darkness, and observing the huge waves that occasionally washed the upper deck. He had not slept a wink during the night, though he had reclined an hour on the divan in the pilot-house. He was not alarmed for the safety of his ship, but he looked out for her very carefully in heavy weather.

He was particularly interested in the conduct of the Blanche. She had taken a position to windward of the Guardian-Mother, and appeared to be doing quite as well in the heavy sea as her consort. She had been built with all the strength and solidity that money could buy; and she was as handsome a craft as ever floated, not even excepting her present companion on the stormy sea, and she was proving herself to be an able sea-boat.

"Good-morning, Mr. Scott," said the commander, as the young officer touched his cap to him.

Scott had been temporarily placed in the watch with the first officer, and his post of duty was at the after part of the ship.

"Good-morning, Captain Ringgold," replied Scott, as he halted to ascertain if the commander had any orders for him. "The gale does not appear to have moderated since I turned in, sir."

"On the contrary, it blows fresher than ever. I did not expect such a nasty time as we are having of it," added the commander.

"According to Captain Haines of the Indian navy, we may expect it to last five days longer, for we have had nearly one day of it."

"Not quite so bad as that, Mr. Scott. If we had stayed in the vicinity of Kuria Muria Bay, we might have got five days more of it; but this is a local storm, and we shall doubtless run out of it in a day or two at most, and come again into the region of the north-east monsoon."

"I hope so for the sake of those in the cabin; and I did not think of the local feature you mention."

"The deck is well officered now," added the captain with a gape, "and I will take a nap in my cabin for an hour or two. Mr. Boulong will have me called if the storm gets any worse."

The commander went to his cabin, and Scott walked aft to the compass abaft the mainmast. The binnacle was lighted, and he looked into it. The course was all right, though the ship yawed a good deal in the trough of the sea, the gale pelting her squarely on the beam. Though it was not an easy thing even for a thorough seaman to preserve his centre of gravity, the young officer made his way fore and aft with the aid of the life-lines which had been extended the evening before. He watched the motions of the Blanche, for there was nothing else to be seen but the waste of angry waters.

Far ahead the light of the breaking day began to penetrate the gloomy black clouds. It was a pleasure to come out of the deep darkness, and he observed with interest the increase of the light. While he was watching the east, the lookout man in the foretop hailed the deck. He listened and moved forward to the foremast to hear what passed between him and the first officer.

"Steamer on the port bow, sir!" reported the man aloft.

Scott saw the vessel, but she was too far off to be made out. She passed and disappeared; but about the moment he lost sight of her, he thought he heard the report of a musket, or some other firearm, to the northward of the ship. He listened with all his ears, and then distinguished very faintly shouts from human voices. He waited only long enough to satisfy himself that he had not mistaken the roar of the sea for calls for help, and then went forward to the pilot-house, where he announced that he had heard the shots and the cries.

"Are you sure of it, Mr. Scott?" asked the first officer.

"Very sure, sir."

"We have heard nothing, and the lookouts have not reported anything," added Mr. Boulong.

"On deck, sir! Wreck on the port beam!" yelled the lookout aloft.

"Call the captain, Mr. Scott," said the first officer, as he went out on deck.

He made out the ominous sounds, and judged that they came from a point not more than a mile distant. The commander and Scott appeared immediately; and with the increased daylight they discovered several men clinging to what appeared to be a wreck.

CHAPTER III

A REVIEW OF THE PAST FOURTEEN MONTHS

The Guardian-Mother had sailed from New York about fourteen months before she appeared in the waters of the Arabian Sea. She was a steam-yacht of 624 tons burden, owned by Louis Belgrave, a young man who had just entered his eighteenth year. His native place was Von Blonk Park, in New Jersey, most of whose territory had been the farm of the young gentleman's grandfather, who had become a millionaire by the sale of his land.

The terrors of the War of the Rebellion had driven the old man to convert his property into gold, which he had concealed so effectually that no one could find it. His only son, more patriotic than his father, had enlisted in the loyal army, and had been severely wounded in the brave and faithful discharge of his duty, and returned to the home of his childhood a wreck of his former self.

His father died during his absence, and Paul Belgrave, the soldier, was his sole heir. His physical condition improved considerably, though he never ceased to suffer from the effects of his wound. The homestead of his father, which had not been sold with the rest of his land, afforded the invalid a sufficient support; and he married Maud Nashwood, the only daughter of one of the small magnates of Von Blonk Park, which had now become a thriving town, occupied mainly by business men of New York.

Paul Belgrave was a millionaire without any millions; for he was never able to find the large property of his deceased parent. For ten years he dug over the cellar bottom of the old house, and the ground in the vicinity; but the missing million entirely eluded his search, and he died as soon as he gave up all hope of finding the treasure..

Mrs. Belgrave was left with their son, then eight years old; but the estate of her husband, with the property of her father, supported her comfortably. The widow had been married at sixteen; and she had the reputation of being the prettiest woman in the Park after her husband died. She had many suitors, but she finally married a handsome English horse-trainer, who called himself Wade Farrongate, though that was not his real name.

For some reason not then apparent, this man at once became the enemy of Louis Belgrave; and the war between them raged for several years, though the young man did all he could to conciliate his stepfather. The man was a rascal, a villain to the very core of his being, though he had attained a position of considerable influence among the sporting gentry of New York and New Jersey, mainly for his skill as a jockey, and in the management of the great races.

Louis discovered a plan on the part of Farrongate to appropriate the stakes and other money dependent upon the great race of the season, and escape to England with his wife and stepson. In this scheme Louis, after he had obtained the evidence of the jockey's villany, went on board of the steamer which was to convey them all over the ocean, and succeeded, with no little difficulty, in convincing his mother of the unworthiness of her husband; and she returned with her son to Von Blonk Park. The young man went back to the steamer, and by skilful management obtained all the plunder of the villain, who sailed for England without his treasure.

Farrongate, or rather John Scoble, which was his real name, was a deserter from the British army. He was arrested on his return, and compelled to serve out the remainder of his term of service. The death of an uncle in India recruited his finances, and he returned to New York. It afterwards appeared that he had some clew to Peter Belgrave's missing million, and he was therefore anxious to recover the possession of the wife who had repudiated him.

A successful conspiracy enabled him to convey her to Bermuda. At this stage of the drama, Captain Royal Ringgold, an early admirer of the pretty widow, became an active participant in the proceedings, and from that time he had been the director of all the steps taken to recover Louis's mother.

In the interim of Scoble's absence, Louis, assisted by his schoolfellow and devoted friend, Felix Mc-

Gavonty, had accomplished what his father had failed to achieve in ten years of incessant search: he had found the missing million of his grandfather, and had become a millionaire at sixteen. The young man fancied that yachting would suit him; and he proposed to Squire Moses Scarburn, the trustee of all his property, to purchase a cheap vessel for his use.

The spiriting away of his mother gave a new importance to the nautical fancy of the young man. Captain Ringgold condemned the plan to buy a cheap vessel. He had made a part of his ample fortune as a shipmaster, and had been an officer in the navy during the last half of the War of the Rebellion. He advised the young man's mother, who was also his guardian, and the trustee to buy a good-sized steam-yacht.

A New York millionaire had just completed one of the most magnificent steamers ever built, of over six hundred tons' burden; but his sudden death robbed him of the pleasures he anticipated from a voyage around the world in her, and the vessel was for sale at a reasonable price. The shipmaster fixed upon this craft as the one for the young millionaire, declaring that she would give the owner an education such as could not be obtained at any college; and that she could be sold for nearly all she cost when she was no longer needed.

This argument, and the pressing necessity of such a steamer for the recovery of Mrs. Belgrave, carried he day with the trustee. The vessel was bought; and as she had not yet been named, Louis called her the Guardian-Mother, in love and reverence for her who had watched over him from his birth. After some stirring adventures which befell Louis, the new steam-yacht proceeded to Bermuda, where Scoble had wrecked his vessel on the reefs; but the object of the search and all the ship's company were saved.

The Guardian-Mother returned to New York after this successful voyage, though not till Captain Ringgold had obtained a strong hint that Scoble had a wife in England. The educational scheme of the commander was then fully considered, and it was decided to make a voyage around the world in the Guardian-Mother. She was duly prepared for the purpose by Captain Ringgold. A ship's company of the highest grade was obtained. The last to be shipped was W. Penn Sharp as a quartermaster, the only vacancy on board. He had been a skilful detective most of his life, and failing health alone compelled him to go to sea; and he had been a sailor in his early years, attaining the position of first officer of a large Indiaman.

The captain made him third officer at Bermuda, the better to have his services as a detective. He had investigated Scoble's record, and eventually found Mrs. Scoble in Cuba, where she had inherited the large fortune of an uncle whom she had nursed in his last sickness. Scoble had come into the possession of the wealth of a brother who had recently died in Bermuda. He had purchased a steam-yacht of four hundred tons, in which he had followed the Guardian-Mother, and had several times attempted to sink her in collisions.

Officers came to Cuba to arrest him for his crimes at the races, and he was sent to the scene of his villany, where the court sentenced him to Sing Sing for a long term. The court in Cuba decreed that his yacht belonged to his wife; and her new owner, at the suggestion of the commander of the Guardian-Mother, made Penn Sharp, to whom she was largely indebted for the fortune to which she had succeeded, the captain of her. The steam-yacht was the Viking, and Mrs. Scoble sailed in her to New York, and then to England, where she obtained a divorce from her recreant husband, and became the wife of Captain Sharp, who was now in command of the Blanche, the white steamer that sailed abreast of the Guardian-Mother when the wreck in the Arabian Sea was discovered.

From a sailing-yacht sunk in a squall in the harbor of New York, the crew of the steamer had saved two gentlemen. One was a celebrated physician and surgeon, suffering from overwork, Dr. Philip Hawkes. He was induced to accept the commander's offer of a passage around the world for his services as the surgeon of the ship. His companion was a learned Frenchman, afflicted in the same manner as his friend; and he became the instructor on board.

Squire Scarburn, Louis's trustee, who was always called "Uncle Moses," was a passenger. Mrs. Belgrave had taken with her Mrs. Sarah Blossom, as a companion. She had been Uncle Moses's housekeeper. She was a good-looking woman of thirty-six, and one of the "salt of the earth," though her education, except on Scripture subjects, had been greatly neglected. Felix McGavonty, the Milesian crony of Louis, had been brought up by the trustee, and had lived in his family. The good lady wanted to be regarded as the mother of Felix, and the young man did not fully fall in with the idea.

When Louis recovered the stolen treasure of the jockey, he had applied to one of the principal losers by the crime, Mr. Lowell Woolridge, then devoted to horse-racing and yachting, for advice in regard to the disposal of the plunder. All who had lost any of the money were paid in full; and the gentleman took a fancy to the young man who consulted him. For the benefit of his son he discarded racing from his amusements. He invited Louis and his mother to several excursions in his yacht; and the two families became very intimate, though they were not of the same social rank, for Mr. Woolridge was a millionaire and a magnate of the Fifth Avenue.

The ex-sportsman was the father of a daughter and a son. At fifteen Miss Blanche was remarkably beautiful, and Louis could not help recognizing the fact. But he was then a poor boy; and his mother warned him not to get entangled in any affair of the heart, which had never entered the head of the subject of the warning. When the missing million came to light, she did not repeat her warning.

After the Guardian-Mother had sailed on her voyage all-over-the-world, Miss Blanche took a severe cold, which threatened serious consequences; and the doctors had advised her father to take her to Orotava, in the Canary Islands, in his yacht. The family had departed on the voyage; but before the Blanche, as the white sailing-yacht was called, reached her destination, she encountered a severe gale, and had a hole stove in her planking by a mass of wreckage. Her ship's company were thoroughly exhausted when the Guardian-Mother, bound to the same islands, discovered her, and after almost incredible exertions, saved the yacht and the family.

The beautiful young lady entirely recovered her health during the voyage, and Dr. Hawkes declared that she was in no danger whatever. The Blanche proceeded with the steamer to Mogadore, on the north-west coast of Africa, in Morocco. Here the ship was visited by a high officer of the army of Morocco, who was the possessor of almost unbounded wealth. He was fascinated by the beauty of Miss Blanche, and his marked attentions excited the alarm of her father and mother, as well as of the commander. He had promised to visit the ship again, and take the party to all the noted places in the city.

The parents and the captain regarded such a visit

as a calamity, and the steamer made her way out of the harbor very early the next morning, towing the yacht. The Guardian-Mother sailed for Madeira, accommodating her speed to that of the Blanche. The party had been there only long enough to see the sights, before the high official, Ali-Noury Pacha, in his steam-yacht come into the harbor of Funchal.

The commander immediately beat another retreat; but the Fatimé, as the Moroccan steamer was called, followed her to Gibraltar. Here the Pacha desired an interview with Captain Ringgold, who refused to receive him on board, for he had learned in Funchal that his character was very bad, and he told him so to his face. When the commander went on shore he was attacked in the street by the Pacha and some of his followers; but the stalwart captain knocked him with a blow of his fist in a gutter filled with mud. Ali-Noury was fined by the court for the assault, and, thirsting for revenge, he had followed the Guardian-Mother to Constantinople, and through the Archipelago, seeking the vengeance his evil nature demanded. He employed a man named Mazagan to capture Miss Blanche or Louis, or both of them.

Captain Sharp, who was cruising in the Viking with his wife, while at Messina found the Pacha beset by robbers, and badly wounded. The ex-detective took him on board of his steamer, procured a surgeon, and saved the life of the Moor, not only in beating off the robbers that beset him, but in the care of him after he was wounded. They became strong friends; and both the captain and Mrs. Sharp, who had been the most devoted of nurses to him, spoke their minds to him very plainly.

The Pacha was repentant, for his vices were as contrary to the religion of Mohammed as to that of the New Testament. Captain Sharp was confident that his guest was thoroughly reformed, though he did not become a Christian, as his nurse hoped he would. Then his preserver learned that the Pacha had settled his accounts with Captain Mazagan, and sold him the Fatimé.

It appeared when Captain Sharp told his story to the commander of the Guardian-Mother at Aden, that Mazagan had been operating on his own hook in Egypt and elsewhere to "blackmail" the trustee of Louis. The Pacha had ordered a new steamer to be built for him in England; and when she arrived at Gibraltar, he had given the command of her to Captain Sharp, to whom he owed his life and reformation.

At Aden, Captain Ringgold discovered the white steamer, and fearing she was the one built for the Pacha, as Mazagan had informed him in regard to her, he paid her a visit, and found Captain Sharp in command of her. The Moor was known as General Noury here, and he made an abject apology to the visitor. Convinced that the Moor had really reformed his life, they were reconciled, and General Noury was received with favor by all the party.

The Blanche was sailing in company of the Guardian-Mother for Bombay when the wreck with several men on it was discovered. And now having reviewed the incidents of the past, fully related in the preceding volumes of the series, it is quite time to attend to the imperilled persons on the wreck.

CHAPTER IV

FIRST AND SECOND CUTTERS TO THE RESCUE

It was still but a dim light when the commander appeared on deck. He could not have slept more than an hour, but he was as wideawake and active as ever before in his life. He had a spyglass in his hand, with which he proceeded to examine the wreck as soon as he had obtained its bearings; for he never did anything, even under such desperate circumstances as the present, until he had first ascertained what was best to be done.

"How long is it since you made out the wreck, Mr. Boulong?" he inquired, still looking through the glass.

"Mr. Scott reported cries from that direction not ten minutes ago, and the lookout aloft hailed the deck a minute or two later," replied the first officer.

"Make the course north by east," added the captain.

"North by east, sir," replied Mr. Boulong, mounting the promenade, and giving the order to the quartermaster through the window. "Steer small till you get the course, Bangs."

The captain and the third officer remained on the promenade deck, still observing the persons on the wreck, who continued to shout and to discharge their firearms till they saw the head of the steamer slowly turned to the north, when they appeared to be satisfied that relief was at hand.

"They are in a very dangerous position," said the commander. "I cannot make out what they are clinging too; but it is washed by the sea at every wave, and they cannot hold out long in that situation. I wonder that all of them have not been knocked off before this time."

"They must have some strong hold on the thing that floats them, whatever it is, for they are under water half the time," replied Scott, who was also using a spyglass. "I can't make out what they are on; but it looks like a whaleback to me, with her upper works carried away."

"There are no whalebacks in these seas," replied the captain.

"But I saw one in New York Harbor; and I have read that one has crossed the Atlantic, going through the Welland Canal from the great lakes."

"They have no mission in these waters, though what floats that party looks very much like one. Call all hands, Mr. Boulong, and clear away the first cutter."

By this time the Guardian-Mother was on her course to the northward. The storm was severe, but not as savage as it might have been, or as the steamer had encountered on the Atlantic when she saved the sailing-yacht Blanche from foundering. The ship had been kept on her course for Bombay, though, as she had the gale on the beam, she was condemned to wallow in the trough of the sea; and stiff and able as she was, she rolled heavily, as any vessel would have done under the same conditions

The change of course gave her the wind very nearly over the stern, and she pitched instead of rolling, sometimes lifting her propeller almost out of the water, which made it whirl like a top, and then burying it deep in the waves, causing it to moan and groan and shake the whole after part of the ship, rousing all the party in the cabin from their slumbers. The ship had hardly changed her course before Louis came on deck, and was soon followed by Felix McGavonty.

"What's the row, Mr. Scott?" asked the former.

"Are ye's thryin' to shake the screw out of her?" inquired the Milesian, who could talk as good English as his crony, the owner, but who occasionally made use of the brogue to prevent him from forgetting his mother tongue, as he put it, though he was born in the United States. "Don't ye's do it; for sure, you will want it 'fore we get to Bombay."

"Don't you see those men standing upon something, or clinging to whatever floats them? They are having a close call; but I hope we shall be able to save them," replied the third officer.

The captain had gone to the pilot-house, from the windows of which the wreck could be seen very plainly, as its distance from the ship was rapidly reduced. By this time the entire crew had rushed to the deck, and were waiting for orders on the forecastle. Mr. Boulong, with his boat's crew, had gone to the starboard quarter, where the first cutter was swung in on her davits. The boat pulled six oars, and the cockswain made seven hands.

With these the cutter was quickly swung out, and the crew took their places in her, the bowman at the forward tackle, and the cockswain at the after. It was the same crew with which the first officer had boarded the Blanche when she was in imminent peril of going down, and he had entire confidence both in their will and their muscle. He stood on the rail, holding on at the main shrouds, ready for further orders.

In the pilot-house, with both quartermasters at the wheel, the captain was still observing with his glass the men in momentary peril of being washed from their insecure position into the boiling sea. Felix had gone aft with the first officer, and had assisted in shoving out the first cutter from the skids inboard, and Louis had come into the pilot-house with Scott.

"Has any one counted the number of men on the wreck, or whatever it is?" inquired the commander.

"There are eleven of them," promptly replied Scott, who, as an officer of the ship, was in his element, and very active both in mind and body.

"Too many for one boat in a heavy sea," added Captain Ringgold. "You will clear away the second cutter, Mr. Scott, and follow Mr. Boulong to the wreck."

"All the second cutters aft!" shouted the third officer from the window; and the crew of this boat rushed up the ladder to the promenade deck, and followed the life-line to the davits of the cutter.

"Bargate, who pulls the stroke oar in the second cutter, has the rheumatism in his right arm, and is not fit to go in the boat," interposed Mr. Gaskette, the second officer.

"Let me take his place, Captain Ringgold!" eagerly exclaimed Louis Belgrave.

"Do you think you can pull an oar in a heavy seaway, Mr. Belgrave?" asked the commander, who always treated the owner with entire respect in the presence of others, though he called him by his given name when they were alone.

"I know I can!" replied Louis very confidently.

"I do not object, if Mr. Scott is willing."

"I am very willing, for Mr. Belgrave's muscle is as hard as a flint."

"Very well. Hurry up!" added the captain.

Four other men were sent aft to assist in the preparations for putting the second cutter into the water; and in as short a time as Mr. Gaskette, who usually went in that boat on important occasions, would have required to do it, the cutter was ready to be dropped into the water when the order was given.

The captain and the second officer continued to

watch the party on the wreck, expecting every moment to see some of them swept into the savage waves that beat against their frail support. The ship went at full speed on her course; for the commander would not waste an instant while the lives of so many human beings depended upon his action.

"Can you make out what they are clinging to, Mr. Gaskette?" asked the commander of the only person besides the two quartermasters who remained with him in the pilot-house.

"Yes, sir; I am just getting an idea in regard to it, though the thing is awash so that I can hardly make it out," replied the second officer. "I think it is the bottom of a rather small vessel, upside down; for I see something like a keel. The party have two ropes stretched the whole length of the bottom, to which they are clinging."

"You are right; that is plainly the bottom of a vessel, and I wonder that the craft has not gone down by this time. How she happens to be in that situation, and why she has not sunk, are matters yet to be explained. Go aft, if you please, and see that both cutters are ready to be lowered into the water, Mr. Gaskette. It is not prudent to go much nearer to the wreck, for the gale may drift us upon it."

The second officer left the pilot-house, and found the crews all seated in their boats, with everything in readiness to obey the order to lower away; and he reported the fact to his superior.

"Starboard the helm, Bangs, and steer small!" said

Captain Ringgold as soon as the officer returned with the information he had obtained.

To "steer small" is to move the rudder very gradually; for if the course were suddenly changed a quarter of the circumference of the compass in such a sea as was then raging, it would be liable to make the steamer engage in some disagreeable, if not dangerous, antics.

"Steady!" added the captain when the steamer was headed a point south of west.

This position brought the starboard side of the ship on the lee; that is, this part of the ship was sheltered from the fury of the wind and the waves, and it was the proper situation in which to lower a boat into the water; for on the windward side these two powerful forces would be likely to stave the cutter against the side of the steamer.

After the commander had struck the gong to stop her, he gave the order to the second officer to lower the first cutter; and he left the pilot-house for this purpose. Mr. Boulong was an exceptionally skilful officer in the handling of a boat in a heavy sea. Watching for the favorable moment, he gave the order to the cockswain and bowman to lower away, with the aid of the oarsmen near them.

"Cast off the after fall, Stoody!" said he sharply to the cockswain; and the order was promptly obeyed. "Cast off your fall, Knott!" he added almost instantly. "Let fall! Give way!"

A receding wave carried the boat away from the

side of the ship, precisely as Mr. Boulong had calculated. The six oars dropped into the water as one, and the men began to pull, getting a firm hold on the receding wave, which sent the cutter to a safe distance from the ship. As soon as she was clear, the commander, who had remained in the pilot-house, rang the gong to go ahead. When the steamer had gathered sufficient headway, she was brought about as cautiously as before.

The second cutter was on the port quarter of the vessel, and this movement placed the boat under the lee. Mr. Gaskette had remained aft, and when the ship had stopped her screw and nearly lost her headway, the captain shouted to him through his speaking-trumpet, which the roar of the waves and the escaping steam rendered necessary, to "Lower away!"

"Lower away when you are ready, Mr. Scott!" repeated the second officer.

Though Scott was only eighteen years old, he was an intuitive sailor, and had a good deal of experience for his years. He had never before occupied his present position; but his nautical genius, fortified by sundry combats with wind and waves, made him feel quite at home. As the first officer had done, he seized the auspicious moment when the retiring wave promised its efficient aid, and gave the orders to cast off the falls.

The six oars grappled with the water on the smooth side of a great wave, and carried it to the apex of the next billow; and she went off as handsomely as the first cutter had done. Mr. Gaskette saw these manœuvres successfully accomplished, and then started for the pilot-house, to report to the captain. On his way he could not help giving an inquiring loȯk at the manner in which the substitute for Bargate performed his duty.

At eighteen Louis was a healthy, vigorous, athletic fellow, developed by an active life on the ocean, and weighing one hundred and fifty pounds. In any trial of strength he was more than the equal of any other member of the "Big Four," as the four young men berthing in the cabin called themselves, borrowing the name from a combination of railroads in the West. He was well trained as an oarsman, and the second officer was satisfied that he was doing his full share of the work.

As Mr. Gaskette reached the pilot-house there was a commotion there, and it was evident to him that something unlooked for had occurred. He glanced at the two cutters; but they were all right, and were steadily making their way to the locality of the wreck.

"The wreck is going down, sir!" exclaimed Bangs with startling energy just before the second officer reached the door.

"It is all up with that craft!" added Twist, the other quartermaster.

Captain Ringgold said nothing, but calmly surveyed the men who were now struggling in the water. They seemed to be all able to swim; but it was a closer call than they had had before. The two cutters appeared to be their only possible salvation, and they were still at a considerable distance from the scene of peril.

It was a terribly exciting and harrowing spectacle; but the commander looked as impassable as ever. He rang the gong for the ship to go ahead; and Mr. Gaskette wondered what he intended to do, though he was not left more than a moment in suspense.

CHAPTER V

THE TITLED GENTLEMEN OF THE TRAVANCORE

THE first and second cutters of the Guardian-Mother were struggling bravely with the huge billows, but not making very rapid progress, though the gale was in their favor. The eleven men floundering in the water where the wreck had disappeared under them were provided with life-preservers, it was now discovered, and their chances were somewhat less desperate than they were at first taken to be. But the waves rudely knocked them about, and sometimes upset them so as to require a struggle to regain their upright position.

"The Blanche is close aboard of us, Captain Ringgold," said Mr. Gaskette. "She is running at full speed for a position on our port hand."

"Very good," replied the commander. "That is the right thing for her to do, if she don't come too near us."

"She is at a safe distance, sir, and her starboard quarter-boat is manned and ready to drop into the water."

"Captain Sharp will do the right thing at the right time," replied the commander, whose gaze was riveted upon the struggling party in the water.

"I trust we shall be able to save the whole of them."

"The chances are good for it," answered the second officer.

"How is the second cutter doing?" inquired Captain Ringgold.

"She is doing very well, sir, though she is some distance behind the first cutter, for she got away from the ship later. Mr. Belgrave is pulling a stroke as vigorous as the rest of the crew. The Blanche is coming about, and she will have her starboard boat in the water in a few minutes more."

As her head swung round to port she stopped her screw, and then backed for a few moments, till she had killed the most of her headway; for Captain Sharp knew better than to drop the boat into the water while the vessel was making sternway. In a very short space of time the six-oar craft was pulling with all the muscle of her British tars for the scene of peril, and not more than two cables' length astern of the second cutter of the Guardian-Mother.

Captain Ringgold observed the boats with the most intense interest as they approached the unfortunate men in the water. The Blanche came about again, and her other quarter-boat was soon pulling after the first. Possibly there was some feeling of rivalry among the crews of the boats in the good work in which they were engaged, for they were all putting their utmost vigor into their oars.

But no boat appeared to gain on the others, and

the one which had started first continued to maintain her advantage till the work of rescuing the sufferers actually began. By this time the action of the waves had separated the party, so that they were scattered over a considerable surface of the breaking billows. Mr. Boulong could see that some of the men in the water were nearly exhausted; for many of them had wasted their strength in useless struggles.

The first cutter was approaching a man who was at the extremity of the western wing of the party. He was a European of thirty years or less; and though his head, hair, and beard were dripping with salt water, there was something in his expression, as he bestowed a single glance upon the boat now close to him, which commanded the respect, and even admiration, of the first officer. He was cool and self-possessed in spite of the peril of his situation, and was observing with painful solicitude the struggles of a person about ten fathoms from him.

"Stand by to lay on your oars!" said Mr. Boulong with energy, when the first cutter was within a boat's length of the individual. "Hold water! Stand by to haul him in, Knott!" he added to the bowman. "Stern all!"

These orders were given as the boat came within her length of the man; and Knott was unshipping his oar, when the stranger raised his left hand, pointing to the struggling person he had been observing in spite of the near approach of the cutter.

"Save that man first, for he is drowning!" he

shouted in tones full of anxiety, if not positive suffering. "I can take care of myself for a while longer."

Mr. Boulong's vision had taken in the drowning man, and he fully realized that the person's situation was desperate, if he was not already hopelessly lost. He had struggled and twisted himself in his involuntary efforts, till his life-preserver had worked its way down to his hips, and then it overthrew him; for he turned a somerset, and disappeared under a coming wave. He had utterly "lost his head," and was like an infant in the fury of the billows.

The men were still backing water with their oars, in obedience to the order of the officer; but as soon as the oars would go clear of the self-possessed gentleman, Mr. Boulong gave the command to "Give way!" and again the cutter went ahead.

It required but a few strokes to give the necessary headway to the boat; and Knott was again ordered to stand by to haul him in. The great wave ingulfed and swept over him, and again left him aimlessly battling with the killing billows. The bowman was in position, and leaned over so far to reach the sufferer, that the officer ordered the next two men to seize him by the legs, to prevent him from being dragged overboard.

Knott grasped him by his upper garment, and drew his head out of the water. He held on like an excited bulldog, in spite of the erratic vaulting of the boat and the struggles of him whom the deep sea seemed to have chosen as its victim. But the bowman was a muscular seaman of fifty, and he won the victory over the billows, and hauled the man into the cutter. He was a person of rather swarthy complexion, dressed in Hindu costume. He was passed along through the oarsmen to the stern-sheets, where Mr. Boulong proceeded to lift him up with his feet in the air, to free his lungs from the salt water he must have imbibed.

By this time the second cutter came up to the scene, and Scott in command wondered why the first officer had passed by one man to save another; for in the commotion of the waves he had not been able to realize the condition of the Hindu, as he appeared to be. But the cool gentleman had been over-confident; and instead of waiting for one of the boats to pick him up, he had disengaged himself from his life-preserver, and attempted to swim to the first cutter. Mr. Boulong was so occupied with his treatment of the first man rescued, that he did not see him, or hear his shout above the noise of the savage waves, and had directed the cockswain to steer for the next man, who seemed to be an older person than either of the others.

The Hindu had not entirely lost his senses; and when he was disburdened of the load of salt water he had swallowed, he looked about him, though still in a somewhat dazed condition.

"Dr. Ferrolan!" he exclaimed. "Oh, save him!" He pointed to him as the stern of the boat rose on

"A ready seaman seized him by the arm." — Page 45.

a billow; and he proved to be the person towards whom the cockswain was steering the boat. "Where is Lord Tremlyn?" he asked, as he surveyed the surrounding waters. "There!" he screamed wildly, as he pointed over the stern, where the person indicated was swimming for the first cutter.

"The other boat is close aboard of him, and will soon pick him up," said Mr. Boulong, turning his attention to one ahead of the cutter.

As he spoke, a booming billow struck Lord Tremlyn, as the Hindu had revealed his name, just as Scott was running his boat up to take him on board. He was caught just in the comb of the wave, and it upset him, making him turn a complete somerset, as his companion had done; but he was master of himself, and when he came up, he appeared to dive through the crest of another billow, and came out close alongside Scott's boat, near the bow. A ready seaman seized him by the arm, and, with the aid of another, hauled him into the boat, where he was passed into the stern-sheets.

"Was Sir Modava saved?" he asked, with no little excitement in his manner, as he spit the salt water from his mouth.

"Don't know him, sir; but they just hauled a man into the first cutter," replied Scott.

"Which is the first cutter?" asked Lord Tremlyn, looking about him.

"The one just ahead of us, sir."

"Thank God, he is saved!" ejaculated his soaked

lordship. "Kindly pull up to her, and let me be sure of it."

"That is easier said than done, sir. The first cutter has just picked up another man, and now she is pulling for all she is worth for the next one. I couldn't overhaul her if I tried, and just now our business is to save those in the water," answered the third officer.

"You are right, Mr. Officer," added Lord Tremlyn, as he seated himself in the place pointed out to him.

There were still eight others in the water, and all of them were to the north of the boats. Those from the Blanche had noticed this fact, and were pulling in that direction. Mr. Boulong had directed his boat, after taking in Dr. Ferrolan, as the Hindu called him, to the person the farthest to the eastward, leaving the others to be saved by the boats nearer to them.

It is enough to say that all the wrecked party were saved, without giving the details of the picking up of each of them. The vessel in which they had foundered had entirely disappeared, and nothing was seen belonging to her. Against the head sea all the boats pulled back to the two steamers. The first cutter of the Guardian-Mother had saved three, the second three, and the two boats of the Blanche had picked up five.

"Now give three cheers, Mr. Scott," said Louis Belgrave in a low tone, as the second cutter, ahead of the first on the return, approached the ship. "The captain will understand from that we have saved all the party."

Scott approved the suggestion, and the cheers were given with a will, and repeated by the crew of the first cutter, not far behind. They were returned from the ship; and the voices included those who belonged in the cabin, as well as the officers, seamen, and waiters, while the ladies, clinging to the rails of the promenade, vigorously waved their handkerchiefs, as the sun rose clear from the eastern waves, though it soon disappeared in the clouds. It was evident to the officers that the gale was breaking; or perhaps, as the commander put it, the ship was running out of it.

Each of the boats got under the lee in turn; the falls were hooked on, and both cutters were hoisted up to their davits, as they had come from the scene of their exploits. Mr. Gaskette was directed to get the ship on her course again; and Captain Ringgold went aft to welcome the shipwrecked mariners, or whatever they were.

The seamen assisted the dripping passengers to the deck; and the masculine tenants of the state-cabin crept along the life-lines to take part in the scene, or at least to witness it. As the steamer was headed to the eastward, the second cutter was the first to be hoisted up. The first person to be assisted to the deck was Lord Tremlyn, though those who had saved him were not yet aware of his quality. The commander extended his hand to him, and it was cordially grasped.

"I congratulate you, sir, on your escape from the wreck of your ship," said he. "I thank God most earnestly that we have been able to save all your party. I hope none were lost before we made you out on the wreck."

"Not one, Captain; and I join with you in reverent gratitude to Him who rules the sea in calm and storm, for our preservation from certain death, which would have been our fate, one and all, but for the care and skill with which you have worked out our salvation. I thank you and the brave and noble officers and crews of your boats with all my mind and heart. I speak not for myself alone, but for all the ship's company of the Travancore, now gone to the bottom," replied Lord Tremlyn, again grasping the hand of the commander.

In a short time the saved from the first cutter joined the others on the promenade deck, and the Guardian-Mother proceeded on her course to Bombay.

"Were you the captain of the Travancore, sir?" asked the commander.

"I am only an amateur sailor," said his lordship; "but I was in command of the unfortunate vessel, which was a steam-yacht of small dimensions, in the service of the Indian government. Ah, Dr. Ferrolan," he continued as those from the first cutter crossed the deck; and he grasped the hand of the person addressed, "let us thank God first, and then the commander of this ship, that we have been preserved, — all the ship's company, I am informed."

"I join you most heartily, my Lord," replied the doctor. "Captain ——"

"Captain Ringgold," prompted Mr. Boulong, by whose boat he had been saved.

"Captain Ringgold, I am your debtor for life;" and he proceeded to express his obligations more at length. "Permit me to present to you Lord Tremlyn, a gentleman who came to India on semi-official business."

"I am happy to know you, Lord Tremlyn," replied the commander; but the title did not appear to make a very profound impression upon him.

"Captain Ringgold, allow me to introduce my particular friend, Sir Modava Rao, a gentleman high in the favor of the Indian government, and I may add of all the native princes."

"I am very happy to make your acquaintance, Sir Modava," replied the commander, taking his dusky hand.

The captain then invited the two titled gentlemen and the doctor of the party to the cabin, while the two engineers were turned over to Mr. Sentrick, the chief engineer.

CHAPTER VI

THE GENERAL INTRODUCTION IN THE CABIN

It was still early in the morning, and the cabin party were not disposed to remain any longer on the promenade deck; for it was almost impossible for some of them to stand up, even with the aid of the life-lines and the rails, and all of them retreated to the boudoir and music-room. None of them had been introduced to the strangers; for they had asked to be excused, as they were not in a presentable condition.

The trio of distinguished individuals who had been conducted to the main cabin by the commander were of course soaked with water, and chilled after remaining so long in their involuntary bath; and for this reason no questions were asked of them to bring out an explanation of the cause of the disaster of which they had been the victims. There were three vacant state-rooms, to which they were assigned, and each of them had a bathroom connected with it. The two cabin stewards had already been ordered to prepare these rooms for the occupancy of the newcomers. Warm baths were ready for them when they took possession of the apartments.

"All this is more luxurious than we have been

accustomed to lately," said Lord Tremlyn, when the commander ushered him into No. 11, which was provided with everything belonging to a suite of rooms in the best hotels of the United States.

"I hope you will be able to make yourself comfortable, sir; but your greatest need at the present moment appears to be dry clothing, when you have restored your limbs to their normal condition in the bath, and I will endeavor to supply this want," replied the commander.

"You are very kind, Captain Ringgold, and I shall never cease to be grateful to you for the service you have rendered to me and my companions; for all of us would have perished when the wreck of our steamer went down, without the prompt assistance you rendered to us," said the principal personage of the party, who was still shivering under the influence of the chill he had received in the cold waters of the sea.

The captain retired, closing the door of the room. He went to No. 12, to which Sir Modava Rao had been shown, and then to No. 13, which had been appropriated to Dr. Ferrolan. He assured both of them that dry clothing would be provided for them, and both of them stammered forth their obligations very profusely from between their chattering teeth. The doors were closed upon them after they had been instructed to call upon the stewards outside for anything they needed.

The commander had taken the measure of the trio,

and knew where to apply for the clothing needed. The surgeon of the party was about the size of Mr. Sage, the chief steward of the ship; and he was asked to supply a full suit, including undergarments, shirt, socks, collar, and cravat. His lordship was about the size of Mr. Woolridge, who was more than happy to provide for the needs of this gentleman. Professor Giroud was a rather slender person; and from his wardrobe came the suit and other furnishings for the titled Hindu. The clothing of each person was placed on a stool at the door of his room, and he was notified where to obtain it.

"Mr. Sage, you understand by this time that we have sixteen places to be taken at the table," said Captain Ringgold to the chief steward.

"I think I had better set two tables, for sixteen would be rather crowded in the space we use now," replied Mr. Sage, who was a Napoleon in his calling. "I propose to arrange them as they were at the big dinner you gave at Aden."

"And while you are about it you may arrange for nineteen places at the tables," replied the captain; but he did not explain who were to occupy the three he had added to the number.

The commander went to his private cabin, after he had visited the pilot-house, and made a diagram of the two tables, assigning places to each of the party and the guests, but leaving three of the end places vacant. He showed it to Louis and Mrs. Belgrave, and they made no objection to the new arrangement. It was handed to the chief steward, who put a card with the name of the occupant of each seat on the plate in front of it. The revolving chairs at the tables had to be all changed, and more added to it; and Stevens the carpenter, with his assistants from the crew, were busy for an hour making the change.

When the commander visited the music-room, he was unable to answer any of the questions of his passengers as to the details of the wreck of the Travancore, though he gave the names and quality of the three gentlemen who had been invited to go below. The sleepers in the cabin had been aroused by the erratic movements of the steamer before daylight, especially by the change from rolling to pitching. There was a thundering roar of escaping steam at times, and all of them had "turned out" to ascertain the cause of the commotion. Felix and Morris had been the first to go on deck, and they had informed the others of the nature of the event which had caused the commotion on board.

The regular passengers had seen the strangers as they came down to the promenade deck from the cutters. They were naturally filled with curiosity to ascertain who and what the trio were. One was a lord, another a sir, and the third a surgeon; and this was all that was known to any one.

"Have we really a live lord on board, Felix?" asked Mrs. Blossom, as they were waiting for breakfast in the music-room.

"He is not a dead one, sure," replied the Milesian, "though he would soon have been a very dead one if we had not happened along when we did."

"One of them was a colored man," added the good lady.

"Sir Modava Rao!" exclaimed Felix. "He is not more than a shade darker than you are, Aunty; and he is a great man in the country we visit next. But dry up; the captain is going to say something."

The commander gave the names of the three distinguished persons who were then in the cabin. It was very nearly breakfast-time, and the trio had had abundant time to dress themselves in the garments provided for them, and he requested all the party to descend to the cabin, leading the way himself. They found the rescued party seated on the divans between the doors of the state-rooms, and they all rose to their feet as soon as the commander appeared.

They presented an entirely different appearance from what they did in their drabbled garments; for those who had supplied them with clothing had brought out their best clothes, and the three gentlemen seemed to be in condition to go to church. Lord Tremlyn hastened to the captain with extended hand as he stepped down upon the floor of the cabin.

"I desire to express my gratitude anew to you, and to the gentlemen who have made us capable of coming into your presence in proper condition," said his lordship, as the commander took his offered hand, which was wrung with the utmost cordiality.

"So far as I am concerned, my Lord, I have done nothing but my duty; for I am a sailor, and the true son of the ocean is always ready to sacrifice even his life to save a shipwrecked brother of the sea," replied the captain.

"Then you are a true son of the ocean, Captain Ringgold, and I shall remember you as long as I live in my prayers!"

"So shall we all!" exclaimed Sir Modava, taking the hand of the commander.

"I indorse the sentiment," added Dr. Ferrolan.

"In regard to the clothing," said the commander, as he threw back his head, elevated his shoulders, and spread out his arms, so as to exhibit to its full extent the height and breadth of his stalwart form, "I was, unfortunately, unable to contribute to the supply of garments for your party; for mine on any one of you would have been like a shirt on a handspike."

"But a London tailor could hardly have fitted us any better," replied the spokesman of the trio.

"I am happy to see you in such excellent condition so soon after the disaster. With your permission, gentlemen, I desire to introduce you to each of my passengers, promising to indicate those whose garments you wear," continued the commander.

"With the greatest pleasure," replied Lord Tremlyn; and the other two bowed their acquiescence.

"This, gentlemen, is Mr. Belgrave, the owner of the Guardian-Mother, the steam-yacht in which he is making a voyage round the world."

"I am extremely pleased to make your acquaintance, Mr. Belgrave," added Lord Tremlyn, as he took the hand of the young millionaire. "We owe our lives to the fortunate presence of your magnificent steam-yacht in this part of the Arabian Sea. Permit me to present to you Prince Modava, who has been knighted for his distinguished services to the British Crown, and who prefers to be known by his English title."

"That's your colored man!" whispered Felix to Mrs. Blossom.

"Good gracious!" exclaimed the motherly lady. "A live prince!"

"It affords me very great pleasure to become acquainted with you, Mr. Belgrave," with a smile so sweet and expressive that it ravished the hearts of the ladies. "I am under a burden of obligation to you which I shall never be able to repay; and I hope I shall be able to render you some slight service in assisting you to see India, for I learn that you are bound to Bombay."

"I thank you, Sir Modava; and we shall gratefully accept any favors you may extend to us."

"Let me add, my Lord, that Mr. Belgrave pulled the stroke oar in the boat which picked you up after you had sent our first cutter to the relief of Sir Modava," interposed the commander.

"Then I shall have an additional reason to remember with gratitude the young gentleman," added Lord Tremlyn.

"Mrs. Belgrave, gentlemen, the mother of our owner," the captain proceeded, as he took the lady by the arm.

"I congratulate you, madam, on being the mother of such a noble son; for not many young men with the fortune he has at his command would pull an oar in such a gale, such a storm, even to save his fellow-beings from perishing in the angry waves," said his lordship, as he took the hand of the lady. "Blessed be the mother of such a boy!"

The members of the Woolridge family were next presented to the trio; and the distinguished strangers had something pleasant to say to each of them. The "live lord" was only twenty-eight years old, and Sir Modava but thirty, while Dr. Ferrolan was forty-six; and all of them seemed to be greatly impressed, and even startled, when Miss Blanche dawned upon them; for she was as beautiful to them as she was to everybody else, and they seemed to be unwilling to allow her to make room for the others to be introduced.

Every person in the cabin seemed to enter into the spirit of the occasion; and the wearers of the borrowed clothing, as the owners of the garments were indicated, brought forth many humorous remarks from both sides, which it would be pleasant to report if space permitted. The ceremony was finished in due time, though it was rather a long time.

"We are not accustomed to the companionship of titled personages," said the commander at its conclusion. "But we are eminently a social party, and we desire our guests to make themselves as much at home on board of the Guardian-Mother as if they owned her, and were running her for their own pleasure."

"Thank you, Captain Ringgold. Titles are not men, and we know that you are all republicans. If we do not make ourselves worthy of the generous welcome you have extended to us, we shall not ask any consideration on account of the titles that have fallen upon us through the nature of our constitutional government. I believe that we all stand on the same level before our Maker; and whatever social distinctions prevail in our country, they do not exempt any Briton from being a gentleman and an honest man," replied Lord Tremlyn. And his remarks were warmly applauded by both English and Americans; and the gentleman bowed his thanks for this appreciation of his sentiments.

At a nod from the captain the bell was rung for breakfast. Taking the "live lord" by the arm, he conducted him to the seat next him on his right. Louis conducted Sir Modava to the place on the commander's left, and placed his mother next to him. It was found impracticable to heed the names that had been placed on the plates, for it would have taken too much time. Louis took Miss Blanche to the place next to his mother, and seated himself at her right.

Dr. Hawkes took possession of Dr. Ferrolan, and placed himself and Uncle Moses on each side of him. The professor took charge of Mrs. Blossom. The captain invited those who remained standing to take such seats as they chose; and when all were placed at the table, he reverently said a brief grace. Everybody was unusually social; but as the commander had announced that the particulars of the wreck of the Travancore would be detailed in due time by Dr. Ferrolan, the subject was ignored, and the voyage of the Guardian-Mother was the general subject of conversation. The chief steward had "spread himself" on the breakfast, and the meal was far more elaborate than usual; and the wrecked trio proved that they had excellent appetites.

CHAPTER VII

DR. FERROLAN'S EXPLANATION OF THE WRECK

WITH the rising of the sun the gale had broken, and by the time the party in the cabin left the table, the north-east monsoon was soothing the ocean with its gentle blast. The angry sea was rapidly becoming good-natured again, though the waves were still high enough to give the ship an uneasy motion. But all the party, and no less the trio added to their number, had their sea-legs on, and no reasonable motion disturbed any of them.

The two engineers from the wreck of the Travancore had been as carefully looked after as the strangers in the main cabin. They had been supplied with clothing, and they had breakfasted in the mess-room on the best the larder afforded. The third person brought in by the second cutter was the Hindu cook of the wrecked steamer; but he spoke English very well, and had been otherwise Europeanized. He had been turned over to Baldy Bickling, the second cook of the ship, who had clothed and fed him, and seemed to be unable to do enough for him.

The three gentlemen in the cabin were as sociable as could be desired; and though it was Sunday morning, the scene at the tables had been very animated.

When the meal was finished, the guests at their own request were shown over the ship; and they were not at all reserved in the expression of their admiration at the elegance with which she had been fitted up, and not less at the convenience of all the arrangements.

Lord Tremlyn was particularly interested in the educational feature of the Guardian-Mother, as Captain Ringgold explained his pet scheme in the library, or study, abaft the state-cabin, as it was called on the plan of the vessel prepared by the gentleman for whom she had been built. The guests looked at the titles of the books, considerable additions to which had been made at Cairo, Alexandria, and elsewhere.

"This is not a library of romances," said his lordship with a smile, as he took in the encyclopædias, books of travel, scientific treatises, and geographical works.

"No, sir; they cover a broad range of useful information," replied the commander. "Those of our company who are disposed to read novels supply themselves with that kind of literature. Quite a number of them are lecturers" —

"Lecturers!" exclaimed the distinguished guest. "Then a large number of your passengers must be scientific people."

"Not at all, sir; the large majority of them are men and women of good education, and Professor Giroud is a learned Frenchman who has been a lecturer at various colleges and schools. Dr. Hawkes is a leading member of his profession, and is sometimes a lecturer in various medical and surgical institutions in New York. Both of these gentlemen are making this voyage to regain their health, injured by over-work."

"You are fortunate in having such men on board," added his lordship.

"But most of our lecturers are persons of fair education, and only three of them have been graduated from the university. We assign subjects to them some time in advance, and they prepare themselves for the occasion. This gives the unprofessional people an interest in the exercises they would not otherwise have. For example, Mr. Woolridge" —

"I beg pardon, but he is the father of the beautiful young lady who was seated at the table next to Mr. Belgrave, is he not?" interposed Lord Tremlyn.

"The same, sir. At first he considered the lectures a bore; and doubtless they were such to him, for he had been a sporting-man and a yachtsman, though he has since abandoned the races. But I gave him as a subject the horses and other animals of Egypt. He did very well with it in his peculiar way; and since that he is one of the most interested in the lectures, — or perhaps I had better call them simply talks," added the commander.

"Then this voyage will create a new taste for him."

"I have no doubt of it. He is a Fifth Avenue

millionaire, and he is able to cultivate any taste he may acquire. Mr. Belgrave is one of our most useful speakers, for he studies his subjects very faithfully. He is a devoted student, speaks French fluently, and gets along very well with Spanish. This voyage is a college course for him."

"Do your ladies take an interest in these lectures, Captain Ringgold?"

"All of them, though I have assigned a subject to only one of them. They all manifest their interest by asking questions. Like myself, Mrs. Belgrave and Mrs. Blossom are Methodists, while the Wooldridge family are Episcopalians, though none of us are bigoted. The sisters of my church are very favorable to religious topics, such as were suggested on the Nile; and when we were near the land of Goshen and the Sinai peninsula Mrs. Belgrave spoke to us in this connection. Mrs. Blossom is one of the "salt of the earth," a very good woman, very religious, and her studies have been confined to the Bible and her denominational newspapers. Her education was neglected, and she is rather tonguey, so that she asks curious questions; but we all esteem her very highly, though her American peculiarities may seem very odd to you."

"I have known similar people in England, and your description of her leads me to respect the lady," replied the titled gentleman, who appeared to be very democratic so far as homely merit was concerned.

Dr. Hawkes had taken his professional brother in

charge, and Louis, Sir Modava, as the commander had Lord Tremlyn, and they were showing them over the ship. We need not follow them or repeat their explanations; but they finally reached the promenade deck, where all the officers were presented to the guests of the steamer. At Conference Hall the three couples met, and the lectures were again commented upon; for this subject was uppermost in the mind of the commander.

"Do you have a lecture to-day, Captain Ringgold?" asked his lordship.

"No, sir; this is Sunday, and we keep the Sabbath in a reasonable manner, and the conference is usually omitted on this day, though when the subject is appropriate for the day the lecture is given. The professor is a Roman Catholic; but we have not had the slightest friction in regard to any man's creed. The owner and voyager in our consort, the white ship abreast of us, whose boat picked up five men of your ship's company, is a Mohammedan, though the captain and his wife are Congregationalists. We have a religious service on board at eleven o'clock, to which your party are invited, though no umbrage will be taken if you prefer to absent yourselves."

"I shall certainly attend," replied his lordship; and his companions said the same. "Have you a chaplain?"

"We have not, and I am obliged to act in that capacity for the want of a better," replied the captain. "We Methodists are all trained to 'speak in meeting,' whether we have the gift or not."

At the appointed time the gong was sounded for divine service, and four whistles were given, that all on board might hear the call. Chairs had been provided for the guests, and all the party were seated when six bells struck. The two engineers of the Travancore were seated on the platform with the cook, and all the officers and seamen who could be spared stood within hearing.

Most of the party were provided with tune-books, and the captain gave out "The Life-Boat." Books were passed to the strangers, and the commander led off in the singing. Lord Tremlyn and Dr. Ferrolan joined in with vigorous bass voices. Captain Ringgold then followed with an extemporaneous prayer, in which he poured forth his thanks to the God who rules the sea and the land for the mercy that had spared their brothers from other lands from the mighty power of the raging billows. Instead of reading a printed sermon as usual, he gave an impromptu address relating to the event of the early morning. Its bearing was very religious, and it was as eloquent as it was homely compared with studied discourses.

After the singing of "Nearer, my God, to thee," the service closed; but the people were invited to keep their seats. Without any explanation of what was to follow, the captain introduced Lord Tremlyn.

"Mr. Commander, and ladies and gentlemen, I am

utterly unable to express my high appreciation of the religious service in which we have all assisted. It went to my heart, and I am sure we who have been saved from perishing in the stormy billows joined heartily with him who officiated in giving thanks to God for our preservation," his lordship began.

"We are all profoundly impressed by the kindness, the unbounded hospitality, which have been extended to us in our unfortunate, I may say our forlorn, condition; and I am sure that not one of us, from the amateur captain of the Travancore, to the coolies who were saved by the Blanche, will ever cease to bless the commander, the officers, the crew, and the passengers of the Guardian-Mother for the overwhelming kindness and care they have all bestowed upon us. Though we are not at the festive board, I venture to propose to you the health of Captain Ringgold, as the representative of all to whom we are so gratefully indebted."

"For he's a jolly good fellow!
For he's a jolly good fellow!
For he's a jolly good fellow!
So say we all of us!"

To the astonishment, and perhaps to the disgust, of the two Methodist ladies, Dr. Ferrolan struck up this refrain, singing with a vigor which proved his earnestness. Sir Modava, the engineers, and the cook immediately joined in with him. Dr. Hawkes, Uncle Moses, Mr. Woolridge, and others, because they approved the sentiment of the words, struck in at the second line, and it became a full chorus before the last line was reached.

It is an English custom to follow a toast to a distinguished personage with this refrain, as expressive of the sentiments of the company; and though it was not adapted to Sunday use, it was sincere and heartfelt on the part of all who sang it. Captain Ringgold rose and bowed his thanks, and Lord Tremlyn spoke again:—

"It is very natural that you should desire to know something about the guests who have been so fortuitously cast into your kindly embrace, and especially in regard to the calamity which has made us the recipients of your generous hospitality; and Captain Ringgold gives us this opportunity to gratify your reasonable curiosity. I am no orator, like my brother, the commander of the Guardian-Mother, and I shall call upon my friend and secretary, who has been travelling with me in India for his health, to give you the desired information." Though it was Sunday, even the commander joined in the applause that greeted the doctor when he mounted the rostrum.

"Mr. Commander, and ladies and gentlemen, I beg to inform you that my Lord Tremlyn is quite as capable of speaking for himself as I am for him; but as I am called upon to make this explanation, I shall do so with pleasure. I have the honor to be the secretary of the Right Honorable Viscount Tremlyn, the son of the noble earl who is Secretary of State for India. He has been on a mission in the interests of his father to obtain certain information, though he holds no official position.

"Sir Modava Rao has held several official positions in India, and is perhaps more familiar with the country and its British and native governments than any other man. He has been travelling with Lord Tremlyn, to assist him in obtaining the information connected with his unofficial mission. My lord has completed the work assigned to him; but the viceroy wished him to visit the Imam of Muscat unofficially for a certain purpose I am not at liberty to state.

"In a small steam-yacht owned by Sir Modava, the most devoted friend of his lordship, in which he had been all around the peninsula, and up several of its rivers, we embarked for Muscat, and safely reached that country. Then the viscount decided to proceed to Aden, where he had important business; for he intended to return to England by the Euphrates route, in order to inform himself in regard to the navigation of the river. We sailed for Aden, believing we should have the calm and pleasant weather of the north-east monsoon.

"Yesterday we encountered the gale from the south-west, which was very unusual. But the Travancore was an able seaboat, and we went along very well until we were run into by a steamer in the darkness and mist early this morning. The side of the little steamer was stove in, and she began to fill. We put on our life-preservers, and prepared for the worst. We stretched a life-line fore and aft, and listened to the gurgling waters below deck. Suddenly, when she was partly filled with water, she capsized. We clung to the life-line, which unhitched forward.

"Of course we expected she would go down; but she did not for several hours. We had our life-preservers on, and we made fast the lines forward, which saved us from being washed off the bottom of the vessel. I had a revolver in my pocket, and when I saw the port light of your steamer, I fired it, and we all shouted at the top of our lungs.

"We could hear the air and the water bubbling and hissing under us at times, and it was understood that the confined air above the water in the hull had kept her afloat. But this air had all escaped as the Guardian-mother approached us, and with no warning she went to the bottom. We were floated by our life-preservers till your boats picked us up, though we were fearfully shaken and tossed about by the waves. Our gallant saviours know how we were rescued — all honor and glory to them!"

The doctor finished his explanation and took his seat.

CHAPTER VIII

AN INTERVIEW IN THE CAPTAIN'S CABIN

"Our log-book indicates that we passed a steamer to the northward of us at four bells in the mid-watch," said Captain Ringgold, when Dr. Ferrolan finished his narrative. "She was headed about west by south; and very likely it was the one which ran into the Travancore, for no other was reported."

"She was a vessel of about four hundred tons," added the viscount. "I was in the pilot-house at the time, though the weather was so thick that I could hardly make her out as she slipped off from our starboard bow, and went on her course."

"Didn't she hail you, and offer to stand by you?" inquired the commander.

"I heard something like a shout coming from her, and in a moment she was beyond hailing-distance. I supposed we were going to the bottom in a few minutes, and had my hands full, so that I had no time to look out for her, though I supposed she would come about and render assistance; but we did not hear from her again."

"It is possible that she did so, and was unable to find you, for it was very dark, and the sea was very rough," suggested the commander. "But her conduct looks heathenish, and I will warrant that she was not an English steamer; for the British tars never pass by their fellow-beings on the ocean in distress without rendering assistance."

"It was a new experience to me," added his lordship, "and perhaps I neglected something I ought to have done."

"I think not; for your first and supreme duty at that time was to look out for the safety of your own vessel," replied Captain Ringgold.

"So far as that was concerned, I believe I did all I could do to repair the mischief," continued the viscount. "The chief engineer reported to me that the side of the yacht was stove in near the bow, and that the water was pouring into the hull. He suggested that a double sailcloth be hauled under the vessel. We had no sails, but we promptly made use of an awning, and we succeeded in drawing it under the bottom, and covering the aperture."

"That was precisely the right thing to do," said the commander.

"Probably it enabled us to float a short time longer than we should otherwise have done; but the yacht had taken in too much water before we applied the remedy, for suddenly, on the top of a huge wave, she made a heavy roll, capsized, and came up with her keel in the air. I am only afraid that I did not do all that might have been done."

"I could have done no more if I had been there with all my ship's company," the commander declared; for the amateur captain of the Travancore was a conscientious man, and desired to relieve his mind of all blame for his conduct; and he had really done all that could be done, though the remedy applied was a failure.

"My chief engineer was an experienced man, and I followed his counsels in everything," added the viscount.

"His lordship did all that it was possible for any man to do in such a case," interposed the chief engineer of the Travancore, who was seated on the platform. "I can only thank God that we were all saved, and I am sure that no one is to blame."

"I am told that our cabin waiter and four coolies were picked up by the other steamer," said Lord Tremlyn, as he looked about him.

"That is true, sir," interposed Mr. Boulong, who stood on the deck by the platform. "Sir Modava told me there were eleven persons on board of the wreck. I saw that number saved myself."

The details of the wreck of the Travancore were fully explained, though individuals continued to talk about it until lunch-time. At the mid-day repast the commander gave up his plan of seating the party, and invited the members of it to select their own places; and they all took those they had occupied at breakfast. In the afternoon the rough sea had almost entirely subsided under the influence of the north-east monsoon, and the motion of the steamer was easy and pleasant.

The company assembled in the music-room after a walk on deck, and the captain, with the three notable guests, joined them after they had finished their cigars; for all of them smoked. The "Gospel Hymns" and other hymn and tune books were distributed. It was the usual time for singing, and the trio from the Travancore contributed largely to the volume of tone on the occasion. The new third officer had been stationed in the watch with Mr. Boulong, and Scott had the first part of the afternoon watch. The officers and engineers not on duty, as well as the members of the party from the wreck, gathered at the windows of the music-room, and the commander invited them to take seats in the apartment, thus adding still more to the volume of the harmony. The music was all sacred, and nothing purely secular was permitted by the captain.

Dr. Ferrolan, who had a fine bass voice, was invited to sing "Rocked in the Cradle of the Deep," at the suggestion of Lord Tremlyn. His lordship sang "Oh that I had Wings!" and Mrs. Belgrave, who was the pianist of the occasion, gave a solo, while Sir Modava sang the "Missionary Hymn," which is still a favorite in England and America, translated into the Hindu language. The party who could not understand him followed in the hymn-books.

"I wonder who wrote that beautiful hymn," said Mrs. Blossom, when there was a pause as the singer finished. "It says Heber in my book, but I don't know who he was."

"Reginald Heber was an English clergyman and poet, born in 1783. He was a student in an Oxford college; I forget which," replied Sir Modava.

"Brasenose," prompted the viscount.

"As a student in this college he wrote 'Palestine,' for which he obtained the prize; and it still holds a place in the literature of England. He soon obtained a living, and occupied a prominent position among the clergy of his native island. In 1823 he was made Bishop of Calcutta.

"Three years later, in the midst of his zealous labors in the service of his Master, he died at Trichinopoly of apoplexy, greatly lamented. Perhaps

> 'From Greenland's icy mountains,
> From India's coral strand,'

which you have sung this afternoon, is the widest-known of Bishop Heber's hymns; but will you indulge me if I ask you to sing another of them, which I find in the book I hold in my hand? —

> Brightest and best of the sons of the morning,
> Dawn on our darkness, and lend us thine aid.'"

The hymn was sung to Mozart's music by about twenty voices, and the effect was exceedingly agreeable. Sir Modava seemed to be in a rapture, as the piece was his favorite, and came from one who was connected with his native land.

He was a rather tall and slender man, and all the ladies declared that he was very handsome; and his slightly dusky hue added to, rather than took from, the beauty of his countenance. He wore a small mustache, but no other beard. He was a nervous and highly sensitive person, and there was always a smile on his face. He had already become a favorite among the gentlemen as well as the ladies.

Another meeting was held in the evening, which was varied by some speaking on the part of the gentlemen, including the guests, Uncle Moses, Dr. Hawkes, and the commander. At the conclusion of the exercises, Sir Modava begged the company to close by singing another of Bishop Heber's verses, which he repeated from memory, though it was in one of the books: —

"God that madest earth and heaven,
Darkness and light;
Who the day for toil hast given,
For rest the night, —
May thine angel guards defend us,
Slumber sweet thy mercy send us,
This livelong night!"

With this musical prayer on their lips, the company retired. Most of them went to their staterooms; for the guests were very tired, and the regular inmates of the cabin had left their berths at an unusually early hour in the morning. All of them, whether technically religious or not, had been greatly impressed by the music and the speaking of the evening. Dr. Ferrolan was a more inveterate smoker than his companions in misfortune, and he went with the commander to the deck, and was invited to the captain's cabin, where he was provided with cigars.

"As you have already learned, Doctor, I am greatly interested in the educational feature of my ship," said Captain Ringgold, after they had conversed a while. "I desire to make it as attractive as possible, and I have studied to vary it all I could."

"You have turned your ship into a noble and useful institution," replied the guest. "Lord Tremlyn and Sir Modava have both spoken in the highest terms of this feature. And these lectures are mainly for the benefit of Mr. Belgrave, your owner?"

"The plan was introduced principally on his account; but it has grown into an exercise for all the cabin party, and most of them are speakers as well as listeners; for it makes all of them feel a greater interest in the conferences," replied the commander. "To-morrow we are to begin upon India, dwelling upon its geography, civilization, government, and history. Now, I wish to ask you, Doctor, if there would be any impropriety in my asking the members of your party berthed in the cabin to take part in these exercises?"

"Not the slightest, Captain Ringgold."

"Probably you are all better informed in regard to the affairs of the peninsula than any three other men I could find if I were to search for them here and in England," added the commander.

"You are not far from right, sir, as far as my associates are concerned; for officially or unofficially they have visited every part of India, and studied up in detail everything relating to the people, the country, the army, and the institutions, both native and British."

"As you have been with Lord Tremlyn in his travels, you must be very familiar with the affairs of India, Doctor."

"Reasonably familiar; but not so well acquainted with them as my companions," answered the physician. "Perhaps I do not violate any confidence in saying that his lordship and his Hindu friend had a conversation just before dinner to-day, in which they were discussing in what manner they could best assist you in seeing India. As you suggest, they are the two men who know more of India than any others I think of, not excepting the governor-general and his subordinates."

"I came to this conclusion when I learned the nature of their mission."

"Sir Modava is personally acquainted with all the native princes; and he and his lordship are regarded by them as second only to the viceroy, as he is often unofficially designated. Every door in India, except those of a few mosques and Parsee temples, open to them, and procure for them and their friends all the privileges that can reasonably be expected. We respect the religious exclusiveness of the sects, and do not ask them to exempt our people from the operation of their rules and customs. The British government rules India in the spirit of kindness and toleration, and interferes with the religious, or even political, institutions only so far as humanity and progressive civilization require. Both of them propose to volunteer to attend you in your travels in the peninsula, if agreeable to you."

"We should be delighted to have such conductors, and I shall gladly pay all the expenses incurred," the commander declared, with an earnestness that attested his sincerity.

"The expense is a matter of no consequence to the two gentlemen; for both of them would be multi-millionaires in America, though pounds don't count so numerously as dollars. I am not at all sure they wouldn't gladly pay the expenses of your party as well as their own; but I am not authorized to speak on this point. I advise you not to mention expense to either of my associates. But you can form no idea of the depths of gratitude in the hearts of the three quartered in your cabin for the timely and skilful service you rendered in saving us from certain death. I base my views on what I have heard them say, and what I feel myself," said the doctor with enthusiasm. "I am certain that any suggestion in regard to expense would hurt the feelings of my friends and companions."

"I thank you, Dr. Ferrolan, for the frankness with which you have spoken, and I shall assuredly profit by what you have said," added the commander.

"In what I said about expense I have been moved by what I should do myself if I had the control of the matter, and were as able as Sir Modava and his lordship to incur a heavy outlay; though I have a sufficient income to support a bachelor, I am a poor man compared with them."

The interview closed, and the doctor retired at the end of his cigar. The next morning Captain Ringgold obtained the ready assent of the two gentlemen to take part in the conference appointed for half-past nine, and later that of Dr. Ferrolan.

CHAPTER IX

CONCERNING THE GEOGRAPHY OF INDIA

"Ladies and gentlemen, it affords me very great pleasure to present to you Sir Modava Rao, who has kindly consented to give you a lesson on the geography of India," said Captain Ringgold when the company were seated in Conference Hall.

This announcement was greeted with unusually stormy applause, in which the ladies joined, and then flourished their handkerchiefs as an additional welcome to the handsome Hindu.

"I have also the pleasure to inform you that Lord Tremlyn and Dr. Ferrolan have indulgently permitted me to call upon them for the instruction in regard to India which they are so abundantly competent to give us," continued the commander with a very pleasant smile upon his dignified countenance. "Their subjects have been arranged, and I congratulate you and myself upon the satisfaction with which we shall all listen to these able exponents of the present condition of this interesting country. Sir Modava Rao, ladies and gentlemen."

The Hindu gentleman was again received with vigorous and long-continued applause. His handsome face, the expression of which was intensified by the fascinating smile that played upon his black eyes and around his finely moulded mouth, was not wasted upon the ladies, or even upon the gentlemen; and it was a considerable time before the plaudits of the company permitted him to speak; and he stood upon the rostrum bowing so sweetly that he was irresistible to the assembly.

"Mr. Commander, ladies and gentlemen," he began, "I have no claim upon you for the exceeding warmth of the reception you have given me, and I thank you with all my heart for all your kindness to me, a shipwrecked stranger on board of your ship. I shall give you as briefly and clearly as I can what I know about the geography of India. I understand that this was the subject to be treated by Captain Ringgold; and I am confident that he could have done it quite as well as I can, though I am 'to the manner born.' But I will proceed with the subject, without wasting any more of your valuable time.

"India is a vast territory, forming the southern peninsula of Asia, with a population, including the native states, of very nearly two hundred and fifty-four million people," continued the speaker, taking a paper from his pocket. "I have received a hint from your worthy commander that I ought to give a comparison of my figures with those of the United States, and our population is about four times as great as that of your country.

"The area in square miles is more than a million and a half, enough larger than your country to cover the State of Georgia;" and the speaker indulged in a cheerful smile. "I did not know what I am saying now till this morning; for I have been studying the 'Statesman's Year-Book,' in order to comply with the commander's request.

"The name of India came originally from the Persians, and was first applied to the territory about the Sindhu River, its Sanscrit name, the early literary language of India. A slight change, and the river was called the Hind, which is still the language of the natives, while the country around it is Hind, from which comes Hindu, and Hindustan; but these designations really belong to a province, though they are now given very generally to the whole peninsula," continued Sir Modava, turning to the enormous map which had been painted by Mr. Gaskette and his assistants.

"Hind, or Hindustan, is the territory near the Jumna and Ganges Rivers, of which more will be said later," as he pointed out these great watercourses, and then drew his pointer around Sind, now called Sinde, on the border of Beloochistan.

"How do you spell Hindustan, Sir Modava?" inquired Mrs. Belgrave. "We used to write it Hindoostan when I went to school."

"I think the orthography of the word is a matter of fashion, for the letter *u* in most European and Asiatic languages is pronounced like the English *oo;* but it is now almost universally spelled with a *u*. It is now almost generally absorbed in the name of

India, and the application of the term to the whole of the peninsula is entirely erroneous; and English authorities usually pronounce it so.

"The name India is now given to the peninsula lying to the eastward of the Bay of Bengal. Siam and Tongking are in native possession, or under the protection of France, while Burma is a part of the British Indian Empire. It was only last year that the French had a brush with Siam, and materially strengthened their position there; and it will not be a calamity when all these half-civilized nations are subjected to the progressive influences which prevail in India proper, in spite of all that is said about the greed for power on the part of the great nations of the world.

"But I am wandering from my subject. India is about 1,900 miles in extent from north to south, and 1,600 in breadth in latitude 25° north. The boundaries of this vast country, established by nature for the most part, are the Bay of Bengal (now called a sea in the southern portion) on the south-east, and the Arabian Sea on the south-west. On the north the Himalaya Mountains separate it from China, Thibet, and Turkestan; but some of these countries are called by various names, as Chinese Tartary, Mongolia, Eastern Turkestan, and so on. On the west are Beloochistan and Afghanistan, and on the east Siam and China, though the boundaries were somewhat disturbed last summer in the former."

"We used to pronounce the name of your great

northern range of mountains Hi-ma-lay′-a; you do not call it so, Sir Modava," said the commander.

"I have always called it Hi-mal′-a-ya, the *a* after the accented syllable being very slightly sounded; this is the prononciation of all the Indian officials," replied the speaker, with his pleasant smile. "These mountains consist of a number of ranges; they extend 1,500 miles east and west, and are the sources of the Indus, Ganges, and Brahmaputra. The highest is Mount Everest, the loftiest mountain in the world, 29,002 feet; and I could mention several other peaks which overtop any of the Andes. Himalaya means 'the abode of snow,' and the foot-hills are the resorts of the wealthy to obtain a cool climate in the summer.

"India is remarkable for its fertility, and its luxuriant growth of plants of all sorts, from the productions of the torrid zone to those of the temperate in the hilly regions of the north. It is abundantly watered by the Ganges, the Brahmaputra, the Jumna, the Indus, the Godavari, and other great streams. The Ganges, though it does not vie with the great rivers of America, is 1,557 miles in length. To the natives it is a sacred river, and the land through which it flows is holy ground. To bathe in its waters washes away sin; to die and be buried on its shores procures a free admission to the eternal paradise of heaven.

"The Ganges Canal, constructed in 1854, is 445 miles long, and is used for both navigation and irrigation. Doubtless you will sail upon it, and learn more about it. Near the Indus are two deserts, one 500 miles long, and the other 400, though the grains may be cultivated in the valleys and other low places; and perhaps these regions will be reclaimed by artificial irrigation. In ancient times gold-mines were worked in the south-west, and the currency consisted of this metal instead of silver, as at the present time; but the veins were exhausted, and the Mysore mines are all that is left of them.

"I suppose you Americans have been accustomed to regard India as an exceedingly hot country; and this is quite true of a considerable portion of it. In a region extending from the almost tropical island of Ceylon, nearly 2,000 miles to the snow-capped summits of the highest mountains in the world, there must necessarily be a great variety of climate. India has three well-defined seasons,—the cool, the hot, and the rainy. The cool months are November, December, January, and a part of February.

"The rainy season comes in the middle of the summer, earlier or later, and ends in September. Winter is the pleasantest season of the year; but autumn, unlike England, is hot, moist, and unhealthy. Monsoon comes from an Arabian or Persian word, meaning a season; and you have learned something about it by this time. It is applied to the south-west winds of the Indian Ocean, changing to the north or north-east in the winter. This wind produces rain, and when they infrequently fail, portions of the country are subjected to famines.

"At an elevation of 7,200 feet the temperature is an average of 58° Fahrenheit, as I shall give all readings of the thermometer. At Madras, on the south-east coast, it is 83°; at Bombay, 84°; Calcutta, 79°; and in Delhi, in latitude 29° (about the same as the northern part of Florida), it is 72°. These annual average temperatures will not seem high to you; but I beg you not to form a wrong impression, for the heat of summer is generally oppressive, and the average temperature is considerably reduced by the coolness of the winter months. In Delhi, quoted at 72°, the glass often indicates over 100°.

"The rain varies greatly in different regions. In the north-east it exceeds 75 inches, and in one remarkable year 600 inches fell at an observatory in north-east Bengal. In some of the western parts it is only 30 inches, while it is hardly 15 on the southern shores of the Indus. I think I must have sufficiently wearied you, ladies and gentlemen."

"No! No! No!" almost shouted the company with one voice; and perhaps there was something so fascinating in the manner of the distinguished Hindu which exorcised all weariness from their minds and bodies.

"Thank you with all my heart; but really you must permit me to retire, for I am somewhat fatigued, if you are not, and I shall be happy to contribute to your entertainment at another time," replied the speaker; and he retired from the platform.

"I shall next call upon Mr. Woolridge, who will speak to you of the fauna of India," said the commander.

The magnate of the Fifth Avenue, not much accustomed to speaking in public, was somewhat diffident about addressing the company in the presence of those who were so well versed in Indian lore; but he conquered his modesty, and took his place on the stand. In expressing his appreciation of the last speaker, he mentioned that he occupied a difficult position in the presence of those who knew India as they knew their alphabet, and begged them to consider his talk as addressed only to the Americans of the party. The guests declared that they should be very glad to hear him; and he bowed, smiled, and proceeded with his remarks: —

"Fortunately I have not much to say, for it will consist mainly of the mention of the names of the principal animals in the fauna of India," he began.

"Are all the animals fawns?" asked Mrs. Blossom, who evidently mistook the meaning of the term used.

"No, madam; some of them are snakes. But I shall refer the serpents to Sir Modava; for I am very anxious to hear the views of a native on that subject. The cattle are cows, buffaloes, and oxen, the two latter used as draft animals, and as agricultural workers. Bulls and cows are sacred beasts, and the Hindus never kill them for food."

"Except Christianized natives, like myself," interpolated Sir Modava.

"Thank you. The native breeds of horses have been greatly improved under the direction of the horse-fancying Briton; but they are never used on the farm. Ponies, donkeys, and mules are in use for various purposes. There are plenty of sheep and goats — so there are of hogs; but the higher of the middle class, like the Jews, regard them as unclean beasts, and would as soon take poison as eat the flesh of a pig. I don't sympathize with them, for I like roast pork when it is well brought up and kept clean.

"Monkeys are as tame as they are mischievous; and doubtless they are tame because they are held to be sacred, and have a better time than they do in Africa and elsewhere. But all the fun of the fauna is concentrated in the wild animals, such as the tiger (about the gamiest 'critter' that exists), the panther, cheetah, boar, bear, elephant, and rhinoceros. Two kinds of crocodiles (not alligators) live in the mud and water of the rivers; and I suppose they snap up a man or woman when they get a chance, as they do in the Philippine Islands and other countries. I advise you all to give them a wide berth; for their bite is worse than their bark, like that of some men we know of.

"There are plenty of deer to furnish a dainty and

healthy diet for the meat-eating wild animals, including the lion, which is not much of a king of beasts here, the hyena, the lynx, and the wolf. All of these last take a back seat compared with the tiger. Game and other birds would make a hunter's paradise if it were not for the snakes and tigers, which are unpleasant to an American when his piece is loaded with only birdshot.

"In the towns on the sea the fish are excellent, and an important industry is curing and smoking them for the markets. In the mountain streams the fishing is very good; but in the warm waters of the streams on the plains, as in Egypt, the fish are soft, and neither palatable nor healthy. Leaving the snakes to the tender mercies of the gentleman from Travancore, I will make my bow," which he did, and stepped down.

He was politely applauded, and the strangers seemed to enjoy his discourse more than the rest of the party.

CHAPTER X

THE FLORA AND THE SNAKES OF INDIA

The middle of the day was devoted to recreation. It was a very pleasant day after the storm, and the ship had again struck into the north-east monsoon. While most of the company were planking the promenade deck, it was observed that Lord Tremlyn and Dr. Ferrolan had retired to the library; for though they were very familiar with India and its people, they desired to freshen their memory among the books.

Miss Blanche was walking the deck with Louis on one side of her, and Sir Modava on the other. All the ladies had declared over and over again that the latter was a very fascinating man; but he was a person of discernment, and he could not very well help seeing that the young millionaire had a special interest in the beautiful young lady.

Like a small boy, the young couple ate sugar because they liked it, and not to swell the saccharine importance of the article, and probably never gave a thought to the natural results of their daily intimacy. It is absolutely certain that they had never indulged in any actual "spooning;" for Louis had never proceeded far enough to call the fair maiden by her given name, without "Miss" before it, precisely as everybody else in the cabin did. They were entirely respectful to each other, and she invariably addressed him as Mr. Belgrave.

They were not as familiar as brother and sister, and doubtless neither of them reasoned over the situation, or considered to what it might lead. Though Miss Blanche was with Louis most of the time when they were on deck, and walked and rode with him when they were on shore, she was just as kind and pleasant with all the members of the "Big Four;" and when Louis was engaged in a special study, as when he was preparing his "talk for the conference," Scott or Felix found a chance for a promenade with her. But everybody else on board understood the situation better than those the most intimately concerned. But no one had any objection, not even Mrs. Belgrave or the parents of Miss Blanche.

At half-past three in the afternoon the signal was given for the meeting in Conference Hall. The ladies would have been glad to hear Sir Modava again; but the commander invited the speakers, and kept his own counsels, so that the party did not know whom they were to hear first.

"There is still a great deal to be said about India, and I am trying to dispose of some of the dryest subjects first. Dr. Ferrolan has very unselfishly consented to make a martyr of himself in the treatment of one of these topics, though I hope another time to assign him something more to his mind. Dr. Ferrolan."

This gentleman was received almost as enthusiastically as the handsome Hindu; for the Americans were disposed to treat all their guests with uniform courtesy, though it was hardly possible not to make an exception in favor of Sir Modava.

"Ladies and gentlemen, I have to admit that, with the limitations the excellent commander has put upon me, there is force in what he said about the dryness of the subject. I delight in botany; and it will not be my fault that I fail to interest you, especially the ladies, who are always and everywhere fond of flowers. But I bow to the mandate of the supreme authority here, and will do the best I can with the broad topic with which I am to struggle. But I will do you the justice to believe that you all want to know something more about the fauna of India.

"I have to observe in the first place that almost one-half of this great region is tropical, though not a square foot of it is within three hundred and fifty miles of the equator. In the Himalaya Mountains we have regions of perpetual snow; and in the country south of them it is more than temperate; it is cold in its season. You can see for yourselves that in a territory extending from the island paradise of Ceylon to the frozen regions of the highest mountain in the world, we have every variety of climate, and consequently about every production that grows on the surface of the earth.

"Our tropical productions are not quite equal to

those that grow on the equator. The coffee, sugar, tobacco, and spices are somewhat inferior to those of Java, Sumatra, and Celebes. Rice is the staple food of the common people, and has been raised from prehistoric periods. Maize, which I believe you Americans call Indian corn" —

"Simply corn, if you please," interposed the commander.

"But corn covers grain of all kinds," suggested the doctor.

"Not with us; we call each grain by its own name, and never include them under the name of corn. It is simply the fashion of the country; and if you spoke of corn in Chicago, it would mean maize to the people who heard you."

"I shall know how to speak to an American audience on this subject hereafter; but *corn* and millet are raised for the food of some of the animals. Oilseeds, as flax for linseed, are largely exported. The cultivation of wheat has been greatly improved, and all the grains are raised. In the Himalayas, on the borders of China, teas are grown under European direction; and you will excuse me if I suggest that they are better than those of 'the central flowery nation.' Dye-stuffs, indigo, and lac are noted for their quality and their quantity.

"The native flowers are not so rich as you would expect to find; but the white lilies of the water are as pretty as anywhere, and the flowering shrubs are beautiful. Of course, if you went out to walk in the jungle you would find wild-flowers enough to make a bouquet."

"But who would do it?" asked Mr. Woolridge.

"I would for one," replied the doctor. "Why not?"

"The cobra-de-capello!" exclaimed the magnate.

"They are not agreeable companions; but we don't make half so much of them as you do, sir. I will not meddle with this subject, as it is assigned to another, and I have no desire to steal his thunder-box. We have all the flowers of Europe, and probably of America; but they are not indigenous to the soil, though they thrive very well.

"Especially on the coast, but of course not in the north, you will find stately palms of all varieties. The banian tree (the English write it banyan) grows here, and I might talk an hour about it. Something like it is the peepul, or pipal, though its branches do not take root in the ground like the other. Its scientific name is the *Ficus religiosa;* for it is the sacred fig of India, and it is called the bo-tree in Ceylon.

"The peepul is considered sacred by the Hindus, because Vishnu, the Preserver, and the second person in the Brahminical trinity, was born under it. This tree is extensively planted around the temples of the Hindus, and many religious devotees pass their lives under its shade for its sanctifying influence. It is useful for other purposes; for the lac-insect feeds upon its leaves, and the women get a kind of caoutchouc from its sap, which they use as bandoline."

"What in the world is bandoline, Mister?" asked Mrs. Blossom, who had listened with half-open mouth after the doctor called the tree sacred.

"It is quite English, I dare say," laughed the speaker, while Mrs. Belgrave was tugging at the sleeve of her friend in order to suppress her. "I venture to say you have used something of the kind, madame. Our women make it of Irish moss, and use it to stiffen the hair, so as to make it lie in the right place.

"I must not forget the bamboo, which is found all over India, and even 12,000 feet up the mountains. Of course you know all about it, for the slender stem is carried to all Europe and America. As you look at it you observe that it has the same structure as some of the grasses, the same joints and cells. It is not sugar-cane, but at some seasons a sweet juice flows from the joints, which is here called Indian honey. I have no doubt my young friends have used the bamboo when they went fishing; and the most expensive fly-rods are made from its material, as well as canes, and scores of other useful articles.

"The original forests which once covered hills and plains have been recklessly cut away; and long ago this source of wealth was driven back into the mountains, to the vast injury of the climate and the water supply for the nourishment of the arable lands of the country. But the British government has taken hold of this matter since the middle of the present century, and has made considerable progress towards the restoration of the forests. Not less than 100,000 square miles of land are now under supervision to this end.

"India is a vast territory; but it is estimated that not more than one-third of it is under cultivation, or used for pasturage. Doubtless there is much more of it available; but a considerable of it consists of steep mountain-sides, of deserts, and the beds and overflow of the rivers. With your permission, Mr. Commander, I will retreat from this prominent position, after doing the best I could with a meagre subject;" and the doctor bowed to the audience, while they were applauding him warmly.

"I think you had better make no apology for your treatment of your subject. I can always tell by the expression of the company whether or not the speaker is interesting the party; and I am sure you have succeeded admirably. The next feature to which I call your attention is Sir Modava Rao, on snakes."

The gentleman was received quite as warmly as before; but Mrs. Belgrave was sorry that such a fine-looking gentleman should have to talk about snakes.

"I fully believe that the Good Father of us all distributed poisonous snakes over India for a good and wise purpose, though I do not know what it was; and if I had the power to do so, I should not dare to kill or banish them all, for I know not what injury I might do my country by removing them. Many thousand natives die every year from snake-bites. Statistics say that 20,000 perish in this manner. But that is only one in 14,361; and a single malignant disease has destroyed more than that in the same time.

"The old woman who was accused of cruelty in skinning live eels, replied that she had been doing so all her life, and the eels must be used to it by this time. We are used to snakes in India, and we don't mind them half as much as you think you would if you lived here. The government offers rewards for killing harmful animals, and thousands of snakes are destroyed every year."

"Do you think it is right to kill them if God put them here for a good purpose, Sir Modava?" asked Mrs. Belgrave.

"Certainly I do. God gave us fire: is it right, therefore, to let the city burn up when the fire is kindled? God suffers sin and evil to remain in the world, though he could banish them by a wave of his mighty arm! Shall we not protect ourselves from the tempest he sends? Shall we permit the plague or the cholera to decimate our land because God punishes us in that way for violating the laws he has set up in our bodies?

"This subject is too large for me to pursue it in detail. I need not describe the cobra, for you will see no end of them about the streets of the cities in the hands of the snake-charmers. He is five feet or more in length. His fangs are in his upper jaw. They are not tubed or hollow; but he has a sort of groove on the outside of the tooth, down which the deadly poison flows. In his natural state, his bite is sure death unless a specific or antidote is soon applied. Thanks to modern science, the sufferer from the bite of a cobra is generally cured if the right remedy is applied soon enough. I have been twice bitten by cobras. The medicine used in my case was the *Aristolochia Indica.*

"There is such a thing as a snake-stone, which is applied to the wound, and is said to absorb the blood, and with it the poison; but medical men of character regard it as not entitled to the credit claimed for it. A chemical expert pronounced it to be nothing but a charred bone, which had probably been filled with blood, and again subjected to the action of fire. It is possible that the bone absorbs the blood; but that is not a settled fact, and I leave it to Dr. Ferrolan."

"I believe it is a fraud," replied the doctor.

"The color of the cobra varies from pale yellow to dark olive. One kind has something like a pair of spectacles on the back of his hood, or it looks something like the eyes with which ladies fasten their dress. This hood or bonnet is spread out by the action of the ribs of the creature, and he opens it when he is angry.

"I had a tame mongoose, a sort of ichneumon. This animal, not much bigger than a weasel, is a great cobra-killer, and he understands his business. This snake is given to hiding himself in the gardens around the bungalow for the purpose of preying on the domestic fowls. I found one once, and brought out the mongoose. He tackled him at once, and killed him about as quick as a rifle would have done it. I think you will learn all you want to know about snakes as you travel through India."

Sir Modava retired with the usual applause. As the company returned from the platform, a gun from the Blanche attracted their attention.

CHAPTER XI

A PLEASANT DINNER-PARTY AT SEA

The Blanche was on the starboard beam of the Guardian-Mother, or, in shore parlance, she was on the right-hand side of her as both ships sailed to the eastward. She chose her own position, and it varied considerably at different times, though it was generally about half a mile from her consort. At the present time she had come within less than a quarter of a mile, as the sea was quite smooth.

"Why, the Blanche is all dressed up as though she were going to a ball!" exclaimed Mrs. Belgrave, as the booming gun attracted the attention of the entire party.

"So she is," added the commander, as he observed her altered appearance for the first time; for he had been giving his whole attention to the lecture. "Captain Sharp is evidently getting up some sort of a frolic."

The first gun was followed by a second, and then by a third; and they continued till thirty-one of them had been discharged. Four pieces were evidently used, and they were fired with considerable rapidity, proving that the British tars who formed her ship's company had seen service in the navy.

"What does all that mean?" queried Captain Ringgold, as the party gathered about him for an explanation, though he was as much puzzled as any of them. "It is not a national salute, so far as I know, and I am utterly unable to say what it means."

But as soon as the firing ceased a signal number went up to the fore-peak. Bangs was the signal officer, and he had his book open as soon as he saw that it was needed.

"What is it, Bangs?" asked the commander at the window of the pilot-house.

"'Stop; I have something to communicate,'" replied the quartermaster.

"All right; give her one bell," added the commander.

Bangs gave the proper signal for the affirmative, after he had struck the gong. The letting off of the steam was enough to inform the captain of the Blanche that his request was complied with, and it was seen that he had a boat all ready to drop into the water. The screw of the ship ceased to revolve; and then, to save time, the commander of the Guardian-Mother ordered the quartermaster to ring to back her, and the Blanche followed her example. As soon as the headway was nearly killed, the quarter-boat went into the water, with an officer in uniform in the stern-sheets. The cutter pulled to the American's side, and a ladder was dropped.

The officer was a very trim-looking man of forty,

and was promptly conducted to the commander on the promenade deck. He was as polite as a French dancing-master.

"I have not the honor to be acquainted with Captain Ringgold, but I beg to introduce myself as Mr. Bland, first officer of the Blanche," said the visitor, with all necessary flourishes.

"I am glad to make your acquaintance, Mr. Bland. My friend Captain Sharp appears to be engaged in a frolic this afternoon," replied the commander, shaking hands with the officer.

"This is General Noury's birthday, sir, and Captain Sharp is taking proper notice of it," replied Mr. Bland, as he took from his pocket a note, and delivered it to Captain Ringgold.

"The general's birthday!" exclaimed the commander. "I wish him many happy returns of it;" and he opened the note.

It took him but a minute to read it, and then he looked extremely good-natured, as though he was more than ordinarily pleased; for he knew that its contents would afford a great deal of satisfaction to his passengers.

"By particular request of General Noury, in whose honor the guns were fired and the Blanche is dressed as you see her, Captain Sharp invites all the cabin party of the Guardian-Mother, including the guests, to dine on board of the Blanche on this happy occasion. Shall the invitation be accepted? Those in favor of accepting it will please raise the right hand,

and keep it up till counted," continued the commander, who was in a merry mood for him. "Our honored guests are expected and requested to vote; for we could not think of leaving them alone on board of the ship. That would be neither decent nor hospitable, and the invitation specially includes them. Please to vote, all."

The hands all went up; and the party seemed to be greatly amused at the operation of voting. The presiding officer declared that it was a unanimous vote, and the invitation was accepted.

"Not quite unanimous, Mr. Commander," interposed Louis Belgrave. "Mr. Scott did not vote."

"You wish to vote in the negative, Mr. Scott?" inquired the captain.

"I do not intend to vote at all, Captain," replied the third officer. "It would be a little cheeky for me to vote to leave the ship without the permission of the captain or of the first officer."

"'In colleges and halls in ancient times there dwelt a sage called Discipline;' and a very good old fellow he was to have about, and quite as good on board ship as in institutions of learning. Do you wish to accept the invitation, Mr. Scott?" asked the commander.

"I should be exceedingly happy to do so."

"Then ask Mr. Boulong's permission."

"Granted!" shouted the first officer, who stood within hearing.

"Mr. Bland, give my compliments to Captain Sharp, and inform him that his invitation is unanimously accepted by both passengers and guests, and we will be on board at five o'clock," said Captain Ringgold, addressing the officer from the Blanche; and he went over the side into his boat.

"You don't give us much time to get ready, Mr. Commander," said Mrs. Belgrave, as all the ladies hurried away to the cabin to prepare for the grand occasion that had so suddenly dawned upon them.

"Elaborate toilets are hardly expected at sea, out of sight of land. Claw-hammer coats are not imperative, gentlemen," said the captain.

Though the two steamers were not in a hurry, both of them resumed their course as soon as the Blanche's boat was hoisted up to the davits; for it is part of the shipmaster's gospel to "keep moving" under all possible circumstances, and to lose no time in arriving at his destined port. All the passengers went below to prepare for the dinner. The Blanche had come within fifty yards of her consort, as the sea was quite smooth.

"Where is that music, Mr. Boulong?" asked the captain, opening the door from his cabin to the pilot-house.

"From the Blanche, Captain."

"But it seems to be a band. Is it an orchestrion?"

"Not at all; there are eight pieces of music on the promenade deck. It seems that His Highness has a small band on board, though I have not heard it before," added the first officer.

The commander thought the music was very fine,

and he concluded that Captain Sharp was running near the Guardian-Mother for the purpose of giving the band an introduction to the consort. Besides the ship's company, there was no one on board of the Blanche but the general and Mrs. Sharp; and the Pacha, accustomed as he was to merriment and revelry, must have been rather lonesome. But it was already proved that he was a reformed man, and had entirely changed his manner of life.

The barge, which was a large eight-oar boat, had been made ready to lower into the water, and the gangway had been rigged out. Though it was winter, the ship was in 18° north latitude, and the weather was as mild and pleasant as in midsummer. There was no spray, and the ladies could go to the Blanche as comfortably as in a carriage on shore.

At quarter before five the gong was sounded in the cabin and on deck to call the party together in the boudoir, where they were to assemble. The ship stopped at the mandate of the captain, and the barge was lowered, and brought to the gangway. The boat was as handsome as anything that ever floated, and the stern-sheets were luxurious enough for a fairy craft. The crew of nine were all dressed in their white uniforms, and sat with their oars tossed, except the cockswain, who stood bolt upright abaft the back-board.

There were sixteen in the party, and the "Big Four" made their way to the fore-sheets; the ladies were handed into the stern by the three guests, and the barge shoved off. The Blanche had taken a position on the beam of the Guardian-Mother, her band playing for all they were worth. Captain Sharp was on the platform of the gangway, and took every lady by the hand as he assisted her to disembark. At the head of the gangway on deck stood General Noury, who received the ladies, all of whom he had met before; and the distinguished guests were presented to him, after which he shook hands with every other member of the party. He was especially respectful, and even reverential, to the commander of the Guardian-Mother, who had forgiven so much in his past conduct.

Mrs. Sharp came in for a large share of the consideration of the visitors. An hour was spent in the drawing-room, as they called the deck cabin, which was as large as the boudoir and music-room of the Guardian-Mother. The band had laid aside their brass instruments, and organized as an orchestra, stationed in a sort of recess in the forward part of the cabin. The general conversed with every person in the party; and when Scott addressed him as "Your Highness," he protested that he did not wish to hear the expression again.

He talked French with Louis, Italian with Sir Modava, and Spanish with Lord Tremlyn; for it was understood that he spoke at least half a dozen languages besides his own, and the guests found he was equally fluent in all they knew. To Miss Blanche he was very polite; but he did not give a moment more to her than to the other ladies, much to the satisfaction of her parents.

The dinner was fully equal to Mr. Sage's best efforts, and the occasion was as hilarious and as pleasant as it could be. Possibly the English guests missed their wine on such an occasion. Lord Tremlyn declared that he seldom drank it at all, and Dr. Ferrolan said the same; and Sir Modava was the strictest sort of a teetotaler, having been engaged in preaching this doctrine among the Sepoys as opportunity offered. The captain of the Blanche informed the commander of the Guardian-Mother that the general had never touched wine since he came on board.

After dinner several of the gentlemen sang songs, and the general gave one in Moroccan, which amused the party, though they could not understand a word of it. Later in the evening Captain Ringgold made a speech complimentary to General Noury, and wished him many happy returns of the occasion they celebrated. He was followed by Dr. Hawkes, Uncle Moses, Professor Giroud, and then by the three distinguished guests from the Travancore.

The general replied to all of them at the close of the entertainment. He was a pleasant speaker, and his handsome face added a great deal to his words. The affair was declared to be a great success for a dinner-party at sea, and the commander of the Guardian-Mother invited all their hosts to assist him in a similar one on board his ship, the signal for which was to be the American Union Jack when the weather was suitable.

The party returned to their ocean home; and the commander spent the rest of the evening in telling his guests the story of General Noury, and especially of his wonderful reformation.

"Then Captain Sharp really saved his life?" added Lord Tremlyn.

"No doubt of it. The two ruffians in a street of Messina had disabled the general, and would certainly have finished him if the captain had not wounded one with his revolver, and tackled the other. He owes his life to Sharp without a doubt. Mrs. Sharp took care of him for quite a time while he was recovering from his wound, and she made a deep impression upon him. He is a Mohammedan, and he sticks to his religion; but even that is capable of making a better man of him than he was before."

"I was much pleased with Mrs. Sharp, not because she is an English woman, but because she is a very worthy person," added his lordship.

"You are quite right, my lord, and she has had a romantic history;" and before they retired he had told the whole of it.

At the usual time the next day the company were assembled in Conference Hall; and when the commander announced that Lord Tremlyn would address them on the general subject, "The People of India," they manifested their interest by a liberal salvo of applause.

CHAPTER XII

THE POPULATION AND PEOPLE OF INDIA

"Ladies and gentlemen, I am happy to appear before you, and to look you all in the face," his lordship began as the applause subsided. "The task befaw me is to put a gallon of fluid into a pint pot. It cawn't be done. I shall not attempt to do what is quite impossible. I can only put in what the vessel will hold. I cawn't say all there is to be said about the people of India in an hour, or even two or three hours."

The noble gentleman was an easy, pleasant, and fluent speaker, evidently quite accustomed to addressing public assemblies; but he had certain peculiarities of speech, a very few of them, which sounded just a little odd to the Americans, as doubtless some of their pronunciation did to the Britons. But there is hardly a perceptible difference in the pronunciation of highly trained speakers of one nation and the other. It is not necessary to indicate any farther the slightly peculiar speech of the accomplished gentleman.

"I can only select from the mass of material before me what I think will be most interesting and useful to you; for I have been warned that I must not talk all day," continued the viscount.

"We leave that to your lordship's own judgment," added Captain Ringnold.

"I will be merciful, Mr. Commander; as merciful as possible. Next to China, India is the most populous country on the globe; and without Nepaul, it numbered, in 1891, 287,223,917, or more than one-seventh of the people on the face of the earth; and the increase in the last decade was almost 28,000,000, — enough to populate about a dozen of your larger States.

"In spite of its vast population, India cannot be said to be a very densely peopled region; 184 to the square mile for the whole country. The mountain territory is quite thinly settled. All the native states have but 108 to the square mile, though the plains of the Ganges show about 400. About Benares and Patna the average is about double these figures. I was looking at the 'Year-Book' in your library, and I saw that the average in the States, including Alaska, is about 18 to the square mile; but the nine States in the north-east have 107.

"The little bit of a State of Rhode Island leads in the density of its population, with 318, while Massachusetts comes next with 278. New Jersey has 193, Connecticut, 154; the big States of New York and Pennsylvania have respectively 126 and 117. In the United Kingdom the average in England is 541; in Scotland, 135; in Wales, 206; and in Ireland, 144. The density of India, therefore, is quite respectable by comparison.

"By the census of 1891, India has seventy-five towns with over 50,000 inhabitants, and twenty-eight with over 100,000; but unlike three cities of the States, it has not one with over a million, though Calcutta and Bombay are likely to reach that distinction in another decade. You have not a monopoly of the fast-growing cities in the States."

"We have found out that Berlin has increased faster than Chicago," said Uncle Moses with a chuckle; "and Glasgow has got ahead of Liverpool."

"Quite true, Mr. Scarburn; but the States have not all the fast-growing cities of the world, wonderful as the increase has been in some of them. Europe, Asia, and Australia are alive. The nearest approaches to a million in India are Calcutta, 861,764, and Bombay, 821,764; but I dare say you are all quite tired of statistics by this time."

"Not at all, Lord Tremlyn; as you present them they are quite interesting." said Mrs. Belgrave.

"Thank you, madam," replied the speaker, bowing low, with his hand on his heart. "Now I am going to speak of the people as other than mere numbers; and if I wished to entangle you inextricably, I should go back about 4,000 years, and tell you about the people down to the present time. I spare you the infliction in full. Four groups of languages are spoken among the natives, and from these the original races that spoke them are traced out.

"I mention one as a specimen, the Kolarian

language, spoken by those who first settled in the hilly regions of the central part. The others are the Aryan, Dravidian, and Tibeto-Burman, all of which you will find in 'Chambers's' in your library.

"The word Hindu is generally used in a very broad sense to cover all the native population of Hindustan or India; but it is really applicable to a religion, and belongs only to those of the Hindu, or the faith of the Brahmins; but, like most others, it consists of a great number of sects. Of this belief there are about 200,000,000 people. They are divided into four grand classes, called castes. The Portuguese called them *casta* in their own language, from which the present name comes. I call them grand classes, or castes, because they are divided into many sub-classes.

"When the Aryans, who came from Europe, and Asia farther north than India, obtained a foothold here, and established themselves, they looked down upon other people in the land, and called themselves the twice-born, or born again, as some modern sects have it. They claimed to have experienced a second, or religious, birth, indicated by a certain cord with which they were invested at a particular age. The natives of the soil and all other outsiders were the once-born.

"In the lapse of time the twice-born were divided into three classes, the Brahmins being the priestly class, the Kshatriyas the ruling military, and the Vaisyas the agricultural classes. These were of the upper grade; and all the once-born were called Sudras. These four classes are the origin of caste, though the divisions have been greatly changed. The Vedas are the four oldest sacred books of the Hindus, otherwise the Hindu Scriptures.

"Derived from their holy books is the allegorical idea that the Brahmin, or priest, was the mouth of the original man; the warrior his arms; the agriculturist his thighs; while the Sudra, or common people, sprang out of his feet. The duties and relations of the four castes are defined and stated in the laws of Manu."

"We have not been introduced to him," suggested Mrs. Woolridge.

"He is regarded as the author of the most noted law-book among the Hindus; but there is so much that is mythical and contradictory said of him, that I will say nothing more about him; but he is authority among the Brahmins. In modern caste the Brahmin is the minister of religion; he alone mediates between God and man, makes sacrifices, and teaches the sacred Veda. His life is portioned off into periods of special duty. As a student he learns the Veda; then he gets married, becomes a householder, and must every day perform the appointed sacrifice. Some of them live in the woods, as hermits, or live like monks, till they are said to be absorbed into Brahma.

"The soldier's sphere is in connection with the State, to support the Brahmin, and execute the laws he makes or interprets. The third class cultivate the soil as proprietors, and engage in trade and commerce. The Sudra is the servant of all the others. Resulting from the intermarriage of members of different castes there are various mixed classes. The lowest is the child of a Brahmin mother and a Sudra father, though in Southern India the Pariah is still lower.

"Of the vast population of India, three-fourths are Hindus in religion. The Buddhists are mostly in Burma, and there are over 57,000,000 Mohammedans. The number of Christians by the last census was 2,284,380; and I am sorry there are no more of them. The Sikhs and the Jains are Indian sects which flourish in certain localities; as there are nearly two millions of the former in the Punjab, and over half a million of the latter in Bombay, and approaching that number in Rajputana, with comparatively few elsewhere. The Parsees, or Parsis, who were driven from Persia by the Mohammedans, number 76,774 in Bombay,—not the city, but the presidency.

"In the small state of Travancore, where my friend Sir Modava was born, there are said to be four hundred and twenty different castes. The distinction is sometimes the result of occupation, branch of trade, or some accidental circumstance. Let me read a short extract from a book from your library:—

"'Among the lowest classes caste has degenerated into a fastidious tenacity of the rights and privileges of station. For example, the man who sweeps will not take an empty cup from your hand; your groom will not mow a little grass; a coolie will carry any load, however offensive, on his head, but even in a matter of life and death would refuse to carry a man, for that is the business of another caste.

"'When an English servant pleads that such a thing is not his place, his excuse is analogous to that of the Hindu servant when he pleads his caste. When an Englishman of birth or profession, which is held to confer gentility, refuses to associate with a tradesman or mechanic; or when members of a secret society exclude all others from their meetings; or when any other social distinction arises, it would present itself to the mind of the Hindu as a regulation of caste.'

"It is a barrier to the progress of Christianity in many ways. It is generally thought that a Christian convert cannot be restored to his caste if he should backslide; and the superstition of the low-class natives is a rhinoceros shield, which it is still difficult to penetrate; but in the end the Cross will come off conqueror, as it always has and always will.

"Caste does not now compel a native to pursue his father's calling, except, perhaps, in the case of Brahmins. For that matter, Brahmins serve in the army, and even act as cooks and in similar occupations. Men of all castes have risen to exalted positions, just as poor men, with none of the advantages of high birth, have in England. The loss of caste has been regarded by the ignorant native here as the most terrible thing that could possibly happen to him; but it is not so in practice, for it has been accomplished by giving a very indifferent supper.

When an outcast enters another caste, he is well and heartily received as a convert. As you proceed through India you will learn more about this stumbling-block of superstition and ignorance.

"The 57,000,000 Mohammedans, of whom 23,658,000 are in Bengal, and over 6,000,000 in Bombay, are either descendants of emigrating Asiatics, or Hindus converted to that faith. Their religion is a mixture of the doctrines of the Prophet and local idolatry; for they have been somewhat infected by the prevailing worship of the natives. The Parsees are an educated mercantile class, the great body of them being found in Bombay. They are fire-worshippers; and their creed is that of Zoroaster, who flourished not less than 800 years before Christ. The Zend-Avesta is the sacred book of the sect, containing their religion and their philosophy. The Caliph Omar conquered the Persians, and established Mohammedanism there, persecuting all who would not believe. The obstinate Parsees fled to India.

"The Parsees of the present day are their descendants, and still cling to their ancient faith. Like all sects, they are fully tolerated by the British government, and are considered one of the most respectable and thriving classes of the community. They are largely merchants and land-owners, and bear the highest reputation for honesty, industry, and as peaceful citizens. They are quite prepossessing, and many of their ladies are remarkably beautiful, though I have seen a fairer American than any one of them.

"Some of them have studied law in England, and all are forward to avail themselves of the advantages of education. A merchant-prince of this sect was noted as a philanthropist; and for the vast sums of money he gave for benevolent institutions, the Queen knighted him, as she did Sir Modava for his public service. This gentleman is Sir Jamsetjee Jejeebhoy He died in 1859.

"Parsees do not eat anything cooked by a person of another religion, and reject beef and pork, especially hams. They are not permitted to marry outside of their own sect. Their dead are not buried or cremated, but are committed to what is called the Tower of Silence. The bodies are exposed on an iron grating, where the carniverous birds of the air can get to them until the flesh has all disappeared. Then the sun-dried bones fall through into a receptacle, from which they are removed to a cavern in the earth."

"How horrid!" exclaimed the ladies with one voice.

"The Parsee does not think so; and perhaps he has the same view you have of our manner of disposing of the dead. In spite of the awe and respect with which the Parsees regard fire, they are about the only eastern people who do not smoke. But I think you need a rest by this time, and I will retire for a little while."

The company applauded as usual, and then began to pace the promenade deck.

CHAPTER XIII

LORD TREMLYN DISCOURSES MORE ABOUT INDIA

The delightful weather of the forenoon charmed the party as they walked the deck. It was midsummer in the middle of the winter, as they looked at it; for the almanac of home lingered in their minds, though the days were longer. The sun was rather warm on both sides of noon, though it was not oppressive, and the abundant awnings protected the passengers from its more searching rays.

Statistical as the lecture had been, the viscount had made it interesting by softening the figures with his comparisons; and some of his points, even in regard to the States, were new to them, and especially in regard to the United Kingdom. In about half an hour they were summoned to Conference Hall again for a continuation of the lecture.

"From the vast emigration to your country, ladies and gentlemen, I suppose there must be a great variety of people on your territory. The Germans, the English, the Irish, the Scandinavians, the Italians, and other nationalities, in the process of assimilation, although very many of them have become as American as Americans themselves, take the manners and customs, the national peculiarities, of the fatherland with them.

"The Irish drink whiskey, the Germans beer, and the Italians are apt to have a stilletto about them. Then the antecedents, climate, politics, and other influences, have made the East differ from the West, and the South from both of them. Lynch law prevails to a considerable extent in the latter, never in the Eastern and Middle States, and very rarely in the West. But all Americans speak the same language; and foreigners are compelled to learn English in order to get on at all, and it has become one of the bonds of your union.

"In India there are not less than twenty-seven languages and dialects in use; and they indicate so many different kinds of people, for we can hardly call them nations, though in many respects they are such. This excellent map behind me, which is worthy of the highest praise as a home-made production, will enable me to give you a better idea of my subject.

"The ingenious artist has colored the different divisions so that you can make them out. The three presidencies are the most notable divisions, and they include all the inferior ones. The Bengal Presidency includes the north-eastern part, from Afghanistan to Burma. The Madras, the south-eastern part, with most of the peninsula. The Bombay covers the greater part of the west coast. The Deccan is a portion of the peninsula.

"It would take me three weeks to describe all the divisions of India, and I shall not attempt to do it. It would be better done as you travel over the country. Eighteen of them are directly governed by the English, and thirteen of them are still under the nominal control of the native princes; but all the latter have a British resident as the adviser of the reigning rajah.

"The English-speaking people of India are a mere bagatelle compared with the enormous population, being only 238,499; but with the army they have been able to hold the country in subjection. The British government takes a fatherly interest in the native states, and they have been loyal without exception in later years, though the history of India will show that not all of them have always been so.

"Until the year 1858 the government was in the hands of the East India Company, of which you will learn more in the history of India. In 1877 her majesty, the queen, assumed the title of Empress of India, and she is the ruler of the country. The government of the highest resort in the affairs of India is a secretary of state, residing in London. He is a member of the cabinet, and has an under-secretary. He is assisted by a council of ten or fifteen members.

"The executive government, administered in India, is the governor-general in council. He is the viceroy of the crown, and is assisted by six members of the executive council, each of whom has his function in the affairs of the state; and the commander-in-chief of the army is *ex-officio* a seventh member. This body is really the cabinet of the viceroy. The laws are made by this council, with from six to a dozen members appointed by the viceroy. This is the way the machine is operated.

"The civil service of the government is rendered mainly by Europeans, though the natives are eligible to office as employees. The English system in the appointment of its officials prevails, and all candidates are regularly examined. Those of you who have looked over Bradshaw's 'Guide to India' will find descriptions of the several examinations for various employments."

"I wish the English system could be transferred to the United States," said Uncle Moses with great unction.

"You have made a beginning, and perhaps you will come to it in time. The civil service prevails in the provinces and states of India as well as in the general government, though the competition is open to the natives.

"The soldiers of the East India Company became the military force of the British crown when the government was assumed. The English army in India now consists of 74,033 men of all arms, and the native army of 144,735, a total standing army of 218,786, which is its strength at the present time. It is a curious fact that, as the native troops are recruited by voluntary enlistment, all castes and races, including Brahmins, are drawn in by the good pay and the pension promised.

"The navy of the East India Company was superseded by the royal navy in 1863; and a dozen or fifteen ships of war are stationed in these waters, with an admiral as commander-in-chief, whose headquarters are at Bombay. The Indian treasury contributes annually to the expense of this force. The great steam navigation companies are available to recruit this branch of the defence of the country.

"The laws are made, and the institutions of India are regulated, by Parliament; and the administration of law and justice is substantially the same as in the United Kingdom. The regular police consists of 160,000 officers and men; and a portion of the expense of this force is defrayed by the towns, the large cities mainly. Besides the city police, there are 560,000 in charge of the villages. The constabulary are natives, with European officers, one to every seven square miles and 1,300 inhabitants, indicating peaceful communities. About 12,000 of the 82,000 persons under sentence are in the convict colonies at the Andaman Islands.

"The educational institutions are progressive, and 400 newspapers are published in various languages, most of them with small circulations, 20,000 being the largest in India. The post and telegraph systems are well cared for; and 17,564 miles of railway are in operation, with others in process of construction. The manufactures, both in metal and fibre, have always been remarkably fine, and the quality is still kept up. Cotton factories have been established, with native labor, which promise great results to the industry of the country.

"The loss of life on account of famine, caused by the failure of the monsoon rains, has been terrific in some years. Canals and reservoirs for irrigation as well as navigation have been built in order to remove this evil. In 1874 £16,000,000 was expended in the relief of sufferers by the government. Since that time a famine fund has been established; and in years of plenty a million and a half sterling has been set aside for this object.

"The excessive density of the population has induced the government to favor emigration; and over a hundred thousand have gone to British Guiana and the West Indies, and other countries. The currency of India will be likely to bother you a little. The silver *rupee* is the unit; though when you see 'R. x.' over or at the left of a column of figures, it means tens of *rupees*. The nominal value of a *rupee* is two shillings, about half a dollar of your money; but it is never worth that in gold, the standard of England in recent years. It was some years ago at a premium of twopence, but for the last three years it has averaged only 1*s.* 5⅛*d.* Its value varies with the gold price of silver in London.

"There is also a government paper currency in circulation, amounting to £16,000,000 sterling. The smallest copper coin is the *pie*, worth half a farthing, equal to a quarter of a cent of your money. Three of them make a *pice*, a farthing and a half, three-quarters of a cent. Four *pice* make an *anna,* a penny and a half, three cents. Sixteen *annas* make a *rupee.* Sixteen *rupees* make a gold *mohur.*"

"Those small pieces are about as insignificant as those of Egypt," suggested Mr. Woolridge.

"There are not many millionaires among the natives, and these smaller coins are mostly used among them. They are convenient also to the stingy Englishman when the plate is passed around in church," added his lordship with a chuckle, which pleased Uncle Moses more than the remark. India has a public debt of about £200,000,000, contracted for railways, canals, war, and other purposes. The revenue last year was £84,932,100, and the expenditures were £84,661,700. Not a large margin; but you must multiply the pounds by five, or nearly that, to reduce them to dollars.

"The poppy is extensively cultivated in India; and the export tax in Calcutta amounts to six and a quarter millions, in Bombay, to three and a half millions, on the manufactured opium. The producer sends his crop to the government factory, whence it is sold to the exporter; all this to prevent frauds on the revenue.

"Wages and prices have gone up under British rule. The best class of laborers get four *annas* a day, and others not more than two, — six to twelve cents a day. Grain for food is a penny for two pounds, — a cent a pound. Women and children earn small wages. The clothing of the poor is scanty and cheap; fuel costs nothing; and rent for dwellings is hardly known. The masses in the country, not laborers, live on the land as owners or lessees. There has never been anything like a poor-law, and ordinarily there is no need of such.

"It would be quite impossible for me to give the history of India in detail in the limited time at my command, especially as we are now approaching the land. Vasco da Gama, the Portuguese navigator, was the first to reach the East Indies, in 1498; but his countrymen never did much trading here, being more intent upon securing the rich treasures of the Indies. As early as 1600 the English turned their attention in this direction. Companies were formed; but being driven by the Dutch from the islands which they still hold, they began to make settlements on the coast of this peninsula. Madras dates from 1639, Bombay from 1686, Calcutta from 1686. The Company said, 'Let us make a nation in India;' and they went to work at once to do it. They accomplished their purpose, fostered by the government, raised and borrowed money, and in the course of time had an army and a navy, and ruled the country. They defeated the Grand Mogul, drove the French out of the peninsula, and were generally very prosperous.

"In 1833 Parliament revoked all the trading privileges of the company; and their dividends to stockholders were then paid out of the taxes assessed on the people of India. They could not trade and could not govern except under the control of Parliament. All the wars of India have been fought by the British nation. After the mutiny, of which more hereafter, the company was compelled to cede its powers to the crown in 1858.

"The native soldiers of Bengal were called Sepoys, and the name has been applied to all native troops. Some small mutinies occurred in this arm of the service in the presidency. Early in 1857 the garrison of Meerut, near Delhi, revolted, and the British troops failed to suppress it. The Sepoys marched to Delhi, where they were joined by the native troops and the mob. The descendant of the Great Mogul, who lived in the palace of his ancestors under British protection, was proclaimed emperor, and his empire re-established.

"Probably 90,000 soldiers, infantry and cavalry, were in a state of rebellion. In many instances they had murdered their officers and their families. They were spread over a broad country, and held forts, arsenals, and treasuries. They were disciplined troops armed with European artillery and muskets, and supplied with ammunition. In portions of the country the British were isolated, as in the camp before Delhi, and in the works at Agra, Allahabad, and Lucknow. The mutiny extended over an area of 100,000 square miles, with a population of 40,000,000. It came at the worst season of the year; and if it had not been speedily suppressed, it would have spread over the whole country. Many believed that the knell of the empire had sounded.

"At that time there were 40,000 European troops"—

"Land, ho!" shouted the lookout man; and the cry was repeated by the sailors and the officers.

"We will attend to the land now, and I will resume latter," said Lord Tremlyn, as he descended from the rostrum.

CHAPTER XIV

SIR HENRY HAVELOCK AND THE MUTINY

The announcement that land was in sight produced some excitement, and the speaker good-naturedly paused to enable the company to see whatever was to be seen. They looked to the eastward, but they could see nothing. They stood upon the promenade, and strained their eyes to the utmost; but it required a nautical eye to make land out of the dim haze in the distance, for that was all there was of it.

"I can readily understand your desire to obtain the first view of India," said Lord Tremlyn.

"But they will not obtain it yet a while," added the commander.

Louis and Felix had ascended the fore-rigging, and discovered what might have been the land or a bank of clouds. There were a great number of boats and small craft in sight, but none of them were near enough to be seen distinctly. They observed that the Guardian-Mother had reduced her speed.

"We shall not be where you can see anything for an hour or more," continued Captain Ringgold. "We have to pass some rather dangerous rocks in this vicinity, and we shall proceed cautiously till we take a pilot."

"A number of large vessels have been wrecked in this locality," said the viscount; "and in a little while you will get in among the multitude of fishing-craft that swarm off the islands."

When the company were satisfied that there was nothing to be seen, they resumed their seats, and the "live boys" in the fore-rigging returned to their places. All were greatly interested in the viscount's account of the mutiny; and he had suspended his narrative just where cunning writers of exciting stories place the "To be continued."

"I had hardly finished what I had to say, or at least what I intended to say; for there are still a great many points upon which I have not touched, leaving them to be brought up as you proceed on your travels through this interesting country," said Lord Tremlyn.

"Go on! Go on!" said quite a majority of the party.

"I have been here before, and perhaps you will excuse me if I have occasion to leave before your lordship has finished; and with this understanding, I think you had better proceed," added the commander.

"I will do so with the greatest pleasure," replied the speaker, as he took his place on the rostrum again. "I have described the terrible situation to which the English in India had been reduced, with nearly a hundred thousand Sepoys in rebellion, and the troops outnumbered a hundred to one, shut up in camps and forts. The fanatical and blood-thirsty mob, far greater than the body of native soldiers, were eager to fall upon and slaughter all Europeans.

"At this time there were 40,000 British troops scattered over the country; several thousand men on their way from England to China were diverted to this country. Forty thousand from home were on their voyage of 12,000 miles around the Cape of Good Hope to relieve the besieged garrisons. But in the midst of the gloom of this miserable summer there was a gleam of sunshine, and the sad disasters at Cawnpore and elsewhere were partially retrieved. This came on the appearance of Henry Havelock, whose noble example of a true life I commend to my young friends here who are just entering upon their careers.

"Havelock was born in 1795. His father was a merchant, and he was well educated. He was at first intended for the law; but he followed the example of his brother, and entered the army a month after the battle of Waterloo. In 1823 he was sent to India; and on the voyage he became a Christian in the truest sense of the word, and this event influenced his life. He was employed in the Afghan and Sikh wars; but he had learned 'to labor and to wait,' and he was still a lieutenant after twenty-three years' service.

"He was in command of a division of the army that invaded Persia in 1856. The news of the Indian mutiny called him hastily to Calcutta. Following the Ganges to Allahabad," continued the speaker, pointing out the river and the city on the map, "he organized, at this point, a force of two thousand men, and pushed on for Cawnpore, driving the enemy before him. At Fatehpur the rebels made a stand; but they broke before his little band, and he hastened on to his destination.

"Nana Sahib, the native leader of the mutiny, was the adopted son of the former peshwa, or ruler, of the Mahrattas, as certain states in the west and middle of India are called. His foster-father had been deprived of his dominion, and lived on a pension paid by the British. The son had been brought up as a nobleman, with expensive habits. When the father died in 1851, the pension was not continued to the son. He was bitterly disappointed that his income was cut off, and it stirred up all the bad blood in his nature, and there was a good deal of it. He did his best to foment discontent, and succeeded too well; for the mutiny was his work.

"As Havelock and his puny force approached Cawnpore, this miscreant incited the cold-blooded massacre of all the women and children the rebels had captured on the day before the place was taken. The intrepid general found the Sepoys strongly intrenched at a village; but he turned their left, and carried the works by a splendid charge of the 78th Highlanders. Entering Cawnpore, he saw the results of the atrocious massacre in the mutilated bodies of the women and children with his own eyes.

The sight inspired the little band of heroes with renewed courage, and Havelock began his march upon Lucknow.

"After fighting eight victorious battles, his little force was so reduced by sickness and fatigue that he was forced to retire to Cawnpore. In September General Outram arrived there with additional troops, and operations against Lucknow were renewed. The general in command of this force outranked Havelock, and the command belonged to him; but with a noble generosity he waived his claim, and served in the expedition under his victorious subordinate as a volunteer.

"Havelock's army now numbered 2,500 men, with seventeen guns. He encountered the enemy, and scattered them several times. They reached the thickly settled town where each house was a fortress, and with valor equal to anything on record, fought their way to the Residency, where they were rapturously received by the beleaguered garrison.

"But with all that could be mustered they were only a handful of men compared with the hosts that surrounded them, and in turn they were at once besieged by the rebels. They were not the men to yield to any odds; and they held their own till November, when Sir Colin Campbell, with 4,700 regulars, forced his way through the enemy, and relieved the place. He was one of the bravest and most distinguished generals of modern times. He fought in the United States in 1814, and in many other parts of the world. He was in the Crimea, and Alma and Balaklava are called his battles; for he did the most to win them.

"In India he completed the work which Havelock had begun, and the following year announced to the viceroy that the rebellion was ended. Just before he had been created Lord Clyde. On his return to England he was made a field-marshal, and received a pension of £2,000.

"To return to Havelock, great honors were bestowed upon him. He was made a baronet, created a Knight Commander of the Bath, and a pension of £1,000 was awarded to him. But he did not live to enjoy his rewards and honors, or even to see the end of the mutiny at which he struck the first heavy blows. In that very month of November when Sir Colin came to the rescue, Havelock was taken with dysentery, died on the twenty-second, and was buried in the Alum-Bagh, the fort containing a palace and a fortress, which he had carried in his last battle.

"Havelock was very strict in his religious principles, and a rigid disciplinarian in the army. He was like the grave and fearless Puritan soldier, somewhat after the type of 'Stonewall Jackson' of your Civil War, though not as fanatical. In his last moments he said: 'For more than forty years I have so ruled my life that when death came I might face it without fear.' This he did; and England will never cease to remember the Christian hero, Sir Henry Havelock. In Trafalgar Square, in London, you may see the statue erected to him by the people of his native country.

"Aside from the mischief done by Nana Sahib, which seems to have had only a limited effect, what were the causes of this mutiny, Lord Tremlyn?" asked Dr. Hawkes.

"There were many causes that produced independent rebellions, such as the greased cartridges served out to the Sepoys, though this was only insignificant. There were too many Bramins in the ranks, and they were fanatics; and biting off the cartridge brought their lips in contact with the grease, which was religious pollution to them. A score of provocatives might be mentioned, but all of them would not explain it. The natives had been transformed into trained soldiers, and they felt the power that was in them.

"Before the mutiny, one British soldier to six Sepoys was about the proportion between them in numbers. The small discontents clustered around this grand error, and broke out in the mutiny. After its suppression, one of the first reforms of the government was to change the proportion of the soldiers; and now they are as one European to two natives. The government is liberal in the introduction of improvements. Now all the strategetic points are under the control of our own soldiers; and at present they constitute nearly the whole of the artillery force of the country. Peace and order have reigned since 1858, and it is not now believed that a rebellion is possible. I expect and hope to be with you for some time to come, and my companions and myself will do our best to inform you in regard to everything in which you may feel an interest."

The viscount bowed very politely to his audience, and was hailed with all the enthusiasm which could be gathered up by a baker's dozen Americans. All of them testified that they had been exceedingly interested in his address, especially that part relating to the mutiny.

"We shall be exceedingly happy in your company, my Lord, as long as you are pleased to remain with us," added the commander. "I have done something towards preparing a route through India; and I should be glad to have the advice of such counsellors as we were so fortunate as to pick up in the midst of the rage of the stormy ocean."

"The time of our party is at your disposal for as long a period as we can be of service to you. We do not wish to force ourselves upon you. We owe our lives to you, and we believe we may contribute to your pleasure and instruction; for we are at home here."

"We did only our duty when we found you on the wreck; and anything in the nature of a recompense for the service which every sailor owes to his fellow-men, or to those who sail on the seas, would be repugnant to me, as it would be to my officers," replied Captain Ringgold.

"I beg you will not regard my proposition as anything in the shape of a recompense; for all our fortunes and all our time for years to come would not be an adequate return for the immeasurable service you have rendered to us," protested the viscount. "We have all been delighted with the manner in which we have been entertained on board of the Guardian-Mother; and without regard to our rescue from the very jaws of death, I declare, upon my honor as a gentleman, that you have won our hearts, — you, Mr. Commander, and all connected with you on board."

"Amen!" shouted Dr. Ferrolan in a burst of enthusiasm.

"So say we all of us!" cried Sir Modava.

"Now permit me to say in all sincerity, that if our acquaintance had begun when we set foot on the deck of your ship, and the noble conduct of the ship's company were entirely obliterated from our memories, we should feel as we do now," said Lord Tremlyn.

"So say we all of us," sang the doctor with Sir Modava.

"I may say that if I had gone on board of the Guardian-Mother for the first time in the harbor of Bombay, I should have felt the same, and had just as strong a desire to assist you in seeing India. When gentlemen of education and character come here from England, the officials give them a warm welcome, and do their best to enable them to see the country, its manners and customs, and its institutions, to the best advantage. We should do the same with Americans; and I account myself fortunate in being the first to greet you, and welcome you to India."

The other two heartily responded to the sentiments of the speaker, and the commander could say no more. By this time the steamer was in the midst of the fishing-boats and other craft. Louis called for three cheers for the guests, and they were given with vigor and sincerity. The party separated, and its members gave themselves up to an examination of the surroundings.

CHAPTER XV

ARRIVAL OF THE GUARDIAN-MOTHER AT BOMBAY

THE coast of Bombay was in plain sight, the province, or state, whose capital has the same name. Groves of cocoanut, date, and other palm-trees bordered it; and far back of it was a range of mountains, the Western Ghats, a chain extending for hundreds of miles along the shore, though from twenty to fifty miles from it.

The fishing-boats were Oriental, and nothing new to the tourists; but the men in them were swarthy-looking fellows, not abundantly provided with clothing. The greater portion of India has a warm climate, and the dress of the people is adapted to it. For the most part, the natives are bundled up in loose white cotton cloth, or what was originally white, which they twist about their bodies with a skill acquired by practice. But these boatmen were almost in a primitive condition.

The distinguished guests on board of the Guardian-Mother were perfectly familiar with Bombay and its surroundings, as they were with all of the country, and their services were just now in demand. The Woolridges had attached themselves to Lord Tremlyn; Louis Belgrave was very likely to be in their company most of the time, and the viscount had manifested no little interest in the young millionaire. He was pointing out the country, and describing it, to this group of four.

Dr. Ferrolan was not so much of a ladies' man as his two younger companions, and was rendering similar service to his professional brother, Uncle Moses, and Professor Giroud. They formed a quartet of educated men, and were more in touch with each other than they might otherwise have been. Sir Modava Rao had attracted to his side Mrs. Belgrave; Mrs. Blossom was usually her shadow; and of course Captain Ringgold, when not employed in his duties in the navigation of the steamer, gravitated, not materially but sentimentally, to this group; for wherever Mrs. Belgrave was, the commander was not far off.

Felix divided himself up among the three parties; and, as he was a lively boy, he afforded no little amusement to all of them. The entire company, including the captain and the third officer, who were to take part in the business of sight-seeing, consisted of sixteen persons, which was just the complement for four carriages, if they were large enough to seat four.

The pilot came on board, and was inducted into the pilot-house. He spoke English, and seemed to be a bright fellow so far as his occupation was concerned. The pilots are said to "pool their issues," and divide their fees. They take their own time, therefore, and are very independent. But this one, when informed that the Guardian-Mother was a yacht conveying a young millionaire all-over-the-world, was very respectful and deferential.

"I have heard of this vessel before, and they say here that the young rajah is worth millions of pounds," said he, when he had laid the course of the steamer.

"I suppose he is as well off as some of your Grand Moguls; but I think you had better call it dollars instead of pounds," replied Mr. Boulong, laughing at the absurdity of the story; but the pilot knew nothing about dollars, and perhaps the reports had been swelled by changing the unit of American currency into that of the British Empire.

"Now you can see the islands more distinctly," said Lord Tremlyn to his group.

"I don't see any islands," replied Miss Blanche.

"They are too near together to be distinguished separately. The Bombay to which we are going is an island eleven and a half miles long. The town has an abundant territory; but large as it is, portions of it are very densely peopled, averaging twenty-one inmates to a house," continued the viscount. "Next to Calcutta it is the largest city in India, and comes within 40,000 of that.

"Bombay has had its vicissitudes. Of course you know that your Civil War produced a cotton famine in Europe; but it raised this city to the pinnacle of prosperity. A reign of speculation came here, and it was believed that Bombay would be the leading cotton mart of the world. Companies were organized to develop the resources of the country in the textile plant; and the fever raged as high as it did when the South Sea Bubble was blown up, or as it has sometimes in New York and other cities of your country.

"New banks were started; merchants plunged recklessly into the vortex of speculation. Then came the news of the surrender of General Lee, and the end of the war in America. The bubble burst, even before it was fully inflated, and the business prosperity of Bombay collapsed. The certificates of shares in companies and banks were not worth the paper on which they were written. Even the Bank of Bombay, believed to be as solid as the 'Old Lady' of Threadneedle Street, had to suspend, and the commercial distress was frightful.

"But it left its lesson behind it; and since that time Bombay has patiently and painfully regained its former solid prosperity. It has recovered what it lost, and is now steadily increasing in population and wealth."

"I never heard of the South Sea Bubble of which you speak," said Louis.

"That is not strange, as it was an affair of one hundred and eighty-one years ago," replied Lord Tremlyn. "I have not time now to describe it in full. The floating debt of England at that time was £10,000,000; and the Earl of Oxford concocted a scheme to pay it off, and formed a company of merchants for that purpose. The riches of the South Sea Islands, including South America, were most extravagantly estimated at that time, and the monopoly of the trade was secured by the company formed. The 'South Sea Company' was bolstered up by the pledge of the duties on the imports from these far-off regions, and the shares sold like wild-fire, increasing in price in the most extraordinary manner. Shares at a par of £100 were quoted at £550 in May, and £890 in June.

"The failure of the Mississippi Scheme, projected in France by John Law to develop the resources of the American State of Louisiana, alarmed the shareholders; but the managers declared that they had avoided the errors of Law in their finances, and the enterprise still prospered. A mania for stock-gambling spread over England, and the people seemed to have lost their wits. The most tremendous excitement prevailed. The crisis came, and it was realized that the scheme was a fraudulent one. Some of the biggest operators sold out their stock, and a panic ensued. Consternation came upon the bubble capitalists, and financial ruin stared them and their dupes full in the face.

"The country was stirred to its very foundations. Parliament was called together, and the books of the company were examined. The 'Bubble' had burst, as it did in Bombay. The private property of the directors was confiscated. The ruin brought about by this enterprise, rightly called a 'Bubble,' was beyond calculation; but it taught its lesson, as such affairs always do."

"We are approaching the harbor," said Mrs. Woolridge, who was not much interested in the South Sea Scheme, though her husband and Louis listened to the explanation very attentively.

"We are, madam. You see to the northward of us two peninsulas. The one the more distant has two hills on it. The first is Malabar Hill, and the other Cumballa Hill. This is the aristocratic quarter of Bombay. The huge bungalows of the rich merchants and higher government officials are here. The scenery, natural and artificial, is very fine, and Asiatic magnificence prevails there. That will be one of our first rides. You observe near the point of the peninsula some towers, like pagodas, which will give you your first impression of the temples of India."

Opera-glasses were then in demand, and were brought to bear on the towers.

"They are in the village of Walkeshwar. The peninsula now quite near is Colaba. Indian names are very much mixed in regard to their spelling. The *c* and the *k* are about interchangeable, and you can use either one of them. Hence this point is often written Kolaba, and the hill yonder Kumballa. The southern part of this neck of land is the native quarter. You will visit all these localities, and it is not worth while to describe them minutely."

"That looks like a cemetery," said Mr. Woolridge,

as the steamer approached the point. "There is the lighthouse."

The commander had left his party as the steamer approached the entrance to the harbor, and had gone forward. The ship had slowed down, and the captain spoke to the pilot about a convenient anchorage. The harbor was large enough to accommodate all the navies of the world, and there was no difficulty on this account. Lord Tremlyn had left his party to look at what was to be seen by themselves, and came forward to the pilot-house. The anchorage was settled.

"Captain Ringgold, if you please, we will now exchange places," said the viscount. "Up to the present time we have been your guests; now I will become the host, and you and your party will be my guests. I beg you will raise no objections, my dear sir, and I shall feel very much wounded if you do not accept the hospitality I tender to you. You are at home on the sea as I am in Bombay."

"You have put it in such a way that I cannot refuse to accept," replied the commander, laughing at the corner in which he was placed. "For the present we are your guests, and we place ourselves entirely under your direction."

"I am extremely happy to take you all under my protection; but I cannot submit to the proviso which you have added to my offer, though I will be satisfied to have you 'for the present' as my guests, and we will leave the future to take care of itself. But in whatever capacity we travel over India, or such portion of it as you may elect, it is rather necessary that we fix upon a plan for our operations."

"I am quite agreed that we had better draw up a programme, and I shall depend upon your counsel in the matter," replied the captain. "For the present, will you excuse me until the ship comes to anchor?"

"Certainly, Captain."

"Here is the custom-house boat, and I suppose I must attend to that."

"Leave that to me, if you please."

In another half-hour the Guardian-Mother was at anchor off the Apollo Bunder, the wharf, or landing-place. The custom-house officers came on board; and, as the ship was not one of any regular line, a high official came off with them. As soon as he reached the deck he discovered his lordship, and rushed to him, bowed profusely, and addressed him in the most deferential manner.

"This is a very unexpected visit, my Lord, and in a steamer flying the American flag," said he, as the viscount gave him his hand, a piece of condescension he appeared to appreciate very highly. "What has become of the Travancore?"

"She was wrecked in the Arabian Sea in a collision, and went to the bottom after holding us up for a few hours. We were rescued from certain death by this steamer, and we have been treated with the utmost kindness and consideration," said his lordship quite hurriedly. "Sir Modava Rao and

Dr. Ferrolan are on board. I am entirely devoted to those to whom we owe our lives, and I am in their service as long as they will stay in India. What is your business on board, Mr. Windham?"

"It is in connection with the customs, my Lord."

"You will dispense with everything in that connection, for this is a yacht; and you will oblige me by not subjecting any person on board to any annoyance, Mr. Windham."

"Certainly not, my Lord; and not a trunk shall be opened. But the newspapers will want the account of your shipwreck, and a reporter came off with me," replied the official.

"Refer him to my secretary."

The under-official obtained particulars from the first officer in regard to the steamer for the custom-house, and Dr. Ferrolan gave the reporter an account of the disaster to the Travancore which he had written.

"I propose to land and proceed to our hotel as soon as the ladies are ready," said Lord Tremlyn, when he had retired to the captain's cabin with the commander. "While they are preparing, we will consider the programme of the tour."

"Very well, your Lordship; I will have the party notified. Mr. Scott," said the captain, opening the door into the pilot-house, "inform all the company that we go on shore in half an hour; and you will go with them. Mr. Boulong, lower the gangway, and have the barge ready."

"Perhaps you have arranged a programme yourself already," suggested the new host of the party.

"I have considered the matter. I proposed to see Bombay, and perhaps run down to Poona. Then go to Surat in the steamer, and visit Baroda, and proceed by the ship to Kurrachee. From there I thought I should send the Guardian-Mother round to Calcutta in charge of Mr. Boulong, while we travelled to Lahore, Delhi, Cawnpore, Lucknow, Allahabad, Benares, and Calcutta by railway. From there we will go to Madras and Ceylon by the steamer," said the commander, who seemed to have arranged the whole trip.

"Excellent, Captain Ringgold!" exclaimed the viscount. "I can hardly better that."

He made some suggestions; but this route was substantially adopted.

CHAPTER XVI

A MULTITUDE OF NATIVE SERVANTS

The barge was ready as soon as it was needed, and lay at the platform of the gangway, with the crew in their white uniforms, quite as smart as man-of-war's-men. The coolie boatmen who were seeking a job to put the passengers on shore were disappointed. The clothing of the guests had been taken in hand by Sparks and Sordy, the cabin stewards, dried, cleaned, and pressed. They wore them now, and had returned the borrowed garments.

The party were impatient to see the strange sights on shore; and they were ready at the gangway when the viscount, to whom the commander had abandoned the direction of the company, gave the word. The ladies were assisted to their places, and the "Big Four" went into the fore-sheets. Bargate, the old man-of-war's-man, was the cockswain, and his lordship gave the word to him to give way.

"Pull to the Apollo Bunder, if you please, my man," said he.

"Which, your honor?" asked Bargate blankly.

"I mean the bit of a basin you see nearly abreast of the ship," the new leader explained, pointing out the locality.

The cockswain shoved off the stern of the boat, the oars dropped into the water, and the men gave way. It was a pull of but a few minutes, and the barge shot into the basin, and came to a convenient landing-place. On the shore they found Mr. Windham, one of the chief officials of the custom-house, who had been on board of the ship. He was surrounded by a small mob of young Hindus, neatly dressed in the native garments of white cotton. The ladies were assisted to the shore first. All of the party carried small valises or satchels containing the needed articles for a few days' stay at a hotel; and these natives took possession of them as they landed.

"What is this man, Sir Modava?" asked Mrs. Belgrave, as one of them relieved her of the bag she carried.

"He is your *Khidmutgar*, madam," replied the Hindu knight, with a smile on his handsome face.

"My what?" demanded the lady. "And must I pronounce that word?"

"Not unless you wish to do so. This man is your servant, your waiter."

"But what are we to do with such a lot of them?" inquired Mrs. Belgrave, as she looked upon the group of Hindus.

"There is only one for each person of the company; for every one must have his servant. We are going to the Victoria Hotel, and this *Khidmutgar* will attend upon you at the table, and do anything you require."

"I don't think I shall need him all the time," added the lady, who thought he would be a nuisance to her.

The young Hindus presented themselves to all the passengers as they landed, taking their small baggage, canes, and umbrellas. Some of them had heard Sir Modava's explanation, and Lord Tremlyn repeated it to others. Most of them had decided to take things as they came, and accepted the custom of the country without any friction. Mrs. Blossom looked rather wildly at the satellite who was to attend to her wants; but her good friend told her to say nothing, and she submitted without a word.

"Captain Ringgold," said the viscount, as he brought forward a rather stout man, with spectacles on his nose, and an odd-looking cap or turban on his head, "this is Pallonjee Pestonjee, the proprietor of the Victoria Hotel."

"I am happy to know you, sir," replied the commander, as he took the hand of the gentleman, who was a Parsee, though he did not attempt to pronounce the name.

"We have half a dozen *shigrams* here," continued his lordship.

"What are we to do with them, my Lord?" asked the captain.

"They are two-horse carriages; and, if you please, we will ride to the hotel in them," laughed the distinguished guide.

The party seated themselves in the vehicles, which

were of English pattern; and they saw cabs and omnibuses in the vicinity. Taking Rampart Row, they passed the university, the court-house, and other public buildings, into Esplanade Road, leading to their destination, about a mile from the landing.

"On our right is Byculla, one of the divisions of the city, and a business quarter, where you will find the retail shops, though they are not all here," said the viscount. "This locality is generally called the Fort; for though its walls have been removed, it retains the old name. Just below the Apollo Bunder, where we landed, are the Grant buildings, or warehouses. Perhaps you saw them from the deck of the ship. Below these, at the extremity of the point, is Colaba, the native town, which is largely occupied by commercial buildings. But we shall ride over this ground again, and you will have the opportunity to see the various structures in detail."

But the tourists were not very much interested in the buildings; for they wanted to see India, its manners and customs, and for the last year they had been seeing edifices as noted as any in the world, though they had yet to be introduced to the temples and palaces of this country, which were different from anything they had seen before.

They soon arrived at the Victoria Hotel; and the *khidmutgars*, carrying the light baggage, were not behind them, though they had run all the way from the bunder. The landlord had come in a carriage. Felix McGavonty, who was the captain's clerk, had made out several lists of the passengers, at the request of Lord Tremlyn; and one of them had been sent to the hotel, so that their rooms were already assigned to them. Their servants appeared to be familiar with the Victoria, and they were taken to their apartments at once.

"What the dickens do we want of all these fellows?" asked Scott when they had been conducted to a room with four beds in it. "They will be a nuisance to us."

"We don't need all you fellows," added Louis Belgrave, turning to his servant. "We are accustomed to wait on ourselves. One of you is enough for all of us."

"No, Sahib; no *khidmutgar* waits on more than one gentleman," replied Louis's man, with a cheerful smile, displaying a wealth of white teeth which would have been creditable to an Alabama negro.

"That's what's the matter, is it?" added Scott. "I have learned that no Hindu will do more than one kind of work, take care of more than one person; and no groom will take care of more than one horse. If you have six horses, you must have six hostlers. That is what Sir Modava told me."

"Custom is law here, and we must follow the fashions," replied Louis. "What is your name, my boy?" he continued, turning to his servant.

"Sayad, sahib," answered he.

Scott's was Moro, Morris's was Mobarak, and Felix's was Balaya; but the last two were speedily abbreviated into "Mobby" and "Bally," to which the young Hindus offered no objection. They were all under twenty years of age, and spoke English passably well.

"Here, Sayad! black my shoes," said Louis, determined to make use of his servant.

"I don't clean the shoes," replied the fellow, shaking his head. "I call the porter;" and he did so.

"That is just what Sir Modava told me," added Scott.

But Sayad had opened his master's valise, placed his toilet articles on the bureau, and brushed his coat, which he had taken off. He arranged everything with good taste, and smiled expansively every time Louis looked at him. The shoes of all four were polished in time; and they were ready to begin their explorations of the city, though it was rather late in the day.

"What time is dinner, Moro?" asked Scott.

"Seven o'clock, sahib," replied the boy; and he was more of a boy than a man.

"What time are the other meals?"

"Meals?" queried Moro.

"What time is breakfast?"

"Bring sahib coffee at six in the morning; breakfast at nine; tiffin at one."

"What's that last one, Moro?"

"We had tiffin at Suez, and it means luncheon," interposed Morris.

"I didn't hear the word; but it is all right, and

tiffin it is after this time. Come; are you going down-stairs, fellows?"

"There is a public sitting-room down-stairs, and we will find that first."

The four servants followed them when they went down-stairs. None of the party had yet gone to the public room except Sir Modava, though Lord Tremlyn soon joined him. Their attendants stopped outside the doors.

"We are going to the tailor's now," said the Hindu gentleman. "As you are aware, we lost all our clothes except what we had on, and we must order a new supply."

"May we go with you?" asked Louis.

"Certainly; if you desire to do so. You may find something to amuse you on the way, as we shall walk; for we want to get our sea-legs off," replied Sir Modava. "It is only five o'clock here, and we have two hours before dinner-time. Ah, here is Miss Blanche."

She was followed by her servant, who was decidedly a nuisance to her, though he retreated from her room as soon as he had put things in order, and remained within call outside the door. Louis invited her to take a walk with them, and she went up-stairs to consult her mother. She returned in a few minutes, ready to go out; and she was as radiant as a fairy in her light costume.

They passed out of the hotel; and the first thing that attracted Louis's attention was a palanquin. It

"The young millionaire walked by the side of the vehicle."
—Page 155.

was not a new thing to the travellers, for they had seen such conveyances in Constantinople and elsewhere.

"You must ride in that palanquin, Miss Blanche," said Louis; and he told Sayad to have it brought up to the door.

It was a compartment like a box, about seven feet long, with a pair of sliding doors at the side. It was balanced on a pole, with braces above and below it. It appeared to be so poised, with the pole above the centre of gravity, that it could not be turned over. The four bearers were coolies, with bare legs, cotton turbans on their heads, and not otherwise overloaded with clothing; but they were dressed like all the coolies about the streets and in the boats of the harbor.

The fair young lady had never been in a palanquin, though she had seen them, and she was pleased with the idea of the ride. It was dropped down upon its four legs, or feet, and Louis assisted her to the interior. It was provided with cushions, and Sir Modava instructed her to recline so that she could see out of the open doors. The young millionaire walked by the side of the vehicle, while the others all followed, with their servants at a respectful distance.

"How do you like the motion, Miss Blanche?" asked Louis, after they had gone a short distance.

"It is not as uneasy as the gait of a camel, though I can feel every step of the bearers. But I should prefer a *shigram*, if it only had a better name," replied she.

"You can call it a brougham, or simply a carriage, if you prefer. We are not here to learn the Indian languages, and we can take our choice; and we can talk 'good old United States,' in speaking of things," suggested Louis. "There! what will you call that vehicle, Miss Blanche?"

"That is called a *gharri*," interposed Sir Modava, who was within hearing.

The vehicle was such as none of the Americans had ever seen. It was a sort of two-wheeled cart, with a top like an old-fashioned chaise, in which a man was seated, while a rough-looking fellow rode in front.

"I should say it was an ox-cart, so far as the team is concerned," said Scott.

"Those are not oxen; they are called bullocks in this country. As you see, they have humps like a camel, though much smaller, in front of which is the yoke," the Hindu knight explained.

"But they don't drive oxen in the United States with a pair of rope reins, as this fellow does," said Scott.

"I have seen them do so in North Carolina," added Morris, who had travelled in the South with his parents.

"I give it up, and it's all right. But what is that man in the cart? Is he a Grand Mogul?"

"Hardly," replied Sir Modava, laughing. "The

driver is the lowest caste of laborers, who works for fivepence a day, and supports his family on it. The man inside is the cook of a Parseė merchant I happen to know, and probably he is going to market to buy supplies for the family. But here we are at the tailor's. You can continue your ramble, and your servants can tell you the way, and what the buildings are."

The two gentlemen entered the tailor's shop; for there are no stores here any more than in London.

CHAPTER XVII

A HOSPITAL FOR THE BRUTE CREATION

THE live boys did not care much for the buildings, though most of those of a public character were architecturally very fine. Around a large open space they found the Town Hall, the Mint, and all the great mercantile establishments. At the time of the young people's visit, it was almost entirely abandoned by those who had held possession of it during the day. Business hours are from ten in the forenoon till four in the afternoon.

Before and after these hours the Fort, as the business section of the city is called, is deserted. This quarter was formerly surrounded by walls or ramparts, which have now been removed; but in its limits is concentrated the great wealth of Bombay. There are no dwellings within this territory, which is consecrated to trade and commerce; and both Europeans and natives hasten at the early closing hour to their homes at Colaba, the Esplanade, Mazagon, Malabar Hill, and Breach Candy, the latter on the seashore.

In front of the Grant buildings they found the Cotton-Green, deserted now, though the stacks of bales were still there, with a few sheds and shanties.

A few half-naked coolies and policemen were loitering about the place; but it is not convenient for a thief to carry off a bale of cotton on his back, and a bullock cart in this locality would excite suspicion. In business hours this is a busy place; and the Parsee and native merchants, robed in loose white garments, not all of them indulging in the luxury of trousers, reclining on the bales, or busy with customers, form a picturesque scene.

"I don't think this is the right time to explore this region," suggested Scott. "We had better come down here when there is something going on."

"You are right, Scott," replied Louis; "and I dare say Miss Blanche has had enough of the palanquin, or will have by the time we get back to the hotel, for we are more than a mile from it."

"I don't think I like a palanquin as well as a carriage," replied the young lady. "If you please, I should like to walk back."

She was promptly assisted to alight, and the palanquin bearers were paid so liberally that they did not complain at being discharged so far from the hotel. Sayad and Moro were sent ahead to lead the way, while the other two walked behind. On their arrival at the Victoria, they found all the rest of the tourists assembled in the parlor, to whom they gave an account of what they had seen.

They went to the saloon in which dinner was served, closely followed by their servants; and the scene there was decidedly unique to the Americans, for there were as many servants as guests. The hotel furnishes no attendants, and each visitor brings his own. But as soon as all were seated, order came out of confusion, and the service proceeded. The dishes were somewhat peculiar; but Sir Modava explained them to the commander and Mrs. Belgrave, while Lord Tremlyn rendered a similar service to the Woolridges and Louis, and Dr. Ferrolan to the professional gentlemen of the company.

"I think you will find this fish very good," said his lordship, as the second course came on. "It is the *bummaloti*, sometimes called the Bombay duck, something like both the salmon and the trout. It is a salt-water fish, abundant off this coast, where it is extensively taken, salted, and dried, to be sent to all parts of India."

"It is elegant," said Mr. Woolridge, who was an epicure.

The roast beef and chickens were very good, and the fruit was highly appreciated. The dinner finished, the party returned to the sitting-room, and found themselves very nearly alone. At the suggestion of Captain Ringgold, Lord Tremlyn consented to give the travellers some information in regard to the city of Bombay.

"When I consider what a vast extent of territory you are to explore in India," the speaker began, "I realize that not much of your time must be taken up in long discourses, and especially not in lengthy introductions. Bombay, the western province of the peninsula, includes twenty-four British districts and nineteen native states, the latter governed wholly or in part by Hindu rulers. This word Hindu, I repeat, properly applies to only a portion of this country, but has come into use as a name for the entire region.

"This is the Bombay Presidency, with a governor appointed by the crown, a Legislative Council, a mixed garrison of English and native soldiers, under a local commander-in-chief. That is all I shall say of the presidency, which is one of three in India.

"The city of Bombay occupies the south end of the island of the same name, and is one of a group of several, of which Salsette is the largest, with which Bombay Island, eleven miles in length, is connected by causeways, over which the railway passes. The business part is at the Fort, where we landed, and the bazaars extend from that in the direction of Mazagon, which lies to the north and east of it.

"You will find here many public buildings and commercial structures which compare favorably with similar edifices in any city of the world; and we shall see them to-morrow forenoon. The Princess Dock, where the great steamship lines land their merchandise, cost a million sterling. Three or four miles off this dock, to the eastward, you saw a couple of islands, the farther one of which is Elephanta, with its wonderful cave, which you will visit.

"The western terminus of the Great Indian Peninsula Railway is here, and with its connections it extends all over India. This is the first port usually reached by vessels from Europe, though Kurrachee is nearer. It is the great mail port; and I have seen landed at Dover thirty tons of post-bags, sent from here by Suez and through Europe by the Orient Express.

"Bombay now exceeds Calcutta in the extent of its commerce. The principal exports are cotton, wheat, shawls, opium, coffee, pepper, ivory, and gums; and the chief imports are the manufactured goods of England, metals, wine, beer, tea, and silks. The prominent industries of the city and its vicinity are dyeing, tanning, and metal working. It has sixty large steam-mills. Of the vast population, now approaching a million, not more than 13,000 are British-born. The water here is excellent, for it is brought from a lake fifteen miles north of us.

"Goa is still a Portuguese possession, nearly three hundred miles down the coast; and a year before they captured it they took possession of this island, in 1509. They held it till 1661, when it was ceded to England as a part of the dowry of the Infanta Catharine, who became queen of Charles II. That is all I need say at present."

The next morning after breakfast the carriages bespoken were at the door. The party seated themselves in the vehicles, which were English, and quite commodious, according to their own fancies; and it need only be said that the commander was in the one with Mrs. Belgrave, and Louis with Miss

Blanche. The viscount directed the driver of his carriage to pass through Cruikshank Road to the Parsees' Bazaar, which is just north of the Fort. Most of the Parsees and Bhorahs who do business here reside in the same section; and there were many fine houses there, though they are abundantly able to live at Breach Candy and Malabar Hill, the abode of the *élite*. The vehicles stopped at an attractive point, and the party alighted. They went into several shops, and were treated with the utmost politeness and attention.

In one of them they were invited into a small rear saloon, magnificently furnished, where they were presented by Lord Tremlyn to a Parsee gentleman. He was dignity and grace united. He was dressed in white throughout, except his cap, or turban, which was of darker material. He wore trousers, with white socks and slippers. His shirt appeared to be outside of his trousers, like the Russians, with a sort of vest over it. He wore a long coat, shaped like a dressing-gown, reaching nearly to the floor.

He was kind enough to call in his wife and little daughter. Both of them had pleasing faces. The lady wore a rich dress and a magnificent shawl, with a head-dress of gold and diamonds. The little girl had on bagging trousers like the Turkish women, and a heavily embroidered tunic, and both of them wore Indian slippers, with the toes turned up.

The ladies of the party were presented to the lady. She spoke English correctly and fluently, and the interview between them was exceedingly interesting to both sides. The Americans did not meddle with forbidden topics, as they had been cautioned not to do, such as their religion and burial rites; but they could not help thinking of this elegant lady's comely form being torn to pieces by the crows and vultures in the Tower of Silence with absolute horror.

From the Bazaar the carriages proceeded through the Fort, and the public buildings were pointed out to them. At the Cotton-Green they got out; for the place was now alive with Parsees and other merchants, with plenty of coolies, some of whom were moving bales, and others sorting cotton. From this locality they rode through Colaba, and saw some native dwellings, as well as some fine European residences, with beautiful gardens around them. They alighted near the most southern point, and inspected a "bungalow," which they were politely invited to enter. It was fitted up with a view to comfort rather than elegance, and the interior appeared as though it might be delightfully cool in the heat of summer.

"What do you call that house?" asked Mrs. Belgrave, as they returned to the road, which they call them all over the city, and not streets.

"A bungalow," replied Sir Modava.

"Why do you call it so?"

"That reminds me of the German," interposed Captain Ringgold, laughing heartily. "'Do you know vot vas der reason vy ve calls our boy Hans?'"

"Well, what was the reason, Captain?" inquired the lady seriously.

"'Der reason vy ve calls our boy Hans is, dot is his name.'"

"Well, that is precisely why we call that house a bungalow," added Sir Modava. "It is the house usually occupied by Europeans here. They are one story high, with a broad veranda, like the one we have just visited. Almost always they have a pyramidal roof, generally thatched, but rarely slated or tiled. When the body is of brick or stone, they call them *pucka* houses. Doubtless you wished to know the origin of the word, Mrs. Belgrave."

"That was just what I wished to know."

"They were probably first called Bengalese houses, and the present name was corrupted out of the adjective."

The party collected together on the seashore, for the viscount appeared to have something to say. The captain of the Guardian-Mother called the attention of the company to the shape of the small bay before them, which looked exactly like a lobster's big claw.

"The point where we are is Cape Colaba, and the small point is Cape Malabar," said Lord Tremlyn. "I think we have seen all our time permits, and now we will drive back through the town and the Esplanade. Perhaps you have not yet heard of the Jains. They are a religious sect, and are more influential and intelligent than most of the Hindus.

More than any other sect they hold the lower animals in the highest regard, amounting to a strange sort of tenderness.

"They believe that man should not injure any animal; and more than this, that human beings are bound to protect the lives and minister to the ills of all creatures, even those the most despised. When, therefore, the pious Jain comes upon a wounded creature of the lower order, he stops to attend to its needs, and even takes it into his house to be healed. To forward this charity, the wealthy of this sect have contributed money for the foundation and endowment of hospitals for the care of sick and wounded animals, and even of those permanently disabled."

"What a beautiful idea, if it is heathen!" exclaimed Mrs. Belgrave.

"We will now drive to one of these hospitals. We have to pass through the Esplanade again to reach the Black Town, as it is called, where most of the natives reside; but we will go by a different road."

In about half an hour the carriages passed through the densely populated region of the Hindus, and stopped at the hospital. The party alighted in a large court, surrounded by sheds, in which are a number of bullocks, some of them with their eyes bandaged, others lame, or otherwise in a helpless condition. They were all stretched out on clean straw. Some of the attendants were rubbing them; others were bringing food and drink to them.

Passing into a smaller court, they found it contained dogs and cats in the same unfortunate and suffering condition.

"It would be a mercy to kill them, and thus put them out of misery," said Dr. Hawkes to the native officer with him.

"Do you serve your sick and disabled in that way?" asked the official.

He could not answer this appeal for the want of time, and they passed into a place for birds. Venerable crows, vultures, buzzards, and other bipeds, most of them with their plumage gone, pass the remainder of their lives in peace in this curious retreat. At the end of the enclosure a heron proudly strutted about with a wooden leg, among lame hens and blind geese and ducks. Rats, mice, sparrows, and jackals have an asylum in the Jain hospital.

"I should like to have some of our people take a lesson from this institution," said Mrs. Woolridge as they left the place.

The carriages then conveyed them to a Hindu temple.

CHAPTER XVIII

A SNAKY SPECTACLE IN BOMBAY

On the way to the temple the carriages stopped at a horse bazaar, in which Mr. Woolridge was especially interested, for some very fine animals were to be seen, including some choice Arabians. They were looked over and admired by the party. The best of them were valued at from six hundred to twelve hundred dollars; and the cheapest were hardly less than two hundred dollars. None but the wealthiest people of the city could afford to ride after these animals.

Around these stables were numerous cafés, and a collection of people of various nationalities were gathered in front and within them. Arabs, negroes, Bedouins, and others were consuming spicy drinks; a group of Persians in picturesque costumes were regaling themselves with great dough-balls, made of flour, sugar, and milk; and dirty visitors from Cabul were feeding themselves on dates.

Still in the Black Town, the carriages stopped at the Chinese Bazaar, though the tourists did not alight. It extended to the shore of the bay, and was crowded with all sorts of people. On the quays were no end of Asiatic goods, mostly of the coarser kind,—the horns of cattle, tortoise shells, elephants' tusks, and bags of pepper, spices, and coffee.

"This looks like Constantinople," said Miss Blanche, as four big coolies, bearing a large box of goods suspended from a pole resting on their shoulders, passed them, struggling under the burden they bore.

"Oriental customs are much the same wherever you find them," replied Sir Modava.

"But if they had a hand-truck, such as they use in the stores of our country, they could do their work with far less labor," suggested Scott.

"Those coolies would not use them," added the Hindu gentleman. "I have seen them in London, and these laborers would regard them as an invention of the Evil One to lead them away from their religion."

Parsees and other merchants were circulating in the crowd, making notes of the prices; and the great variety of representatives of different countries was surprising to the visitors. Not far from this bazaar is the great mosque of the Mohammedans. After all the magnificent buildings of this kind the party had visited in Turkey, Egypt, and Algeria, it was not a great attraction. It was not to be compared with many mosques they had seen. As usual, the party were invited to remove their shoes, though the sight hardly paid for the trouble. The scene was the same as in others of the kind. A venerable

Moollah was expounding the Koran to a group of true believers.

His audience were all seated on the pavement, and they seemed to be giving excellent attention to the discourse. Sir Modava explained that the Mohammedans of Bombay were more orthodox, or strict, in the observance of the requirements of their religion than in Bengal; for a considerable proportion are direct descendants from the original stock who had emigrated to India from Persia. They are bitterly opposed to the Hindus, and a serious riot had occurred not long before.

There are many Hindu temples in Bombay, though not many of them are accessible to strangers; but the party drove to one in the Black Town. It had a low dome and a pyramidal spire. Both of them were of the Indian style of architecture, very elaborate in ornamentation. It looked like a huge mass of filigree work.

The visitors next found themselves at Girgaum, which is a forest of cocoanut-trees extending from the Bazaars to Chowpatti, at the head of the Back Bay. Among the trees, as the carriages proceeded along the Queen's Road, they found a great number of Hindu huts, half hidden in the dense foliage. They paused to look at one of them.

The walls were of bamboo and other tropical woods, and the roof was thatched with cocoanut leaves, which required poles to keep them in place. It had several doors, and cross-latticed windows,

There was no particular shape to the structure, and certainly nothing of neatness or comeliness about it. A large banana tree grew near it; a woman stood at one of the doors, staring with wonder at the strangers, and a couple of half-naked coolies were at work farther away. The morality of the residents of this section could not be commended.

"In the evening this grove is lighted up with colored lamps," said the viscount. "Taverns and small cafés are in full blast, the sounds of music are heard, and a grand revel is in progress. Europeans, Malays, Arabs, Chinese, and Hindus frequent the grove. Far into the night this debauchery continues, and I trust the authorities will soon clean it out."

The carriages continued on their way to Malabar Hill, and made a thorough survey of the locality. At the southerly point they came to the village of Walkeshwar, whose pagoda-like towers they had seen from the ship, filled with residences, though not of the magnates of the city. Most of the buildings here were very plain. The hill is not a high one, but along its sides the elaborate bungalows of the merchants and others were erected, all of them with fine gardens surrounding them.

Breach Candy, on the seashore, in front of Cumballa Hill, is the most aristocratic neighborhood, and contains the finest mansions. Tramways, which is the English name for horse-cars, extend to this locality, as well as to most other important parts of the city; and there is a station on the steam railroad near it, though most of the wealthy residents ride back and forth in their own carriages.

The Tower of Silence, in which the Parsees expose their dead to be devoured by birds of prey, was pointed out to them. No one but the priests are allowed to enter it; and the relatives leave the body at the door, from which they take it into the building. It is placed between two grates, which allow the vultures to tear off the flesh, but not to carry off the limbs. It made the Americans shudder when their guides told them about it more in detail than when it was described in the lecture.

Passing by the cemeteries of the English and the Mussulmans on their return to the city, they halted at the Hindu Burning-Ground, on the shore of the Back Bay. Here the natives are burned to ashes. For some distance they had noticed funeral processions on their way to this place. The remains are borne on open litters. A granite platform is the base of the funeral pyre, and the bodies wait their turn to be reduced to ashes; and the cremation is far more repulsive than that in our own country.

Dealers in wood for the combustion sell the article to the relatives. Some of them are cutting up fuel and arranging the pyre, while others seated on the walls play a lugubrious strain on the native instruments. The disposal of the body of an old man was in process while the tourists looked on; and the corpse was placed on the pile, the friends covering it with bits of wood till it was no longer in sight.

Then the eldest son came to the scene, howling his grief and beating his breast. Grasping a torch prepared for him, he set fire to the corners of the pile that covered the remains. The flames rose high in the air, and the attendants fed the fire by throwing on oil. Soon the body reappears, a blazing mass, which is soon reduced to ashes. Water is then thrown on the pyre, and a portion of the ashes cast into the sea.

There is nothing very repulsive in the rite of burning the dead; though the visitors had some difficulty in keeping out of the reach of the foul smoke, which brought with it a disagreeable odor. The carriages continued on their way to the city; and when they entered a street, Lord Tremlyn called the attention of those with him to a couple of native women who had stopped to look at them, for the party excited no little curiosity wherever they went. It had become known by this time that a dozen American ladies and gentlemen were circulating through the place, engaged in sight-seeing.

They had comely features of a brownish hue, and were dressed in the loose robes of the country, reaching to the ground; one of the garments extended to cover the head, though not the face. Both of them wore heavy gold bangles on their arms, but both were barefoot.

"They are not Mohammedans," suggested Mrs. Woolridge.

"They may be for aught I know," replied his

lordship. "The women of this sect here do not veil their faces as a rule."

"They are quite good-looking," added the New York magnate. "What caste or class do they belong to?"

"I should say they were in the Vaisya caste, agriculture and trade. They are well dressed, and therefore not Sudra. Probably they are the wife and daughter of a shopkeeper.

"What is this crowd in the square?" asked Morris, who had been looking about him.

"We will drive over there and see," replied the viscount as he directed the coachman.

"Festival of Serpents," said the driver through the window.

"You have an opportunity to see one of the sights of Bombay; but we shall be obliged to leave the carriages, for it is a great performance, and there will be a large crowd." They alighted at a convenient place, and moved towards the square. The ladies were in doubt as to whether or not they cared to see such an exhibition; but the three gentlemen who were accustomed to them declared that there was no danger.

"This affair is in the nature of a religious festival," said Sir Modava. "There are scores of snakes brought before you; but they have had their poison fangs extracted, and they could not harm you much more than a playful kitten. This is a day appointed to make prayers and offerings to the snakes, in order to conciliate them and to insure immunity from their bites. Though these occasions occur all over India, I don't believe there is a single bite the less for them."

"It is the anniversary of the killing of the great serpent Bindrabund, which was creating terrible havoc on the shores of the river Jumna, an event in Hindu mythology, which is as true as any mythology," added Lord Tremlyn. "You observe that it calls together a great crowd of people of all classes, and you see fat Brahmin ladies here in palanquins, very richly dressed, and looking as sweet as sugar. You notice the rich standards and the torches, the trumpeters, and the girls playing on tom-toms and cymbals. But we must get nearer to the centre of the show."

"Not too near," pleaded Mrs. Woolridge.

The crowd opened for the sahibs and the ladies, treating them with the utmost deference, as though they were superior beings; and they obtained a position where they could see the entire performance. A group of *sapwallahs*, or serpent-charmers, each bearing a basket about fifteen inches in diameter at the bottom, but not more than ten at the top, each containing several cobras, marched into the centre of the crowd. Pious Hindus brought forward bowls of the milk of buffaloes, of which the serpents are very fond, and placed them on the ground. The snakes were released from their confinement, and they made for the bowls of milk without any delay.

Some of the tourists had never seen a cobra, though they are found in Egypt. The ladies shrank back when they appeared, and some of them shuddered at the sight of the reptiles. The body was somewhat enlarged near the head, and the spectacles could be distinctly seen in this part. The instruments played, the standards and the torches were waved; but the snakes continued their milk feast undisturbed.

The principal *sapwallah* had a wand in his hand, which he flourished while he repeated a volume of gibberish which none of the party but Sir Modava could understand. When Mrs. Belgrave asked what he said; he replied that he was uttering invocations to the serpents, and entreating the whole tribe of snakes not to bite the people.

One of the *sapwallahs,* who wore nothing but a turban on his head and a fringed cloth about his loins, went to one of the bowls from which half a dozen cobras were feeding, and taking hold of one of them, pulled him away from the milk. The serpent thus treated was furious with anger, and instantly opened out his hood, showing the spectacles in full. Another cobra was put in his place at the bowl, and his persecutor sat down on the ground with him, fooling with him as though he had been a kitten or a pet dog.

In turn the snakes remaining in the baskets were released, and allowed to feast on the milk as others were removed. There was a great crowd of *sap-*

wallahs in charge of them, and none of them were permitted to escape. The reptiles showed their temper as they were taken from the milk by spreading their hoods; but they were so skilfully manipulated that they had no chance to bite.

"I think I have had enough of this thing," said Mr. Woolridge, with a look of disgust on his face. "There is no fun at all in it, and I should like to make them a target for my revolver."

"It is about time for tiffin, and we had better return to the hotel," added Lord Tremlyn. "I shall keep you busy this afternoon; and while you are resting you shall take in a Nautch dance, which is one of the institutions of this country. After that we shall go to the island of Elephanta."

The live boys of the party were rather pleased with the spectacle, though they had had enough of it; while the ladies, whose flesh had been "crawling" at the uncanny sight, were glad to escape. They all reached the hotel, and were hungry enough after the long jaunt of the forenoon to appreciate the "tiffin."

CHAPTER XIX

THE CAVES OF ELEPHANTA

THE influence of Lord Tremlyn and Sir Modava was enough to procure anything in Bombay, and an apartment that served as a special banquet hall had been prepared at their command, and their guests were introduced to it immediately after tiffin. As the viscount had suggested, they were considerably fatigued after the long jaunt of the forenoon, though they were refreshed by the luncheon they had taken. The hall was furnished with sofas and easy-chairs for the occasion, and they were made very comfortable.

The performers were seated on the floor of the room when the company took their places. A man with a slouched turban and something like a sheet wound around his body, reaching nearly to his ankles, the only clothing he wore, entered the hall. At the entrance of the party the girls rose from the floor and saluted them deferentially.

There were six of them, very modestly dressed, only their arms and feet being bare. Their black hair was parted in the middle, and combed back behind the ears, after the fashion of many years ago in the United States. They all wore ornaments in their ears, and around their ankles. The material of their dresses was various, some of it quite rich, with pearls and gold in places. They looked quite serious, as though they were about to engage in a religious ceremony, though it had no such connection. Some of them were decidedly pretty, though their style of beauty was not entirely to the taste of the Americans. They had black eyes, and they looked the visitors full in the face, and with entire self-possession.

"Now what are these girls, Sir Modava?" asked Mrs. Belgrave.

"They are professional dancers, and that is their sole occupation," replied he. "They are engaged by rich people when they give parties, and for weddings and other festive occasions."

"Is that man the only musician?"

"He is the only one for this entertainment, and he plays the tom-tom with his fingers. I am afraid you do not appreciate our native music, and we did not engage any more of it. They are about to begin."

The musician beat the tom-tom, and the girls rose from the floor, shook out their dresses as any lady would, and then it appeared that the ornaments on their ankles were bells, which rattled as though it were sleighing-time as they moved about. They formed in a semicircle before the audience; one of them stepped forward, and turned herself around very slowly and gracefully, with a quivering of the body, like the gypsy girls of Spain, which caused her bells to jingle.

With eyes half-closed, and with a languishing expression on her dusky face, she made a variety of gestures, posturing frequently as she continued to turn. When this one seemed to have exhausted her material, another advanced to the front, and proceeded to exhibit her variety of gestures and postures, which were but slightly different from those of the first one, though she went through the movements of a snake-charmer. In like manner all the performers went through their several parts, imitating various musicians on different native instruments.

Two of them went through a very lively performance, leaping and whirling very rapidly. The exhibition concluded with a round dance, which was thought to be very pretty, perhaps because it was exceedingly lively. Mrs. Belgrave and Mrs. Blossom had never been to a theatre in their lives, never saw a ballet, and were not capable of appreciating the posturing, though the animated dance pleased them. The Nautch girls retired, and the "Nautch," as such an occasion is called, was ended.

"Perhaps you have seen snakes enough for one day," said Lord Tremlyn; "but I thought you ought to see the performance of the snake-charmers. We will have it here instead of in the open street; and it is quite different from the show you witnessed this forenoon."

As he spoke the door opened, and a couple of old and rather snaky-looking Hindus, folded up in a profusion of cloths, rather than garments, entered the apartment. Sir Modava conducted them to a proper distance from the audience, who could not help distrusting the good intentions of the vicious-looking reptiles. Each of them carried such a basket as the party had seen in the square. The men seemed to be at least first cousins to the serpents the baskets contained, for their expression was subtle enough to stamp them as belonging to the same family.

The performers squatted on the floor, and each placed a basket before him, removing the cover; but the serpents did not come out. The charmers then produced a couple of instruments which Sir Modava called lutes, looking more like a dried-up summer crookneck squash, with a mouthpiece, and a tube with keys below the bulb. Adjusting it to their lips, they began to play; and the music was not bad, and it appeared to be capable of charming the cobras, for they raised their heads out of the baskets.

The melody produced a strange effect upon the reptiles, for they began to wriggle and twist as they uncoiled themselves. They hissed and outspread their hoods, and instead of being charmed by the music, it seemed as though their wrath had been excited. They made an occasional dart at the human performers, who dodged them as though they had been in their native jungles, with their business fangs in order for deadly work. But the Hindu gentleman explained that they could bite, though they could not kill, after their poison fangs had been removed.

Then one of the performers stood up, and seizing

his snake by the neck, he swung him three times around his head, and dropped him on the floor. There he lay extended at his full length, as stiff as though he had taken a dose of his own poison.

"I have killed my serpent!" exclaimed the Hindu with a groan. "But I can make him into a useful cane."

Sir Modava interpreted his remarks, and the fellow picked up his snake, and walked before the audience, using it as a staff, and pretending to support himself upon it. Then he held out the reptile to the visitors, and offered to sell his cane; but they recoiled, and the ladies were on the point of rushing from the room when Sir Modava ordered him off. He retreated a proper distance, and then thrust the head of the creature beneath his turban, and continued to crowd him into it till nothing but his tail was in sight. Then he took off his head covering, and showed the reptile coiled up within it.

Lord Tremlyn looked at his watch, and then carried a piece of money to the chief charmer, which he received with many salaams, in which his companion joined him, for the fee was a very large one. He suggested that the party had had enough of this performance, to which all the ladies, with Mr. Woolridge, heartily agreed. The carriages were at the door of the hotel, and the company were hurriedly driven to the Apollo Bunder, where they found a steam-launch in waiting for them. Lord Tremlyn had arranged the excursions so that everything proceeded like clockwork, and Captain Ringgold wondered what he should have done without his assistance.

The island of Elephanta was about five miles distant, and in half an hour the party landed. Upon it were a couple of hills, and it was entirely covered with woods. One of the first things to attract the attention was a singular tree, which seemed to be a family of a hundred of them; for the branches reached down to the ground, and took root there, though the lower ends were spread out in numerous fibres, leaving most of the roots above the soil.

"This is a banyan-tree," said Sir Modava. "It is a sort of fig-tree, and you see that the leaves are shaped like a heart. It bears a fruit of a rich scarlet color, which grows in couples from the stems of the leaves. They are really figs, and they are an important article of food. In time the trunk of the tree decays and disappears, and temples are made of the thick branches. Some of these trees have three thousand stems rooted in the ground, many of them as big as oaks: and these make a complete forest of themselves. One of them is said to have sheltered seven thousand people; but I never saw one as big as that."

The party proceeded towards the caves, but had not gone far before they were arrested by the screams of some of the ladies, who were wandering in search of flowers. Louis Belgrave was with his mother and Miss Blanche. Sir Modava, who was telling the rest of the company something more about the banyan-tree, rushed to the spot from which the alarm came.

There he found Louis with his revolver in readiness to fire.

"Snakes!" screamed Mrs. Belgrave.

In front of them, asleep on a rock, were two large snakes. The Hindu gentleman halted at the side of the lady, and burst out into a loud laugh.

"The snakes of India seem to be determined that you shall see them," said he. "But you need not fire, Mr. Belgrave; for those snakes are as harmless as barnyard fowls, and they don't know enough to bite."

"I see that they are not cobras," added Louis, as he returned the revolver to his pocket. "But what are they?"

"Those are rock snakes."

"But I don't like the looks of them," said Mrs. Belgrave, as she continued her retreat towards the path.

"I think they are horrid," added Miss Blanche.

"But they do no harm, and very likely they do some good in the world," said Sir Modava; "but there are snakes enough that ought to be killed without meddling with them."

"You see that rock," said the viscount; "and it is a very large one. Can you make anything of its shape? I suppose not; nobody can. But that rock gave a name to this island, applied by the Portuguese two or three hundred years ago. It is said to have been in the form of an elephant. If it ever had that shape it has lost it."

"'Snakes!' screamed Mrs. Belgrave." —Page 184.

After penetrating a dense thicket, the tourists discovered a comely flight of stairs, cut out of the solid rock of which the hill is composed, extending to a considerable distance, and finally leading into the great pillared chamber forming a Hindu temple, though a level space planted with trees must first be crossed.

They entered the cave. On the left were two full columns, not yet crumbled away as others were, which gave the observers a complete view of what a vast number of others there were. Next beyond them were three pilasters clinging to the ceiling. This part of the cavern was in the light from the entrance; but farther along, considerably obscured in the darkness of the subterranean temple, were scores, and perhaps hundreds, of others. The pillars were not the graceful forms of modern times, and many of them had lost all shape.

This temple is said to have been excavated in the ninth century. The walls are covered with gigantic figures in relief. The temple is in the form of a cross, the main hall being a hundred and forty-four feet in depth. The ceiling is supported by twenty-six columns and eighteen pilasters, sixteen to eighteen feet high. They look clumsy, but they have to bear up the enormous weight of the hill of rock, and many of them have crumbled away.

At the end of the colonnade is a gigantic bust, representing a Hindu divinity with three heads. Some say that this is Brahma, as the three symbols of the creator, preserver, and destroyer, forming what is sometimes named the Hindu trinity. But the best informed claim that the figure represents Siva, the destroyer of the triad of gods. All the reliefs on the walls relate to the worship of this divinity, while there is not a known temple to Brahma.

The principal piece of sculpture is the marriage of Siva to the goddess Parvati; and it is identified as such, wholly or in part, because the woman stands on the right of the man, as no female is permitted to do except at the marriage ceremony. The party wandered through the caverns for two hours, and Sayad and Moro, the only servants brought with them, kindled fires in the darker places, to enable them to see the sculpture. Sir Modava explained what needed explanation. He conducted them to an opening, lighted by a hole in the hill, where they found a staircase guarded by two lions, leading into what is called the Lions' Cave.

The tourists at the end of the two hours were willing to vote that they had seen enough of the caverns, and they returned to the hotel in season for dinner. On his arrival Lord Tremlyn found a letter at the office. On opening it, the missive proved to be an invitation for that evening to a wedding for the whole party. They considered it for some time, and as it afforded them an opportunity to see something of native life it was decided to accept it.

CHAPTER XX

A JUVENILE WEDDING AND HINDU THEATRICALS

The note to Lord Tremlyn enclosed sixteen cards printed in gold letters, one for each member of the company, and they were passed around to them. They were to the effect that Perbut Lalleejee would celebrate the marriage of his son that evening, and the favor of the recipient's attendance was requested to a Grand Nautch at nine o'clock. The gentleman who sent out these cards was one of the wealthiest of the Parsee community, with whom the viscount was intimately acquainted, and he strongly recommended the Americans to attend.

The Parsees kept their religious affairs to themselves, and the party were not to "assist" at the ceremony, which would have been an extra inducement to attend. Promptly at the hour named the carriages set the tourists and their volunteer guides down at the magnificent mansion of the father of the young man who was to enter the marriage state that evening.

The street in the vicinity of the house was brilliantly illuminated, and it was covered over with an awning, from which no end of ornamental lamps were suspended. Behind a mass of flowers — cartloads of them — a foreign orchestra was placed. As the carriages stopped at the door, the band began a military march, whose inspiring strains seemed to give an additional lustre to the elaborate decorations. It was easy for the guests to believe that they had been introduced into the midst of a fairy scene. Sahib Perbut appeared at the door as soon as the vehicles stopped, and took his lordship by the hand, and each of the guests were presented to him as they alighted. The host was not an old man, as the strangers expected to find him, since he had a son who was old enough to get married.

He was very richly dressed, and he was a gentleman of unbounded suavity. Taking Mrs. Belgrave by the hand, he conducted her into the house, the rest of the party forming a procession behind them. The Americans had been obliged to make a trip to the Guardian-Mother, to obtain garments suitable for such a "swell" occasion, and they were all dressed in their Sunday clothes.

If the exterior of the splendid mansion had challenged the admiration of the guests, the interior presented a scene of Oriental magnificence which might have astonished even the Count of Monte Cristo. The party were conducted to the grand and lofty apartment where the Nautch was to be given. Immense mirrors reflected the brilliancy of a thousand lights; the floor was covered with the richest of carpets, the luxurious divans and sofas were overspread with the cloths of Cashmere; the elaborate richness of the costumes of the Oriental guests, and the army of servants manipulating *punkas*, or fans, formed a scene not unlike, while it out-rivalled, the grand *dénoûment* of a fairy spectacle on the stage.

The procession of foreign guests were all seated in the most conspicuous divans; for if Lord Tremlyn had been the Prince of Wales, he and his friends could hardly have been treated with greater distinction, as he was the unofficial representative of the predominating influence in the affairs of India near the throne of the United Kingdom and the Empire. The party were immediately beset with servants offering them fruit and sherbets, and they were sprinkled with rose-water from silver flagons.

The Nautch girls were not the same the tourists had seen earlier in the day. There were more of them, and they were of a finer grain; in fact, the gentlemen, who were judges, declared that most of them were really pretty. They were seated on the floor in native fashion. They had great black eyes; their complexion was only the least tawny, and was paler than it would have been if they had lived on a more invigorating diet than rice and fruits.

There were half a dozen musicians, who played upon tom-toms, instruments like a fiddle, and one that was very nearly a hurdy-gurdy, with lutes and flutes. They gave the preliminary strains, and the dancers formed the semicircle. The performance was similar to that the party had seen at the hotel, though it was more finished, and the attitudes and posturing appeared to belong to a higher school of art than the other. But the whole was so nearly like what the strangers had seen before, that they were not absorbed by it, and gave more attention to the people attending the feast; for they were an exceedingly interesting study to them.

After the performance had continued about a quarter of an hour there was a pause, and the dancers retreated to a corner of the room, seating themselves again on the floor. At this moment Sahib Perbut came into the grand saloon leading a boy, who did not appear to be more than ten years old, by the hand. He was dressed in the most richly ornamented garments, and he was an exceedingly pretty little fellow. He was conducted to the viscount.

"Will your Lordship permit me to present to you and your friends my son Dinshaw, in whose honor I am making this feast? This is Lord Tremlyn, my son," said the father, who was evidently very proud of the boy.

"Sahib Dinshaw, I am very happy to make your acquaintance," replied his lordship, as he rose and took the hand of the young gentleman, whom he introduced to every member of his party.

They all followed the example of the viscount, and addressed him as "Sahib Dinshaw," the title being equivalent to "Lord," or "Master," applied by the natives to their employers, and to the English generally. All of them gazed at him with intense interest, not unmingled with admiration. The hero of the occasion spoke English as fluently as his father.

"How old are you, Sahib Dinshaw?" asked Mrs. Belgrave, who was strongly tempted to kiss the little fellow; but she was afraid it would not be in order, and she refrained.

"I am ten years old, madam," replied Dinshaw, with the sweetest of smiles.

"And you have been married this evening, sahib?" continued the lady.

"I should not ask him any questions in that direction," interposed Sir Modava, afraid she would meddle with an interdicted subject; and the young gentleman's father seemed to have a similar fear, for he gently led him away.

He was introduced to the members of the "Big Four," who could hardly keep their faces at the proper length after hearing what passed between the youthful sahib and Mrs. Belgrave, at the idea of a ten-year-old bridegroom.

"Is it possible that this little fellow is married, Sir Modava?" exclaimed the principal lady from Von Blonk Park.

"There can be no doubt of it," replied the Hindu gentleman. "But it is hardly in the same sense that marriage takes place in England and America. The bride will be received into this Parsee family, and the groom will remain here; but everything in the domestic circle will continue very nearly as it was before, and husband and wife will pursue their studies."

"It looks very strange to us," added the lady.

"It is the custom of the country. The British government does not interfere unnecessarily with matters interwoven into the religion and habits of the people, though it has greatly modified the manners of the natives, and abolished some barbarous customs. The 'suttee,' as the English called the Sanscrit word *sati*, meaning 'a virtuous wife,' was a Hindu institution which required that a faithful wife should burn herself on the funeral pyre with the body of her deceased husband; or if he died at a distance from his home, that she should sacrifice herself on one of her own."

"How horrible! I have read of it, but hardly believed it," added the lady; and others who were listening expressed the same feeling.

"It was a custom in India before the time of Christ. Some of your American Indians bury the weapons of the dead chief, food, and other articles with him, as has been the custom of other nations, in the belief that they will need these provisions in the 'happy hunting-ground.' The Hindus believed that the dead husband would need his wife on the other shore; and this is the meaning of the custom."

"It is not wholly a senseless custom," said Mrs. Woolridge, "barbarous as it seems."

"In 1828, or a little later, Lord William Cavendish, then Governor-General of Bengal, determined to abolish the custom, though he encountered the fiercest opposition from the natives, and even from many Europeans, who dreaded the effect of his action. He carried a law through the council, making it punishable homicide, or manslaughter, to burn a widow. In 1823 there were five hundred and seventy-five of them burned in the Bengal Presidency; but after the enactment of the law, the number began to decrease. The treaties with the Indian princes contained a clause forbidding it. The custom is really discontinued, though an occasional instance of it comes to light."

The dancing had been renewed, and this conversation continued till later. At this wedding Lord Tremlyn met a gentleman whom he introduced to some of his party as Sahib Govind. This gentleman had just invited him to visit a theatrical performance at a private house, such as a European can very rarely witness.

"I never went to a theatre in my life!" protested Mrs. Belgrave.

"But this is a representation in connection with the religious traditions of the Hindus," argued his lordship.

It was decided to go, the scruples of the Methodists being overcome by the fact that it was a religious occasion, and not at all like the stage performances of New York. The carriages conveyed them to the house indicated by Sahib Govind, and they were conducted to a hall, at one end of which was a stage, with a thin calico curtain in front of it. The performance was just beginning.

A Brahmin came out in front of the curtain, with some musicians, and set up an image of Ganesa, the god of wisdom; then he prayed this idol to enlighten the minds of the actors, and enable them to perform their parts well, which was certainly very untheatrical, the Americans thought, when Sir Modava had translated the substance of the invocation. The Brahmin then announced that the subject of the play was the loves of the god Krishna.

"Who is the hero of the piece, Sir Modava?" asked Mr. Woolridge, who was a theatre-goer at home.

"He is really Vishnu, one of the Hindu trinity, known as the preserver. Vishnu has a considerable number of forms, or incarnations, one of which is Krishna, the most human of them all."

The curtain rose, and cut short the explanation. The scene, painted on canvas, was an Indian temple. A figure with an enormous wig, his half-naked body daubed all over with yellow paint, was seated before it, abstracted in the deepest meditation. The interpreter told them it was Rishi, a supernatural power, a genius who is a protector to those who need his services. Then a crowd of gods and goddesses rushed on the stage, and each of them made a long speech to the devotee-god, which Sir Modava had not time to render into English, even with the aid of Sahib Govind.

The actors were fantastically dressed. One had an elephant's head, and all of them wore high gilt mitres. Krishna enters, and the other divinities make their exit. He is a nice-looking young man, painted blue, and dressed like a king. His wife enters, and throws herself at his feet. Then she reproaches him for forsaking her, in a soft and musical voice, her eyes raining tears all the time. She embraces his knees.

Then appears the rival in her affections with Krishna, Rukmini, an imperious woman, and tells by what artifices she has conquered the weak husband. Then follows a spirited dialogue between the two women. The rival boasts of her descent from Vishnu, and of her beauty and animation, and reproaches Krishna with his unworthy love. Sir Modava wrote this down in his memorandum book, and handed it to the Americans.

Satyavama, the wife, insists that her only crime was her love for her divine husband. She narrates her early history, when she was a peasant girl on the banks of the Jumna, with her companions, and drew upon herself the attention of the god. Her life had been simple, and she had always been a faithful wife. Yet Rukmini triumphs over her. Her pride is aroused; she rushes off, and returns with her little son.

"Kill us both, since we cannot live without your love!" the interpreters rendered her piteous cry. The rival ridicules her, and, urged on by her, Krishna hands her a cup of poison, which she drinks, and sinks to the ground.

"It is not the poison that rends me; it is that my heart is broken by the ingratitude of one I have so dearly loved." She forgives him, and dies.

But not thus does the Indian love-story end; for the genie enters, and in thundering tones calls Krishna to an account for his deeds. The festive god is tortured with remorse, but has no excuse to offer. He drives Rukmini from him, and implores the yellow-painted god for forgiveness; and, as he is the preserver, it is granted. Satyavama is brought back to life. She presents her son to her husband, who holds out his arms to embrace him; and the curtain drops in a blaze of Bengal lights, and the "Wah! Wahs!" of the Hindu audience.

The interpreters finished their explanations, and the company retired with the salaams of the crowd. It was very late when they retired to rest that night.

CHAPTER XXI

JUGGERNAUT AND JUGGLERS

THE next day was Sunday, and none of the party appeared in the parlor till quite late; not because it was the Sabbath, but because they were all very tired, even the four lively boys, who had done more sight-seeing than the rest of the tourists. They were always on the wing, and while the older ones rested, they always found some novelty which drew them away from the hotel. Of the four servants only two attended upon them. They had practically retired two of them with some difficulty when they were away from the party, for they were a nuisance to them, so many of them.

Sayad and Moro were retained, however; for they were more intelligent than the others, spoke English better, and were more enterprising, frequently suggesting some means of amusement to them. They were interested in the boys and girls, and Sayad told Louis and Felix all about them,—about their homes, their schools, their sports; and Moro did the same for Scott and Morris. On this Sunday they were conducted to a Sunday-school of two hundred scholars, under the direction of the missionaries, though the teachers are mostly natives.

It was a strange sight to them, the variety of races, the strange costumes, and the absence of any considerable portion of costume at all. There were Mohammedans, Chinamen, negroes, Jews, and a few Europeans. They fell in with the missionary from England, who told them a good deal about their work, and how interested they were in it, declaring that they could see the fruits of their labors, detailing a number of instances of conversions. They had a day-school also, and they hired a strict Hindu because he taught English so well. He hated the Christians, and did his work only because he was paid for it; but he had to listen to the prayers and exhortations, and finally he yielded in spite of himself, and became a very useful Christian minister.

This gentleman said that the number of Christians in India had doubled within ten years. He invited the party to come to the church, and the boys hastened back to the hotel to tell their friends about it. They all went to this meeting, including their three distinguished guides. The service was about the same as at home, the clergyman was a native of the Brahmin caste, and he preached a very earnest and sensible sermon. The funds of the mission were increased at least a thousand dollars by this visit.

In the evening the entire company attended the Church of England at the invitation of Lord Tremlyn; and the sermon was preached by the Bishop of Bombay. The Methodists were as much pleased with it as though it had been delivered by one of their own fold. A portion of the day was passed in writing letters to their friends at home, and quite a bundle of them was collected for the post by Louis. They were all sealed, with stamps affixed, and Morris's servant Mobarak was directed to put them in the mail-box. But the fellow shook his head, and declined to obey.

His sahib was proceeding to give him a lecture in rather energetic terms, when Sir Modava interposed, and explained that the servant had religious scruples, knowing that the stamp had been wet on the tongues of the senders, which made it unclean to him, and he could not touch it.

"I have heard of a young man not older than Mobarak who lost his life rather than come in contact with the saliva of a foreigner; but I doubt if many would carry their fanaticism to that extent," he added.

The next morning the party were up at six o'clock, and after they had taken their coffee, carried up to them by their servants, went out to walk by two and threes; but they returned by seven o'clock, and were assembled in the parlor. The sights in the streets had become rather an old story by this time, and there was not much to be said about them.

"Have you recovered from the fatigues of Saturday, Mrs. Belgrave?" asked Lord Tremlyn.

"Entirely, my Lord. I am quite ready for the next item in your programme," replied the lady.

"How did you enjoy the play, madam?" inquired Sir Modava.

"As a religious exhibition, from my point of view, it was a failure."

"It does not convey much of an idea of even the mythology of the Hindus," added Professor Giroud. "If Krishna was a divinity, or even an incarnation of one, he is a very bad representation of the piety and morality of the gods. The affair was well enough as a love-story, but the conclusion looked like a pleasant satire on those authors who insist that their tales and novels shall have an agreeable ending;" and the professor indulged in a hearty laugh as he recalled the manner in which Satyavama had been brought back to life by the divinity in yellow paint.

"I like that kind of a winding up of a story, and I don't like the other kind," added the magnate of the Fifth Avenue. "We read novels, if we read them at all, for the fun of it, with some incidental information in the right direction. When I was a young man I had a taste for the sea, as most boys have, and I read Marryat's novels with immense pleasure. In 'The King's Own,' after following the young fellow in his adventures all over the world, his life terminated just as he was reaching home, and I was disgusted. I have read most of this author's books again, but I never looked into 'The King's Own' a second time."

"I think we all like to have a story 'end well,' though it was a rather violent bringing up Saturday night," said Dr. Hawkes. "But the actresses in that play were all exceedingly pretty girls, and I did not suppose so many of them could be found in all India."

"That was just what I was saying to Govind after the performance, and he laughed as though he would choke himself to death," interposed Lord Tremlyn, laughing rather earnestly himself. "There was not a single female on the stage; for the custom of the theatre here does not permit women to appear, any more than it did in the time of Shakespeare."

"But I saw them!" exclaimed the surgeon. "I think I know a woman when I see one, though I am an old bachelor, and rather a tough one at that."

"Not always, Doctor; for not one of those you call girls was a female. A woman on the Hindu stage is a thing unknown," rallied the viscount.

"I suppose I must give it up, though I would not do so on any less authority than that of your lordship," replied the surgeon good-naturedly.

All the rest of the party expressed their astonishment in terms hardly less strong; and the ladies were even more incredulous than the gentlemen.

"As Govind told me, all the female parts were taken by boys remarkable for their beauty and the sweetness of their voices," added his lordship. "But this is understood to be our last day in Bombay, though the limitation of time does not come from any suggestion of mine; and we must make the best use of what remains. You have not half seen Bombay yet."

"We should need ten years for our trip if we were to exhaust every place we visit," replied Captain Ringgold. "All we expect is to get a fair idea of a city; and I think we have done that here, especially as we shall see the same things, as far as manners and customs are concerned, many times before we finally take our leave of the country at Colombo in Ceylon."

"While we are quietly seated here, I should like to ask for some information in regard to Juggernaut," said Uncle Moses. "I used to read the most horrible stories in my Sabbath-school books about that idol."

"Those stories, as I have been informed by elderly Englishmen, were published in the United Kingdom, and all of them are inventions or gross exaggerations," replied Sir Modava, with his pleasant smile. "Puri, or Juggernaut, is in the district of Orissa, on the western shore of the Bay of Bengal. It is one of the holiest places in India among the Hindus. It contains a temple of Juggernaut, in honor of Vishnu, in which is an idol of this Hindu god, called Jagannath, which is mentioned in history as far back as A.D. 318. Vishnu is the Preserver of the Hindu trinity, and therefore in an especial sense the god of the people; and sometimes 100,000 natives gather at this shrine, bringing offerings to the value of nearly £40,000.

"The town has a population of twenty-two thousand, and it contains six thousand lodging-houses for the pilgrims who visit it. The chief temple has a hundred and twenty others in an enclosure, with a tower one hundred and ninety-two feet high. Juggernaut's car, of which you have read, Mr. Scarburn, is a sort of temple, thirty-five feet square, and forty-five feet high, with wheels seven feet high. The car-festival is the chief of twenty-four held every year, when the idol is dragged to the country house. Though the distance is less than a mile, the sand is so deep in the roadway that it requires several days to complete the journey.

"The idols in the temple are hideous-looking objects, with enormous eyes and crescent-shaped mouths, the horns pointing upwards. But they are very richly ornamented; for the idol has an income of over £30,000 from lands and religious houses. It used to be currently reported and believed that fanatical, crazy devotees cast themselves under the wheels of the car, and were crushed to death, immolating themselves as an offering to the god. But these statements have been strictly investigated, and branded as the calumnies of English writers. Two distinguished savants have declared that self-immolation is utterly contrary to the worship of Juggernaut, the very unusual deaths at the car-festival being almost invariably accidental."

"It is a great pity that these horrible stories were ever poured into the minds of children, and I am thankful that the libraries contain nothing of the kind now," added Uncle Moses.

The company breakfasted with excellent appetites after the exercises of the morning; and then Lord Tremlyn conducted them to the large saloon where the Nautch had been given, and they were astonished to find that one end of it was occupied by no less than fourteen men, not one of whom was more than half clothed, though the tom-tom player had on a pair of short trousers. This fellow began to beat his instrument with frantic energy, moaning and howling at the same time as though he was in great agony.

"Oh, dear!" exclaimed Mrs. Belgrave, putting her fingers into her ears. "Can't you stop that hideous noise, Sir Modava?"

"No more howling!" protested he in Hindu.

The chief juggler declared that they could not go on, and Uncle Moses suggested that they had to overwhelm the senses of the audience to enable the jugglers to deceive them. Their Hindu guide talked with them, and then ordered them to leave the hotel. The performers were not willing to forego the rich reward expected; and a compromise was effected by which the tom-tom was to be used, but the howling was to cease. Lord Tremlyn had announced the nature of the entertainment as they entered the apartment, and most of the tourists had heard of the wonderful skill of Indian jugglers.

A couple of the performers produced two swords twenty-six inches long, and pushed them down their throats to the hilt, and then asked Dr. Hawkes to feel the point in their stomachs. Another put a stone in his mouth, and then began to blow out smoke and a cloud of sparks from his nose as well as his mouth. Turning a somerset, he cast the stone on the floor. One took an iron hoop from a pile of them, and set it to spinning on a pole in the air. He continued to add others, one at a time, till he had eighteen of them whirling above his head.

Another set a lot of small swords circling in the air, till he had ten of them buzzing about his head. At the same time a sleight-of-hand man was doing a variety of tricks very skilfully, and acrobats were mounting on each other's shoulders, and pitching themselves about very promiscuously. While the party were wondering at the skill of the performers, though many of them had seen most of the tricks at home, a boy about eight years old came into the room with a good-sized basket in his hands, which he placed on the floor as the men spread out into a semicircle. The child stepped into the basket, which did not seem to be big enough to hold him, even when reduced to his smallest dimensions.

The drummer played a new tune, and sang in a low tone. The boy seemed to have a fit, and writhed as though he were in convulsions, finally dropping down into the basket very slowly. Mrs. Blossom was sure the basket was not big enough to contain him, and wondered what had become of him. Then the performers threw themselves on the basket, closed the lid, and began to punch it in every direction with long and wicked-looking knives. The ladies were appalled at the sight; but they were assured that it was all right.

The Hindus finally crushed down the basket till it was almost flat, and it did not look as though there was any space in it for a kitten, much less an eight-year-old boy. Then the men formed a circle around the basket, and began a sort of chant. Something like a voice seemed to be sounding in at the open windows. It continued to come nearer, and at last appeared to proceed from the basket, which began to be distended, till it was restored to its full size. Then the lid was removed, and the child sprang out, to the great relief of Mrs. Blossom.

Then one of the jugglers set a top to whirling, placed the point on the end of a stick, and balanced it on his nose. So far it was no new thing; but one of the spectators was asked to say stop at any time he pleased. Captain Ringgold gave this command; and when he did so, the top ceased to whirl, though, upsetting the bicycle theory, it kept its place on the stick. "Go!" added the commander, prompted by Sir Modava; and the plaything began to whirl again, as though its gyrations had not been interrupted. It was stopped and started again several times, till the spectators were satisfied.

The stick and the top were critically examined by the whole party, but not one of them could suggest an explanation of the trick. The last two acts were the most surprising; and the rest of the performance, though skilfully done, did not amount to much. His lordship gave the chief juggler a handful of silver, and they left the hotel with a profusion of salaams; for they did not often make in a month what they got for an hour, the Hindu gentleman said.

CHAPTER XXII

A MERE STATEMENT ABOUT BUDDHISM

"I LOOKED into a Hindu temple this morning while I was walking about," said Louis Belgrave, after the jugglers had been discussed a while. "I saw some very ugly-looking idols; and I should like to ask if they really represent individuals, or are creatures of the imagination."

"Both," replied Sir Modava with a smile; "there are, as you have been told before, a great many different sects, and a system of mythology. About all the gods and goddesses known to the Greeks and Romans have an existence in the Indian mythology more or less similar to them. Indra, the counterpart of Apollo in some of his functions, drives the chariot of fire that lights the day.

"Rhemba was born of the sea, and is the Indian Venus; Cama is Cupid; Parvati, whose image you saw at Elephanta, is Ceres; and so on to the end of the chapter. These divinities are represented in the temples, but they are without form or comeliness."

"They are not much like the beautiful statues of the Greeks," added Louis.

"The most prominent Indian sects are the Saïvas, or worshippers of Siva; the Vaïshnavas, who bow down to Vishnu under his several incarnations, like Krishna, whom you could not greatly respect; and the Jaïns, allied to the Buddhists, found mostly in the northern sections of India. They occupy important positions, and possess wealth and influence. There are subdivisions into sects among them, and it would be quite impossible to follow them through the mazes of belief to which they adhere. There is a great deal of philosophy among many of the sects."

"But what are the Buddhists?" inquired Dr. Hawkes.

"Buddhism is quite as much a philosophy as a religion. It is not as prevalent in India proper as formerly; though it is still dominant in Ceylon, Napaul, Burma, and in the more northern countries of Asia. Its history is somewhat indefinite. Gautama, of whom a great many pretty stories are told, is sometimes regarded as the founder; though some who have studied the history of the sect, or order, do not believe that the Buddha was a real person, but an allegorical figure.

"Those who give a personal origin to the system, now said to be the religion of one-third of the human race, begin with Prince Siddhartha, a young man disposed to be an ascetic, and inclined to retire from the world. In order to wean him from his meditative tendency, his father, in order to cure him, and prevent him from forsaking his caste, married him to a beautiful princess, and introduced him to the splendid dissipation of a luxurious court. A dozen years of this life convinced him that 'all was vanity and vexation of spirit,' and he became a sort of hermit, a religious beggar, and spent his time in dwelling upon the miseries of human life.

"He used up years in this manner, and after much reasoning, came to the conclusion that ignorance was misery. He gave himself up to study, and at last came to believe that he had reached the perfection of wisdom. The tree under which he sat when he reached this result was then called *Bodhidruma*, or the tree of intelligence; and the Buddhists believe the spot where it grew to be the centre of the earth. A tree that passes for this one was discovered by a Chinese, still standing twelve hundred years after the death of the Buddha; and the bo-tree of Ceylon is regarded as its legitimate descendant. You have been told something about it.

"In Benares, having ascertained the cause of human misery, and learned the remedy for it, the Buddha began to preach his peculiar salvation. In the phrase of his religion he 'turned the wheel of the law.' One of his titles is *Chakravartin*, which means 'the turner of a wheel.' The doctrines of the Buddha are written out on a wheel, which is set in motion with a crank, though it is sometimes operated by horse-power; and such machines are sometimes seen in front of religious houses in Thibet, and the monks have portable ones."

"I thought the religion of Thibet was the worship of the Grand Lama," suggested Louis.

"That is a form of Buddhism. The most important of the converts of the Buddha was the Rajah of Magadha, or Behar, on the Ganges, which gave him a good start, and it has since made almost incredible progress. It would take too long to state the doctrines in detail of this sect, and you get an idea of what it must be from what I said of its founder. Its leading doctrine is the transmigration of souls, also called by that tough word, metempsychosis, though other Hindu systems adopt this belief. It seems to include the recognition of the immortality of the soul, which at the death of the body passes into another form of existence, — a man, a woman, a lower animal, or even a tree or other plant. The Buddha claims to have been born five hundred and fifty times, — a hermit, a slave, a king, a monkey, an elephant, a fish, a frog, a tree, etc. When he reached his highest condition of perfection, he could recall all these different states of being; and he has written them out.

"Some of the negroes of Africa have this belief, and when a child is born they decide upon the ancestor whose soul has returned to the flesh in this world. There are one hundred and thirty-six Buddhist hells, regularly graded in the degree of suffering experienced and the length of time it endures, the shortest term being ten million years. A good life secures an elevated and happy life on earth, or as a blessed spirit in one of the many heavens, where existence is continued for a bagatelle of ten billion years. When the *karma* is exhausted" —

"What in the world is that?" asked Mrs. Blossom, who was struggling to understand the subject.

"It is the allotted term of existence, including the manner of living, whether in bliss or misery. The person must be born again, and then become a god, or the vilest creature that crawls the earth, according as he has behaved himself. The Buddhists do not appear to have any idea of a personal God; and they are practically atheists, though there are many good things in their system. They recognize no omniscient, omnipresent, all-powerful Supreme Being, who presides over the universe and all that is in it. They are pessimists, and believe that life, on the whole, is misery, a curse rather than a blessing. I have given you only a faint outline of what Buddhism is. It has points in which it resembles Christianity. Buddha is dead and gone; but his followers put up petitions to him, though there is no one to hear and answer their prayers. But I must stop for the want of time rather than because there is nothing more to be said; and I have done no more than touch the subject."

"But it is not very different from Brahminism," suggested Professor Giroud.

"You are quite right, Professor," replied Sir Modava. "Brahma means the universal spirit; but it is not a personal divinity to be worshipped. I believe there is not an idol or sculpture in all India that represents Brahma. Something that passes for this mystic spirit is represented with four heads."

"But is there not a new church or philosophy of recent date — I mean Brahmo Somaj?" inquired Dr. Hawkes.

"Rammohun Roy, or Rajah Ram Mohan Rai, was a Hindu ruler in the Presidency of Bengal, born in 1772. His ancestors were Brahmins of high birth. He studied Sanskrit, Arabian, and Persian, and was a profound scholar and philosopher. When he began to have some doubt about the faith of his fathers, he went to Thibet to study Buddhism, where he was so outspoken that he offended the priests and others, and his religious belief brought upon him the enmity of his own family. In 1803 he lived in Benares, and held a public office at one time. He published works in the languages with which he was familiar, directed against idolatry, which he labored to uproot.

"He succeeded to abundant wealth at the death of his brother in 1811. His influence assisted in the abolition of the suttee, and in bringing about other reforms. He published 'The Precepts of Jesus,' accepting his morality, but denying his divinity and the truth of the miracles. More than fifty years ago he started an association which became the Brahmo Somaj, which is a living and working society still. He went to England in 1831, and was received with great respect and friendliness. I have great reverence for the man, though I do not accept all his religious views."

"Lord Tremlyn informed this company in regard to the divisions of caste, so that I think we have a tolerable idea of the matter," said Captain Ringgold, reading from a paper in his hand. "But all these sects and castes are divided again into tribes and trade societies. Then there is a considerable portion of the people who, though they are fully recognized as Hindus, are outside of the pale of this multiform organization.

"I should say that all this would make endless complications in business and society. Each of these societies, or whatever you may call them, is independent, and has its own regulations. None of its members can marry into another caste, or even eat with those of a lower rank. A man born into one of these associations having a particular business cannot take up another calling without being pinched by the social law in all that he holds dear in life. His wife deserts him, his children refuse to acknowledge him as their father, and his property is absorbed by his society or caste. All this for no crime, no immorality; and he may be a noble and true man. If he chooses to be a tinker, instead of a trader, all the gods of Hindu antiquity light upon his head, and worry him to the funeral pyre by the shore."

"That is quite true, Captain, and I join with you in condemning this grossly heathen institution," added Sir Modava. "But time and Christianity will yet do their work, and my country will be saved. But I submit, my dear Captain, that there is another side to the question."

"Quite true, and I was about to state it. The man

who remains faithful to the requirements of the society is protected and supported. Wherever he goes, at whatever distance from his country he may be, he finds a roof and a hearthstone which he may make his own for the time. If gone for years, he will find the house and the field of his fathers undisturbed, of which he may take possession. This institution may remove care and anxiety from the mind of the man, and make him, as we find here, calm and contented, but without the ambition of the business-man. I have taken most of this from a book I found in Bombay."

"The most influential caste here are mostly Jains and Buniahs; and though they belong to different tribes, they are united in business matters. They wear their own costumes; but they have done more than any others for the prosperity of the place," said Lord Tremlyn. "They are the speculators in cottons and other goods, and many of them have immense wealth. The Buniahs are always intelligent, and somewhat aristocratic. You may know one of them by his tall turban, like a shako, though sometimes it is rolled like a conch-shell. Around his dress he wears a red band, which he twists about his limbs, and has a long calico tunic closely fitted to his chest. His chosen calling is that of a commercial broker.

"These rich Hindus, while adhering to everything required by their religion, adopt English fashions, and revel in British luxuries. You will see them late in the afternoon on the public roads, in elegant carriages, drawn by the finest horses, and attended by servants in rich liveries. Their houses are magnificent, furnished like the Parsee's we visited the other evening. The social intercourse between them and their European neighbors is very limited.

"The Mohammedans here are an important class of people, and some of them are very wealthy, and are honest and upright merchants. They are very strict in the observance of their religion, and not one of them would eat pork or drink wine or liquors. If it were the beginning of their year, which is different from ours, you might witness a celebration of the day. It is called the Mohurrum, and takes place on the shore of the Back Bay. They construct a great number of temples of gilt paper, and after marching with them in procession through the city, they cast them into the sea. I do not quite understand what it means; but the first month is usually a time of mourning and fasting in commemoration of the sufferings of the two nephews of the Prophet. The ceremony at the water is very ancient.

"The wives of Mussulmans here have more liberty than in most Eastern countries. They go about the streets with their faces uncovered, and are clothed for the most part like the Hindu women. As they appear in the street they are not so neat as the other native females, who spend much time in bathing, and are always clean and tidy. I have nothing more to say at present."

"I have an announcement to make," said Captain

Ringgold. " To-morrow forenoon we shall return to the Guardian-Mother, and sail for Surat."

The party spent the rest of the day in excursions about Bombay in three parties, each under the direction of one of the hosts.

CHAPTER XXIII

THE UNEXAMPLED LIBERALITY OF THE HOSTS

The Blanche, the elegant white steam-yacht of General Noury, which had sailed in company with the Guardian-Mother from Aden, and which had assisted in the rescue of the crew of the Travancore, had come into the harbor of Bombay, and lay at anchor not half a mile from her consort. The owner was a Moor of the highest rank, and a Mohammedan; and he had friends in Bombay, though he had never been there before. He had written to them of his intended visit, and they had taken possession of him on his arrival.

The general had been invited, with Captain and Mrs. Sharp, to join the party of her consort in the business of sight-seeing; and Lord Tremlyn and Sir Modava had united with Captain Ringgold in the invitation. The commander of the Blanche had visited the party on shore; but he was engaged in making some changes on board of his ship which required his attention. The Mohammedan magnates had kept the general very busy, night and day, and *fêted* him like a king.

Lord Tremlyn had taken care of the engineers and other people of the wrecked steam-yacht, and had treated everybody in a subordinate capacity with princely liberality. He and his Indian associate were both multi-millionaires, with fortunes inherited from their ancestors and other relatives; and unitedly they had placed a large sum of money in the hands of the captains of the two steamers, to be equitably distributed among their ships' companies. Captain Ringgold remonstrated against this lavish gift to his own people.

"It is a sailor's duty, and a large part of his religion, to assist those in peril and distress on the sea, the poor and the rich alike, and I dislike to have my men rewarded in money for a service of this kind," said he rather warmly.

"It was the good Father in heaven who sent your ship to our aid when we were perishing; but he works through human agencies, and I feel it to be a solemn duty to recognize my obligations to those so providentially sent to save us," replied his lordship, taking the hand of the commander with much feeling in his tone and manner. "I shall never cease to be grateful to Heaven for this interposition in my favor, and that of my companions; for all of us were in the very jaws of death."

"I can understand your feelings, my Lord; but all my people, as well as myself, may soon require the same service we have rendered to others, and I desire to let what we have done be placed to our credit against the possible debt of the future," added the captain.

"I shall feel better and happier when I have done,

in connection with Sir Modava, what I propose, and I beg you will withdraw your objections," persisted the viscount.

They argued the question for some time; but at last the commander yielded the point. Every seaman, fireman, and waiter received five pounds, and every officer a larger sum, in proportion to his rank, after the manner in which prize-money is distributed on board of ships of war. The same apportionment was made on board of both steamers, and Lord Tremlyn and Sir Modava were most vigorously cheered by the two ships' companies.

Due notice had been given to Captain Sharp of the intention to sail for Surat on Tuesday; and on the day before the cabin party of the Blanche, which included Dr. Henderson, the surgeon of the ship, came to dine with their friends at the Victoria Hotel. General Noury, who had been taking leave of his Mussulman hosts, was attended by three of them, who were at once invited by his lordship to join them at dinner, and the band of the Blanche had been sent on shore for the occasion.

The general had been taken about the city and its vicinity by his host, and they were anxious to retain him longer in Bombay. He was on excellent terms with Lord Tremlyn, who, though a strict Churchman, was not a bigot; and his connection with the affairs of India had brought him into intimate association with men of all religions, and there were about thirteen million Mohammedans in the Punjab.

His lordship renewed his invitation to the general to join the party who were going across India, and he seemed to be inclined to accept it. His Mussulman friends declared that he would be most cordially welcomed by all the people of their faith, especially if attended by such excellent Christian people; and they appeared to have none of the bigotry so often found among the followers of the Prophet.

"I don't quite understand your plan, Captain Ringgold," said Captain Sharp. "You go to Surat, and from there across the country;" for the conductors had decided not to go to Kurrachee. "But what becomes of the ships?"

"The Guardian-Mother will proceed to Calcutta, as soon as we land, in charge of Mr. Boulong," replied Captain Ringgold. "We shall join her there."

The commander of the Blanche shook his head; and after some discussion he declined to join the tourists, and his wife would not go without him. Doubtless he had some strong reasons for his decision, though he did not state them; but probably he had not as much confidence in his first officer as Captain Ringgold had in Mr. Boulong. The question was settled that the general should go, and he insisted that Dr. Henderson should go with him; and with three physicians in the excursion they appeared to be provided for any emergency.

The dinner was a very merry affair. The band played to the delight of all; and one of the general's friends declared that they had no such music in Bombay, to which he replied that he had engaged the best he could find in Italy. The company retired to the parlor, and the band played on the veranda for an hour longer. Some of the most distinguished of the civil and military officers located in the city called at this hour by invitation of the viscount, to pay their respects to the visitors; and Mrs. Blossom declared that she was never so "frustrated" in all her life.

"I should like to take my band with me," said General Noury, when the officials had all departed. "I am very fond of music, and I think it will afford us all a great deal of pleasure; of course I mean at my own expense."

"I beg your pardon, General Noury, but it must be at my expense," interposed Lord Tremlyn. "I was thinking myself what an addition it would be to have such excellent music on our way, and I am sure it will add a great deal to the earnestness of the welcome we shall everywhere receive. As to the expense, I hope and beg that not another word will be said about it. The entire party are the guests of Sir Modava and myself."

"I protest"— Captain Ringgold began.

"Pardon me, my dear Captain; you are all our guests, and protests are entirely out of order," interposed Lord Tremlyn.

It was a very pleasant and friendly dispute that followed, and his lordship had carried his point at the close of it. The commander had been to the landlord, and asked for his bill; but the worthy

Parsee informed him that it had already been paid. He had remonstrated with the hosts; but they had been inflexible. It was finally decided that nothing more should be said about expense; for his lordship declared that it was a very disagreeable subject to him. The captain believed that he was entirely sincere; and though he had never encountered such extreme liberality before, he gave up the point.

"You can tie your purse-strings with a hard knot, Uncle Moses, for you will not have occasion to undo them again for a month," said Captain Ringgold. "I don't quite like it."

"I don't know that I wonder at the generosity of our hosts," replied the trustee, as he put his fat arm around the neck of Louis, who stood next to him. "If this young man had been in the situation of Lord Tremlyn and Sir Modava when you picked them up, I am very sure I should not have grumbled if I had been called upon to disburse a sum equal to what this trip will cost them, if they, or any one, had picked him up. There are two sides to this question, Captain."

"Then you fight on the other side, though you hold the purse-strings," said the commander.

"Would I give a hundred thousand dollars for saving Sir Louis's life? His mother would give ten times that sum, and all the rest of the young man's fortune. That is a matter about which we must not be mean; and the other side take that view of it. I quite agree that not another word ought to

be said about expense," responded Uncle Moses, giving the young millionaire another hug.

"Uncle Moses is not a bit like the miser that could not afford a candle at his death-bed in the night," added Louis. "If they had done as much for us as we have for them, I should be glad to take them all around the world, and pay for an Italian band of music all the way."

"That's right, Sir Louis! Do as you would be done by," chuckled the trustee.

"It just occurs to me, Captain Sharp," said the commander of the Guardian-Mother, as the former was about to leave, "that there is no reason for your going to Surat, for we can take the general, Dr. Henderson, and the band along with us. You have a voyage of two thousand miles before you."

"Which I can make in seven or eight days without hurrying," replied the captain of the Blanche. "I could get to Calcutta before you do if I sailed two weeks hence."

"Just as you please."

But General Noury seemed to like the idea of getting on board of the Guardian-Mother even for a day, and adopted the suggestion of Captain Ringgold.

"There is next to nothing to be seen at Surat, and we shall go from there immediately to Baroda, on our way to Lahore," interposed Lord Tremlyn. "The Maharajah of Gwalior is an old friend of Sir Modava, and I am well acquainted with him. I

have no doubt we shall be very hospitably treated there, and that you will be introduced to many things that will interest you. If Captain Sharp desires to see some Indian sports, he can go with us to Baroda, stay a week, and then return to his ship here by railway."

"I like that idea, as my wife wishes to see a little more of India on shore, though she does not wish to take the long journey you are to make," added Captain Sharp.

This plan was accepted, and the party separated. The next morning the carriages conveyed them to the Apollo Bunder, and at seven o'clock the Guardian-Mother was under way. The band was playing on the promenade, and the party were taking their last view of Bombay and its surroundings. Captain Sharp and his wife were on board. The three doctors formed a trio by themselves, and were discussing jungle fever, which existed in the low lands beyond Byculla.

The sea outside was smooth; and at four o'clock in the afternoon the steamer was among the Malacca shoals, in the Gulf of Cambay, with a pilot on board. She soon entered the Tapti River, fifteen miles from its mouth. The band had scattered after the noon-day concert, and the party took the chairs in Conference Hall.

"I suppose you wish to know something about the places you visit, ladies and gentlemen," said Lord Tremlyn, rising before them, and bowing at the ap-

plause with which he was heartily greeted. "This is Surat, a hundred and sixty miles north of Bombay, on the Tapti River, which you may spell with a double *e* at the end if you prefer. It has a population of a hundred and ten thousand. It extends about a mile along this river, with the government buildings in the centre.

"The streets are well paved, and the houses are packed very closely together. There are four very handsome Mohammedan mosques here, so our friend the general will have a place to go to on our Friday." The Mussulman bowed, and gave the speaker one of his prettiest smiles. "The Parsees, of whom a few families own half the place, are prominent in business, as in Bombay; and they supply the most skilful mechanics, the liveliest clerks, and the quickest boys in the schools. They have two fire-temples here. The Hindus, especially the Buniahs and the Jains, are as prominent as in Bombay. The city was founded before 1512; for then it was burned by the Portuguese, who did it again eighteen years later.

"It had a very extensive commerce in its earlier years, and flourished on its cotton trade during the American war. In 1811 it had a population of two hundred and fifty thousand; but five and thirty years later it had less than one-third of that; but has gained somewhat up to the present time. Nearly a hundred years ago it was the most populous city of India. But I do not propose to exhaust the subject, and now you may see for yourselves."

His lordship and the Hindu gentleman, since their liberality had been whispered through the ship, were exceedingly popular, and both were warmly applauded whenever they opened their mouths. The party found enough to occupy their attention till the ship came to anchor, with its brass band in full blast, off the public buildings. A steam-launch came off for the passengers; for the hosts had written to every place they were to visit, and carriages were in readiness for them when they landed.

They rode over the town after a collation at a club-house, and saw all that was to be seen. They were quartered for the night at private residences, and there was almost a struggle to know who should receive them.

CHAPTER XXIV

THE RECEPTION OF THE MAHARAJAH AT BARODA

India has nearly twenty thousand miles of railroads open and in use, and thousands more in process of construction. As in England, they are invariably called "railways." They do not have baggage, but it is "luggage;" a baggage-car is unknown, for they call it a "van;" and the conductor is the "guard." Our travellers had become accustomed to these terms, and many others, in England, and now used them very familiarly.

Early rising is hardly a virtue in India; for he who sleeps after six in the morning loses the best part of the day, especially in the hot season. The tourists were up before this hour, and had coffee wherever they were. They had been treated with the utmost kindness and consideration, and their hosts could not do enough for them. They were conveyed to the railway station by them, and there found his lordship with a plan of a number of carriages — they are not cars there. On this plan he had placed, with the assistance of the commander, the names of the entire party.

They were to leave at seven; for it is pleasanter to

travel early in the morning than later in the day, and the train was all ready. They were not a little astonished when they were introduced to their quarters in the vehicles, to find them quite as luxurious as a Pullman, though they were constructed on a different plan, and were wanting in some of the conveniences of the American palace-car, though better adapted to the climate of the country.

Each carriage contained but two compartments; but they were suites of rooms on a small scale. The principal one was of good size, and on one side was cushioned to the ceiling, so that being "knocked about" did not imperil the traveller's bones and flesh. Against this stuffed partition was a low couch, which could be made up as a bed at night, or used as a reclining sofa by day.

Over it was a swinging couch suspended by straps, which could be folded up, or be entirely removed, and formed a couch like the one below it. On the other side of the apartment was a toilet-room, with all conveniences required for washing and other purposes, including a water-cooler. In this compartment the traveller takes his servant, and often a cook, for the valet cannot meddle with culinary matters; and they sleep on the floor wherever they can find a place. A reasonable additional price is charged for accommodations in this luxurious style.

The journey to Baroda would occupy hardly more than three hours, and these elaborate arrangements were scarcely necessary for the time they were to be used; but the members of the party looked upon them with especial interest in connection with the long travel to Lahore, and that which was to follow to Calcutta, though they were to break the journey several times on the way.

The "Big Four" had a compartment to themselves, with the two servants, Sayad and Moro, who proved to be such good fellows that the boys liked them very much. Sir Modava had managed to dismiss more than half of the attendants furnished at first, for all the party declared that such a mob of them was a nuisance; and the others had overcome their repugnance to serving more than one person in the face of dismissal, for their perquisites had already been considerable as they valued money.

"This isn't bad for a haythen counthry," said Felix, as he stretched himself on the lower couch. "We'll git to Calcutty widout breakin' ahl the bones in our bodies."

"This is vastly better than anything I expected to find here," replied Louis, as he pushed his crony over against the partition, and lay down at his side.

"But where do the elephants and the tigers come in?" asked Scott, as he called upon Moro to "shine" his shoes. "I haven't seen an elephant since I came here."

"Elephants are not worked in this country," added Morris. "The Moguls use them when they want to go in state, and sometimes when they go hunting tigers; and then the big beast gets most of the hard scratches."

"But the elephant can take care of himself when the mahout allows him to do so," argued Scott.

"Is the mahout his schnout?" asked Felix.

"You know better than that, Flix. The mahout is the fellow that sits on the elephant's neck and conducts him. He is the driver," replied Morris.

"Is he afeerd of schnakes?"

"He needn't be, perched on the top of the pachyderm," answered Scott.

"Who is he? Oi've not been introjuced to 'm."

"Are you going among elephants, Flix, and don't know what a pachyderm is?" demanded Scott.

"Oi see, it's the elephant, and ye's call him so bekase he carries his pack on his bachk; and 'pon me worrud that's the roight place to carry it."

"I wonder if we are to have any hunting out here where we are going," suggested Scott. "How is it, Louis? You are in the ring with the Grand Moguls."

"Sir Modava told me that the Maharajah whom we shall visit at Baroda is a great sportsman, and always treats his guests to a hunt," answered Louis.

"Is it after schnakes?"

"No; but after tigers."

"But I want to hunt some schnakes; I'd loike to bring down a good-soized cobry," said Felix, rising from his reclining posture.

"No, you wouldn't, Flix," sneered Scott. "If you saw a cobry, you would run till you got back to Ireland."

"Is'ht me! Wud I roon from a cobry? Not

mooch! Ain't I a lineal dayscindant of St. Patrick? — long life to him! And didn't he dhrive all the schnakes and toads out of the ould counthree! Jisht show me a cobry, and thin see me roon!"

Before the Milesian could tell how he intended to kill the cobra if he saw one, the train stopped; and a moment later Sir Modava, the commander, and Mrs. Belgrave appeared at the door.

"We have come to make things a little more social," said the Hindu gentleman as they entered the compartment; and the servants brought stools from the toilet-room, so that all were seated, making quite a family group.

"Are there any snakes where we are going, Sir Modava?" asked Felix, before any one else had a chance to speak. "I am spoiling for a fight with a cobra;" and he came back to plain English, which he could use as well as any one.

"Plenty of them, Mr. McGavonty," replied the East Indian. "You will not get badly spoiled before you fall in with all you will wish to see."

"Then I will bag some of them," added Felix.

"No, you won't, Flix; they will be more likely to bag you," rallied Scott.

"But I am in earnest," persisted the Milesian. "I have seen plenty of them in Bombay; and upon my word and honor, I don't feel at all afraid of them. One of them might hit me when I was not looking, for they don't play fair; but I shall be on the watch for them, and I'll take my chance."

"But, Sir Modava, do you really dare to go out where there are cobras?" asked Mrs. Belgrave, looking at her son.

"Certainly we do; we don't think anything at all about them."

"But you are in danger all the time."

"Of course it is possible that one may be bitten when a snake comes upon him unawares. The deaths from snakes and wild animals in all India averages annually twenty-two thousand. About a thousand are killed by tigers. Of a hundred and fifty kinds of snakes, only about twenty are poisonous. The deaths from snakes is one in 13,070; and the chance of being bitten is very small."

"I am afraid your figures lie, Sir Modava," said Captain Ringgold, with a pleasant laugh. "Millions of the people live in cities and large towns where there isn't a snake of any kind."

"Quite true, and, to some extent, the figures do lie; but there are plenty of cobras and other snakes in parts of Bombay, and the figures are not so false as you think, Captain," replied Sir Modava. "But I forget that I was sent here for a purpose by Lord Tremlyn. I am to tell you something about the Mahrattas, which is the name of the people who inhabited the region north of us. They have a long history which I have not time to review, but they have been prominent in the earlier affairs of India. They have always been a warlike people, and wrested the country from the Mogul emperor, sometimes called the Grand Mogul, and made themselves a powerful people.

"The present maharajah rules over the most extensive kingdom of any native prince. He is a Rajput, which is the aristocracy of the Mahrattas. He is the most powerful of the Indian rulers, and one of the most hospitable. I was formerly in his service, and he considers himself under some slight obligations to me. He is an independent prince in the same sense that other rulers are in this country. There is always a British representative at his court, who advises him in some matters of government, and his realm is called a protected state.

"He is a great sportsman; and I have no doubt you will be invited to hunt with him, as well as to witness some exhibitions which may not be agreeable to the ladies."

"Don't we stop at any stations on the road?" asked Louis.

"There is no town of any great consequence between Surat and Baroda, and this is a special express train," replied Sir Modava.

Some of the party looked out the windows, and the intelligent guide explained what was to be seen along the way. Some handsome temples attracted their attention, but they were insignificant compared with what they had been taught to expect in the future. The train crossed a bridge, which brought them into the suburbs of Baroda.

"The outskirts of the town contain a hundred

and fifty thousand inhabitants, far more than the city itself," said the Hindu gentleman. "The streets are very narrow here, and the houses are nearly all of wood; but they are different from any you have seen before, for they are peculiar to Goojerat, the state of which Baroda is the capital. You see at about all the crossings pagodas and idols, with banners flying over them. It is an unhealthy region, the ground is so low; and yonder you see a stately hospital, built by the Guicowar, as the maharajah is called."

The tourists had all they could do to see the strange things that were pointed out to them, and while thus employed the train stopped at the station. Looking out the windows again, they saw several elephants, all handsomely caparisoned, and with howdahs on their backs. A band of native musicians was playing near them, and the party wondered what this display could mean; but Sir Modava was unable to inform them. They got out of the carriages, and found themselves in a handsome square.

A company of cavalry was drawn up near the elephants, at the head of which, surrounded by a numerous staff of officers, sat on a prancing horse, caparisoned with exceeding richness, a person who could be no other than the maharajah. He was dressed in the most magnificent robes of India, covered with jewels in ornamental profusion.

"That is the Guicowar," said the Hindu guide.

"He is doing us great honor in coming out in this manner to welcome us."

As soon as he discovered the party, the ruler dismounted nimbly from his noble steed, and, attended by some high officers, advanced to meet them. A sort of procession was hastily formed with Lord Tremlyn at the head of it; for he was the most distinguished person, and in some sense the representative of the British home government. The Italian band of the general, as soon as the native band ceased, struck up "Hail, to the chief!"

The party encountered the king, who rushed up to the viscount, and seized him by the hand, as not all kings are in the habit of doing. They talked together for a few moments, when his Highness happened to see Sir Modava, and rushed to him, seizing him in a semi-embrace, clasping the Hindu with his right hand while the left encircled his shoulder. The potentate was profuse in his congratulations to the two gentlemen on their escape from death in the shipwreck, and this afforded Lord Tremlyn an opportunity to present Captain Ringgold as the commander of the steamer that had saved them.

"He is my friend, then," said the Maharajah, as he gave him no equivocal shake of the hand.

Then Louis and his mother were presented and described, and received an equally warm welcome. But the prince decided to receive the rest of the party at the palace, and they were requested to mount the elephants. The ladies were timid about it; but Louis told his mother that she must get up into the howdah as though she had been riding elephants all her life, and she did so, the others following her example. Louis assisted his mother first, and then Miss Blanche.

They were all seated on the huge beasts, and the procession started, the Italian band following the native, and playing when they ceased to do so.

CHAPTER XXV

FELIX MCGAVONTY BRINGS DOWN SOME SNAKES

"WELL, what do you think of this?" asked Captain Ringgold, turning to Mrs. Belgrave, as the elephant moved off.

"I don't feel quite at home up here," she replied, holding on with both hands at the side of the howdah.

"I think it is nice," added Miss Blanche. "It seems very much like riding on a camel, only there is more motion."

"It is a good place to see everything there is to be seen," suggested Louis, as he looked about him. "The king is taking us to his palace in high style. If he meant to astonish us, he has hit the nail on the head."

"But where are Lord Tremlyn and Sir Modava?" asked Miss Blanche.

"They are mounted on a couple of as handsome horses as I ever saw in my life," replied the commander. "One of them is on each side of the Guicowar, at the head of the cavalry troop. In England and America the escort goes ahead of the persons thus honored; but here, as a rule, the king cannot ride behind anybody. You remember that when we saw the Sultan going to the mosque in Constantinople he rode at the head of the procession, and all the great officers of state went behind him; and that seems to be the fashion here."

"But is he much of a king?" Mrs. Belgrave inquired.

"They all call him a king, and I suppose he is one. He is a Maharajah, a word written with a capital, and composed of two words, *maha*, which means great, and *rajah*, a king. The definition is 'a Hindu sovereign prince,' and that makes a king of him. He rules over a large territory, and Lord Tremlyn says he is the most powerful of all the native princes. He is certainly treating us very handsomely."

"I think I could get along without quite so much style," said Mrs. Belgrave, laughing; and she seemed to feel as though she was taking a part in a farce.

"All the style is in honor of the distinguished gentlemen we picked up in the Arabian Sea. But excuse me, Mrs. Belgrave, if I suggest that it is not wise and prudent to laugh in the midst of such a spectacle as this. The Hindus are very exclusive until you get acquainted with them, and have a great many prejudices which we cannot comprehend. They are very sensitive, and are very likely to misinterpret the expression and the actions of a stranger; your laugh might be offensive, leading them to believe you were sneering, or making fun of them, as we should call it."

"Then I will be very circumspect," replied the

lady. "But is the Guicowar really a king, when all this country belongs to the English? Victoria is the Empress of India."

"He rules over a protected state; but his powers seem to be almost unlimited. A British officer is always at his court, and is called a 'resident,' who is the representative of the government. But he does not meddle with the affairs of the state unless occasion requires."

The houses the tourists passed were all of Indian style, and there were always towers and pagodas in sight. The region as they passed out of the city was rural; and finally they came to the great gates of the palace, which they entered. The grounds were covered with great trees and gardens, in the midst of which was a palace, where they found the cavalry drawn up and presenting arms. The elephants were made to kneel down as when the party mounted them, and they descended by means of ladders.

A host of servants ushered them into the palace, which Lord Tremlyn said had been appropriated to their use. Their luggage had already been sent to their apartments; and an hour later the company assembled in the grand salon, dressed to receive the Guicowar. His Highness did not "put on any style this time," and was as sociable as any common person. He saluted the commander and Mrs. Belgrave; and then all the rest of the party were presented to him by the viscount, and Mrs. Blossom had nearly shaken herself to pieces during the ceremony.

A bountiful collation was then served in another apartment, at which the Maharajah presided. He spoke English as fluently as any person present, and was very affable to all. The Italian band played during the repast, and the Guicowar declared that it was the finest music he had ever heard. General Noury had been placed on his right as the one highest in rank of any present.

The king proved himself to be exceedingly well informed in regard to the United States, and was even able to talk intelligently with the gentlemen about Morocco. Though he had a wife, a mother, and a young daughter, they were never presented to the gentlemen of the party, though the ladies were permitted to make their acquaintance, and learned more from them about Hindu domestic life than they could have obtained from any others.

"To-morrow will be a great day in Baroda," said Sir Modava to the commander. "It is the great Sowari, a procession such as none of your people ever saw, I will venture to say; and his Highness has provided places for all of you where you can see the whole of it in detail."

The king announced this great state occasion himself before the lunch was finished, and gave the visitors a cordial invitation to witness the procession. The "Big Four," a term of which the viscount and Sir Modava had already learned the meaning, were very impatient to do some hunting. They had brought their guns with them, and Louis informed the Hindu gentleman of their desire.

"Is there any place near the palace where we could find any game?" he inquired.

"Not in the palace grounds, but within a few miles of it a very rugged region may be reached, and a road-wagon will be provided for you. I will speak to the Guicowar about it," replied Sir Modava; and he broached the subject at once.

In half an hour a vehicle was at the door; and the boys were ready, dressed for the hunt, and with their guns in their hands. Two officers were appointed to attend them, and both of them spoke English very well. The vehicle provided was a kind of coach, the floor of which was cushioned, so that several persons could sleep on it during a long journey. It was drawn by four high-spirited horses; and, though the road was bad, it was driven at a high rate of speed; and in less than an hour they alighted in a wild region, where there was not a building of any kind to be seen.

The two officers directed the servants to take some boards from the top of the carriage, with which they stated their purpose to make a platform in a tree, where they could watch for game; but the boys objected to this arrangement, and declared that each of them would hunt on his own hook.

"But suppose you should come across a tiger, for

they have been found here, though I hardly think you will see one," said one of the officers. "What would you do then?"

"Shoot him, of course," replied Scott. "What are our guns for?"

"But you may fire half a dozen balls into him without disabling the beast," added Khayrat, the principal officer. "Tiger-hunting is dangerous sport, and you can't be too careful."

But the boys were very confident, and all of them were good shots; but they had never tried any hunting of this kind. Khayrat said there was plenty of deer in the vicinity, and they had better confine their attention to them. If they approached the foothill of the Vindya Mountains, which he pointed out to them, they might find tigers. With this warning, the "Big Four" separated, and struck into the jungle. Khayrat followed Louis, for he had been informed that he was the most important person in the quartet. Adil, the other officer, kept near Scott, who appeared to be the most reckless of the four.

Felix was not attended by any one; but he had not gone more than a hundred yards before he saw a huge cobra directly in front of him, bestirring himself as though he "meant business." The fellow stood up, and he looked mad enough to chew up the hunter. But before he had time to discharge his piece at the monster, for he looked as though he was six feet long, Felix heard a rustling in the bushes at his left, and a moment later a disturbance on his right.

"He saw a huge cobra directly in front of him." — Page 242.

He looked in the direction of the noises, and saw two more cobras lifting their vicious heads into the air. These were more than he had bargained for; and, believing that discretion was the better part of valor, he climbed a tree in which he saw a convenient resting-place. Between him and the three snakes there was a small pool of water, half concealed by the bushes, and the reptiles had probably come there to drink or to obtain for food some of the amphibious creatures that lived there.

The enthusiastic sportsman had hardly begun to climb the tree before he heard a hissing behind him, and discovered another cobra. Two of the four in sight were much smaller than the other two, and he could easily believe he had come upon a family of them. He got a position in the tree, and lost no time in attacking the enemy. He was a good shot, for he and Louis had both been thoroughly trained in a shooting-gallery in New York. He gave his attention to the one nearest to him, and wondered he had not trodden upon him as he came to the spot.

As this one stood up Felix could see the top of his head, and he decided to use his revolver first. He fired; and, as the reptile was not ten feet from him, so skilful a marksman could hardly help hitting him. He did hit him, and the ball passed through his head. He wriggled a moment, and then stretched himself out at full length, dead.

One of the larger ones was within twenty-five feet of him, and he used his repeating rifle this time. He slipped a little in his perch as he discharged the piece, and the ball went through the snake's body, which was furiously mad, hissed and shook himself. He held still a moment, and then Felix fired again. The ball seemed to tear his head all to pieces, and he dropped down out of sight. He had to fire several times to kill the other two; for, as he expressed it, they "would not hold still."

But he had killed the four, and felt just as though he had settled the snake question. Most of the natives, who are oftener the victims of the cobra than the white people, go about in the dark with naked feet, and it is not strange that they are bitten. He descended from the tree, and went to examine the game he had brought down. Cutting some pliable sticks, he dragged the serpents together, and passed a withe around them behind the hood, and started back for the rendezvous where they were to take the carriage. He was determined to convince Scott that he was not afraid of snakes.

He had already heard several shots, and realized that his companions had found game of some kind. He waited a full hour for them, when Louis returned first, with a very handsome deer slung on a pole with Khayrat carrying the other end. Morris came in with a monkey, which the officers would not have permitted him to kill if they had been near him. Scott came in last with only a couple of birds.

"Did ye's mate ony cobrys, Musther Scott?" asked Felix.

"Not a cobra; and I didn't want to meet any," replied Scott, disappointed at his luck.

"You's air afeered of the schnakes," rallied the Milesian.

"So are you, Flix. If you saw one you wouldn't stop running till you got back to Baroda," returned the third officer of the ship.

"But I have seen four of them in my little walk, and I'm not doing any running just now," said Felix triumphantly.

"Go 'way with you, Milesian, and don't tell any fish stories!" replied Scott, continuing to blackguard him while the servants were putting the deer on the top of the wagon.

"Do you want to carry those snakes back to the palace?" asked Khayrat.

"What snakes?" asked Scott.

"I'll be most happy to introjuce you to four uv 'em I killed," added Felix; and Scott was convinced against his will, and the dead serpents were put on the wagon.

In another hour they reached the palace, and the game was exhibited to a wondering audience. The officers explained how so many of the cobras happened to be together; but Felix had reached a correct conclusion before. Mrs. Blossom scolded him for not running away when he saw the first one; but he declared he had to prove that a boy with Kilkenny blood in his veins was not afraid of snakes.

CHAPTER XXVI

THE MAGNIFICENT PROCESSION OF THE SOWARI

FELIX had to repeat his story, and he was regarded as quite a hero by the Americans, though Sir Modava and other natives thought but little of it. Mrs. Blossom continued to scold at him for not running away from the serpents.

"How could I run away when I was surrounded by the snakes?" demanded Felix, when the worthy lady's discipline became somewhat monotonous to him. "If I had done what you say I should certainly have been bitten. I did better: I climbed the tree, and bagged the whole four at my leisure."

"But snakes can climb trees," persisted the excellent woman.

"I suppose they can, but they don't always; and I knew the one nearest me wouldn't do much climbing with a hole through his head. Besides, they say the cobra does not come at you unless you meddle with him, like the rattlesnake. I suppose I disturbed them, and they hoisted the flags to let me know they were in town. I wanted to reduce the number of the varmints a little."

"But why did Khayrat tell me I ought not to have shot a monkey?" asked Morris.

"Because monkeys are harmless, and the Hindus consider them sacred. Before you get to Calcutta you will find them housed in temples. Besides, the natives are very tender of all animals," replied Sir Modava.

"In the hospital for lame ducks and superannuated bullfrogs we visited in Bombay, do they take in sick cobras?" asked Felix. "Do they nurse lame tigers?"

"They do not; it would not be quite safe to do so. Morris, the monkey you shot will be decently buried," said the Hindu gentleman.

"I am willing; for, though they eat them in some countries, I don't hanker after any monkey-flesh," replied the young hunter. "I met a man at my father's house who had lived for years in Africa, and he said they ate the boa-constrictor there, — the natives did, not the white people."

"So I have heard; but many Hindus never eat meat at all," added Sir Modava, as the party retired to dress for dinner.

The party were to dine at the palace with the Guicowar, and it was to be a state dinner. Though contrary to Hindu etiquette, the ladies were all invited, and they were treated with "distinguished consideration." It was a very elaborate occasion, and a few speeches were made at the last of it. The principal one was by the king himself, who enlarged upon his relations with Lord Tremlyn and Sir Modava, whom he regarded as two of his best friends,

From this point, he dwelt upon his esteem for the commander of the Guardian-Mother, who had rendered a service to India in saving them from certain death, which they, better than he, could understand and appreciate.

Captain Ringgold and General Noury made fitting replies; and the party returned, escorted by a score of torch-bearers, to the "Garden of Pearls" as the summer palace in which they were lodged was called. They appeared early in the morning, and after they had taken their coffee Louis and Felix took a long walk outside the palace walls. At the gate they saw a little animal which seemed disposed to make friends with them. They had brought their guns with them, and Felix was on the point of firing at him when Louis interposed.

"That's a mongoose," said the latter. "Haven't you heard of him?"

"Never did."

"The creature is a sort of ichneumon, with a long body, extending back of his hind legs, which gradually decreases in size till it becomes his tail. His body is long, even without the portion of it which belongs to his caudal appendage. He has a small head and a sharp nose, and is something like a weasel. He has the reputation of being the great serpent-killer of India, and many wonderful stories are told of him. He is very useful about a house in destroying rats and other small nuisances."

The mongoose ran along ahead of the boys while

Louis told what he knew about him. Felix protested that a little fellow like that couldn't do anything with such a cobra as he had shot the day before, for the snake was a trifle more than five feet long. They had gone but a short distance farther before Khayrat stepped out from a tree which had concealed him.

"There's a cobra in here somewhere," said the officer, who was one of the king's huntsmen. "I brought out my mongoose, but the little rascal has left me."

"There he is, just ahead of us," replied Louis. "He seems like a kitten, he is so tame."

"He is my pet, and I am very fond of him, for I think he saved my life once. I was just on the point of stepping on a cobra when Dinky attacked the snake and killed him after a fight," added Khayrat. "I think he is on the track of the enemy, for the serpent killed two chickens last night."

"There he is!" exclaimed Felix, as he brought his gun to his shoulder.

"Don't fire! Let Dinky take care of him; for my pet is spoiling for a fight, as one of the Americans said yesterday," interposed Khayrat.

The serpent was a large one, though not equal in size to the one Felix had shot the day before. He had erected his head, and spread out his hood, and he looked as ugly as sin itself. He knows all about the mongoose, and seems to have an instinctive hatred of his little but mighty enemy.

The little snake-killer made a spring at him, and then skilfully whirled himself around so that the snake could not bite him. Dinky knew what he was about all the time; and though his foe struck at him several times, he dodged him and put in several bites. After considerable manœuvring, the snake appeared to have had enough of it, and deemed it prudent to beat a retreat. He dropped on the ground, and headed for a thicket; but this was just what Dinky wanted. He sprang upon the neck of the cobra, placing his fore-paws on him, and then crushed his spine with his sharp teeth. The serpent was dead, after writhing an instant.

The fight was ended, and Khayrat caressed the victor. Louis declared that the mongoose was a friend worth having, and immediately made a bargain with the huntsman to procure him a couple of them, and send them to Calcutta. They returned to the palace; and at the breakfast-table Louis told the story of the battle, in which all the Americans were much interested. But the business of the forenoon was the great Sowari, or public procession; and the party were conveyed in carriages to the pavilion, from the veranda of which they were to see the spectacle. An abundance of easy-chairs was provided for them, and they were made very comfortable.

It required more than an hour for the procession to pass the point of observation; and when the last of it had disappeared in the distance all the Americans declared that they had never seen anything, even in

Europe, which could be compared with it in variety and magnificence. It was an Oriental spectacle, and the tourists could easily believe they had witnessed a pageant that had stepped out of the pages of the "Arabian Nights."

First came the regular soldiers of the Maharajah, who were sepoys, all under the command of English officers; and they marched like veterans who had been drilling half their lives. They were followed by a company of Arabs, who seemed to have been imported for the occasion. Sir Modava explained what the troops were as they passed. Next came a whole squadron of Mahratta cavalry, which looked as though they were serviceable soldiers of that arm, for they were good riders, well mounted, and were all lusty fellows.

After the cavalry came a troop of dromedaries with small cannons mounted on their backs, with gunners to work the pieces. The military portion of the procession was completed by several regiments of the Guicowar's special army. Following the household troops, apparently acting as an escort, came the royal standard-bearer, a personage of decided importance in an Oriental pageant. He was mounted alone on a huge elephant, magnificently caparisoned and adorned with the royal standard, a flag of cloth-of-gold, on a long staff.

In front of the elephant marched a band of eighteen or twenty native musicians, playing upon all sorts of Indian instruments, including tom-toms, lutes, like flageolets, cymbals, and horns. Surrounding the great beast that had the honor to bear the flag of the Mahratta States were numerous horsemen, all clothed in the richest Oriental costumes, armed with spears and curved sabres, with shining shields, and steel gauntlets on their hands. All these, and all the others, wore white turbans, picturesquely folded.

Behind the standard-bearer were two more elephants, each decked in all the splendor of the East; and mounted upon them were some of the great dignitaries of the court, over whom servants held highly fringed and ornamented umbrellas. In the procession was a troop of camels, all dressed out in the style of the horses and elephants. To say that the Americans were dazzled by the splendor of the scene would be to state it very mildly, for they were literally confounded and overwhelmed; and yet they had not seen the great feature of the spectacle, the Guicowar himself. Sir Modava had to talk very fast to describe the scene as it passed before them.

A dozen men, handsomely dressed like all the others, presently appeared, each bearing on a long pole something that looked like a crown. This was a sort of incense-censor, in which perfumes were burned, and from which a column of blue vapor proceeded. They were immediately before one of the king's elephants, which now came in front of the veranda. He was a gigantic creature, bearing on his back a howdah of solid gold. He was robed like the others, and the portions of his skin in sight were fantastically painted in various designs.

The howdah was surmounted by two pyramidal roofs, one in front of the other, supported by small columns. At the end of the elephant's tusks, which were sawed off square, were attached bouquets of rich feathers. On each side of the huge beast was a platform, suspended at the outside by golden cords, on which stood four men very richly dressed. One of them bears the hook, or pipe, presented to the Guicowar by the viceroy, another waves a banner, and the others flourish fans of peacock feathers. In front of the mahout is planted an ornament reaching nearly to the top of the howdah.

The golden howdah was presented by the Queen and Empress of India, and glitters with diamonds and other precious stones. The two domes make it look like two pavilions, and in the forward one sits the Guicowar in solemn dignity. He wears a tunic of scarlet velvet, which is covered with gold and diamonds. In fact, he seems to have diamonds enough to freight a schooner. Either he or one of his predecessors purchased a brilliant for which he paid the bagatelle of four hundred thousand dollars. Under the rear pavilion, and behind him, is the king's prime minister.

One of the officials at his side is the king's herald, who unfolds a flag of cloth-of-gold, and flourishes it before the people, and there are not less than a hundred thousand of them in the streets. As he does so he announces in good Hindustanee and in a loud voice a proclamation: "*Srimunt Sircar! Khunderao Guicowar! SenaKhas Khel! Shamshar Bahadoor!*"

"Exactly so," said Felix in a low tone.

"I suppose it is not given to outsiders to know what all that means?" added Louis.

"Certainly it is," replied Sir Modava. "It means, 'Behold the King of Kings, Khunderao Guicowar, whose army is invincible, whose courage is indomitable.'"

"Is that in a Pickwickian sense?" asked Scott.

"Not at all, for the Guicowar is as brave a man as ever put a foot into shoe-leather, or went barefooted," replied Lord Tremlyn, "though there is a little exaggeration common to the Orient in the proclamation."

As his Majesty came in front of the veranda the party rose and saluted him with low bows, and the waving of handkerchiefs by the ladies. He responded with a kingly smile and a graceful wave of the hand. The procession passed on, and shortly afterwards the booming cannon announced that the moment of the solemn benediction had come. The attentive officials of the court presently appeared with the carriages, and an invitation to the whole company to dine with the Guicowar again at his table.

They had to wait an hour for the king, but they found enough to interest them in observing the coming of numerous other guests. In an ante-room the floor was almost covered with shoes, many of them of the richest material, even with precious stones upon them. Sir Modava explained that Eastern etiquette required that the visitors going into the presence of the Maharajah should remove their shoes, but that Europeans and Americans were exempt from this requirement.

When the party entered they found the king seated in an apartment open to the air of heaven on two sides. All were barefoot or in their stocking-feet except the Guicowar, who occupied a bench, or platform, at one side. He had removed his state garments, and was dressed in a suit of white linen. Most of the native officials present were seated on the floor; but the gentlemen of the visitors were invited to sit with his Highness, though only Lord Tremlyn and Sir Modava accepted it.

CHAPTER XXVII

VARIOUS COMBATS IN THE GUICOWAR'S ARENA

THE party remained a week at the palace of the Guicowar, and every day had a new pleasure or recreation. The king was as familiar with all the members as though they had belonged to his own household. He was sociable with them, and they ceased to be embarrassed in his presence. Even Mrs. Blossom no longer trembled before him, and he was as jolly with the boys as though he had been one of them.

On the day after the Sowari the gentlemen of the party were conducted to the arena of the elephants, which was a large enclosure, reminding those who had seen them of the bull-rings of Spain. It was surrounded by buildings; and on one side, behind a wall, was a vast area of elevated ground from which the people of the town could witness the scenes presented in the arena.

The ladies of the party had made the acquaintance of those of their own sex in the household, and the sports of the day had been discussed among them. On this day it was to be an elephant fight. The native women did not attend, for they never took part in any public affair. Mrs. Belgrave, as soon as she learned the nature of the entertainment, promptly declined to be present at it, and the others were of the same mind.

To make the best of it, it was a brutal sport. The elephant is a noble beast, so intelligent that he deserves the consideration of man; and to them it seemed barbarous to set them fighting, even if the animals had belligerent instincts, though they never displayed them in their domesticated condition unless under strong provocation. Some of the gentlemen regarded the exhibition as but little better than a prize-fight; though they all attended the occasion, for the more sensitive ones thought it would be impolite to decline the invitation, especially as the exhibition was got up especially for them.

They were ushered into a large apartment, one side of which consisted of lofty arches, through which the display could be witnessed. At either end of the arena was chained a monster male elephant. A number of female elephants were on an elevation near it; and it seemed as though they were placed there for the same reason that the ladies were admitted to the tournaments of the knights in England and France. It was said that these females had a decided taste for such fights, and possibly the sight of them stimulated the male combatants.

There were a number of men, very slightly clothed, in the ring, who seemed like the *chulos* of the Spanish arena, though their functions could hardly be the same; and there were many openings in the walls through which they could escape, instead of leaping over the fence, as the bull-fighters do. Some of them were armed with lances, and others with a stick with fireworks at the end.

The Guicowar entered the spectators' apartment, which was already well filled with nobles and the foreigners. He was dressed in white linen, with an elegant cap on his head. He had a fine athletic form, and wore a short beard. He was not inclined to take the special arm-chair assigned to him, but walked about, speaking to his guests, not omitting the boys, to whom he appeared to have taken a fancy.

His Highness gave a signal, at which the mahouts took their places on the necks of the big beasts, and the chains which secured the combatants were cast off. The monsters roared, and, with their trunks elevated, advanced to the affray. They increased their speed as they came nearer to each other. They rushed together, as Scott expressed it, "head on," and the strangers seemed to feel the shock through their nerves. It was so violent the beasts dropped upon their knees forward.

Then they began to twist their trunks together, and buck with their tusks. For some minutes the giants wrestled together, but the combat proved to be of brief duration. The party could see that one of them was getting the worst of it, and was inclined to "hedge." In fact, he had had enough of it; but he was too wise to abandon his tactics when it was time for him to retreat. Mustering all his power, he made a desperate effort, and succeeded in forcing the other back enough to turn his huge body without exposing his flank to the tusks of the enemy, and then beat a hasty retreat.

The vanquished brute was removed from the arena, and the victor remained alone on the field he had won; but he had only come to the beginning of his troubles, for there was a second act to the affair. The men, who were armed with whips, fireworks, red cloths, and other instruments of torment, assailed him. They pricked him with the javelins, shook the red banners in his face, and fizzed the pyrotechnics before his eyes. They tormented the poor creature till he was furious. He had no adequate weapon for this unequal and unfair warfare.

He chased one assailant and then another, being as often turned aside from his intended victims by the thorning of the other tormentors. As he became a little more accustomed to the game, he ceased to be diverted from his victim and confined his attention to only one. The red banners, the blows from the whips, and the fizzing of the powder, did not affect him. He pursued his victim till the man was glad to save himself by dodging through one of the narrow doors in the wall, where the monster could not follow him. He butted against the wall, and then pounded the earth with his feet in the fury of his wrath.

If the man had far to run he would inevitably be lost; for the elephant, clumsy as he appears to be, develops great speed of foot when he is excited. An incident was related by one of the nobles to Captain Ringgold as the runner disappeared within the door. A young man who was very swift of foot was closely pursued by the elephant, and had reached the door, when he was seized by the arm, tossed in the air, and came down heavily on the ground. The foot of the infuriate beast was raised to crush his skull, when another man flashed a Bengal light in his face, with the flame almost in his eyes, and the giant bellowed and fled.

At the blast of a bugle all the men in the ring suddenly deserted it. The elephant looked about him for any new assailant, and was immediately provided with one. A door flew open, and a fine looking fellow, mounted on a magnificent horse, dashed into the arena. After the manner of the *matador* in a bull-fight, he conducted his steed, prancing in his pride, up to the arch at which the Guicowar stood, and saluted him with the grace of a knight-errant whose head was full of ladies.

The elephant is said to have an especial aversion to a horse; and the tormented beast in the ring at once manifested the prejudice of his race, for he made a dart for him. The horse did not flinch, but stood still till the giant was almost upon him. Then, at the command of his master, he wheeled, and the rider gave the big beast a smart punch with his lance. For a few minutes there was a lively skirmish between them, the horseman pricking him on the trunk or the flanks, and the rage of the elephant was at its highest pitch.

The fleetness of the horse and the skill of his rider kept the latter out of harm's way till the elephant seemed to be exhausted. The Americans thought he had done enough for one day, and the horseman retired. The great beast which had borne the brunt of three combats was allowed to cool off, and then his mahout conducted him to the rest he had bravely won. The nobles in attendance were sufficiently civilized to indulge in betting, and wagers had been made on the various fights in progress. Mr. Woolridge, who was a reformed sportsman, may have been tempted; but he did not feel at home in this kind of sporting, and he did not break through any of his good resolutions.

After the elephant had been removed, there was no little excitement among the assemblage in the veranda, and the betting seemed to be livelier than ever. A dozen officers armed with rifles and lances were stationed about the walls of the arena; and then an iron-bound cage was drawn into the enclosure, which contained a monstrous tiger. The guests wondered if this fierce brute was to be loosed in the arena, and they examined with interest into the safety of the situation. A number of rifles were brought into the veranda, with which the Guicowar and his native guests armed themselves.

"What does this mean, Sir Modava?" asked Captain Ringgold.

"The next battle will be a noble one, and immense wagers are depending upon the result," replied the Hindu gentleman.

"Is that big tiger to fight the crowd here assembled?"

"Not at all; but it is such a battle as has never been fought here, if anywhere. His Highness had long desired to see a bull-fight, and he imported four of the finest Spanish bulls his agent could find. The *toreadors* came with them; but they all refused to fight in this arena, which they declared was not adapted to the purpose, and they went home. Three of the bulls died of disease, and only one was left. A discussion arose as to whether he was a match for a tiger. This battle is to settle the question; and the bets are mostly in favor of the tiger, though the Guicowar, with a few others, places his stake on the bull," Sir Modava explained.

The tiger was released from the cage at a signal from the king. He leaped from the cage, and seemed to be astonished at the sight of so many people. Three officers took possession of the brute's prison, armed with rifles to shoot him if he killed the bull. No person was in the ring, or within reach of the savage animal. The door by which the horseman had entered was thrown wide open, and the bovine, vexed to the highest degree of wrath, came into the arena with a bounding run.

The tiger had advanced quietly to the centre of it, though with the royal mien of the "king of beasts,"

" The striped beast went up into the air." — Page 263.

as he was here, his eyes like a couple of coals of fire. He caught sight of the bull as soon as he appeared, for he had doubtless killed many a bullock in the jungle. He planted himself on the ground in readiness for a spring. His present enemy saw him at the same instant; but he did not halt, or show any signs of fear.

The bull crouched his head, increased his speed, and bounded on the tiger. At that moment the striped beast went up into the air so quickly that the audience could hardly see how it was done. His horned foe showed that he had not wholly escaped, for his head was covered with blood. But the tiger was not yet defeated. He sprang to his feet, and darted furiously at his enemy. He fastened with claws and teeth upon the neck of the bull, and the king believed that his wager was lost.

But the Spaniard shook him off, and turned upon him again, tossing him higher in the air than before. He came down badly disabled; and the bull, as though it was the finest sport in the world for him, gored him with his long horns till the life was gone out of him. The Spaniard was the victor. The people shouted themselves hoarse; but their cries were in honor of the Guicowar, and not the bull. The victor had lost a great deal of blood from a bad wound in the neck, and it was a question whether or not he would die; but he did not; he recovered, and before the tourists left India Sir Modava learned that he had been killed in a battle with a smaller tiger than the first.

Though the guests said but little about it, most of them were disgusted with these spectacles, and considered them cruel and brutal. They remained their week at Baroda. Those who desired to do so were taken to a hunt one day with a cheetah, in which this animal killed deer and other animals; and on another, on elephants, for tigers. Two tigers were killed, and Louis Belgrave had the honor of shooting one of them. Felix brought down a couple of cobras; and killing them seemed to be his forte. Khayrat invited the party to witness a battle between his mongoose and a couple of cobras his hunters had caught; and he killed them both, one at a time.

They all declined to attend a fight between a couple of coolies, with horn spikes attached to their hands, for this was worse than a prize-fight. But there was no end of amusements that were not brutal, and they enjoyed themselves abundantly to the end of their stay. They visited the temples and the palaces of the nobles, where they were received with the utmost attention. Captain Sharp and his wife declared this was the red-letter week of their lives; but the commander of the Blanche insisted that he must take his ship around to Calcutta, and left by train for Bombay the day before the company departed.

The Guicowar resorted to various expedients to retain his guests, with whom he was evidently sincerely pleased; but the commander was inflexible. It was not possible to see a tithe of India, and he felt obliged to leave at the expiration of the time he had fixed for the visit, and he begged Lord Tremlyn and Sir Modava not to place them in any more courts, or they would never get out of India. The train was prepared for their departure, and, in addition to the compartment cars in which they were to pass most of their time, a carriage was fitted up, so that all of them could assemble in it; in fact, it was a conference hall on wheels.

CHAPTER XXVIII

AT THE CAPITAL OF THE PUNJAB

An early breakfast was provided for the travellers, and at this repast the farewells were spoken. Speeches were made by all the principal persons of the party of Americans, and by the Moroccan magnate, expressive of the very great enjoyment of the visit, and in praise of the liberality of the kingly host's hospitality. Captain Ringgold returned his thanks quite eloquently.

The Guicowar again enlarged upon the service the commander had rendered to India in saving the lives of two of his best friends, who had also been the friends of his country, and his only regret was that the Americans could not remain longer. Lord Tremlyn and Sir Modava could not in a lifetime discharge their obligations to their friends who had entertained them like princes on board of the Guardian-Mother.

The ladies did not make speeches; but they expressed their gratitude to his Highness in a less prominent manner for the kindness extended to them, and at the close of the entertainment Miss Blanche advanced to the king, and presented to him a package containing the photographs of the whole company, and that of General Noury, each with the autograph upon it.

"I am very sorry that our party are unable to present to your Highness a gift in keeping with the magnificence of the hospitality extended to us," said the beautiful young lady; "but this package contains the photograph of every member of our company, and we beg that you will accept them as the only tribute of our gratitude for your kindness which is available to us at this distance from our homes. We leave behind us our best wishes for the prosperity, health, and happiness of your Highness."

The Guicowar declared that he should value the gift more than all the gold and gems that could have been gathered together, and he should always remember with delight the fairy who had presented them to him, and it would afford him the greatest pleasure to look in the future upon the faces of those whose presence at the palace he had so greatly enjoyed.

The actual parting was the scene of a great deal of hand-shaking, mingled with pretty speeches. The Guicowar went with them to the station, and saw them seated in the great carriage that had been prepared for them. The train moved off, with handkerchiefs waving at every window, and with a profusion of gestures on the part of the magnificent host. It required some time to talk about the scenes at the court of the king, though all of the party were observing the country through the windows.

It was a strange country to the Americans; and

they found something to look at all the time, though it was a wild and rugged region for the first two hours, with only a single town that was noticeable in that time. As they were passing out of Baroda, the viscount called their attention to a building at some distance from the road, and called it a "travellers' bungalow." It was a very comfortable house, where tourists may find hotel accommodations, though they are hardly hotels. They are provided by the government, and are to be found in all the travelled regions of India. They are sometimes free for the rooms, but the guest pays at a very low rate for his food.

"We are coming now to Ahmedabad, which is in Gujrat, or Goozerat, for you take your choice in regard to many of these Indian names; and this city is its chief town, and the second in the province of Bombay. It was formerly one of the largest and most magnificent cities of the East, as the ruins still indicate. It contains several elegant mosques, but the town has not more than a seventh part of its former population of nine hundred thousand," said Sir Modava, as he opened a travelling-bag, and took from it a large bundle of photographs.

"Oodeypore is the capital of a Rajputana state; and its palace is said to be the largest and most magificent in India, though the town has a population of less than forty thousand. The maharajah entertained the Prince of Wales in it when he made his progress through the country. It is built in the mountains, and it would be a troublesome journey for us to reach it. The next city of any importance to which we shall come is Jeypore, and we shall dine there."

When the train stopped for water a lunch was sent to the compartments, to which all the passengers now retired for the rest of the day. At Jeypore dinner was served, good enough, though not elaborate. At the table Sir Modava passed around some photographs of the place, including the palace of the Maharajah, the Golden Kiosk, and the temples of the valley of Ambir. It was impossible to visit all the wonderful structures on the road without spending at least a year in the country; and a dozen volumes would hardly contain the description of them. The palace at Jeypore is half a mile long, and contains one seventh of the area of the town.

Though the railroad passed within fifty miles of Delhi, the train sped on its way to the north all night and nearly the whole of the next day, arriving at Lahore at five in the afternoon. No towns of any considerable importance were passed during this long stretch of 540 miles. Though Lord Tremlyn and Sir Modava, with their friends, were invited to the residence of the lieutenant-governor, the party went to the Victoria Hotel, for the viscount thought it would be an imposition to quarter them on the chief authority, being eighteen in number.

"We are now in the Punjab, the north-western corner of India," said the Hindu gentleman, when they were seated in the parlor of the hotel. "It is watered by the Indus and five of its branches, on one of which, the Ravi, Lahore is situated. Punjab means five rivers. It has a population of more than twenty-five million; and, General Noury, it has more Mohammedans than the whole of Morocco. I will not give you any more statistics, for I fear you would not remember them."

"Thank you, Sir Modava," added Mr. Woolridge.

"The manufactures of silk, cotton, and metals are very important; for the soil is not very fertile, though cotton, rice, sugar, indigo, and all kinds of grains and fruits, are raised. Lahore is the capital of the Punjab, and has a population of a hundred and seventy-seven thousand, though it once contained a million. At this point we are near the Himalaya Mountains. About a hundred and fifty miles east of Lahore is Simla, nearly eight thousand feet above the sea. This is a noted sanitarium; and in the hot season it is the resort of thousands of people, including the highest officers of the army and the government."

"Is this as near the Himalayas as we are to go?" asked Scott.

"About as near, though at Patna you will be about one hundred and fifty miles from Mount Everest, the highest peak on the earth."

"I should like to go there," added Scott.

"You couldn't climb it; and what good would it do you? I could mention a hundred places in India I should like to visit; but it is not practicable to do so," added the commander. "We can only take along with us a few specimens of the wonderful country, and make the best of them."

After dinner the party divided up according to their own fancy, and went out to walk, though some were too tired to do so. Louis invited Miss Blanche to go with him; and she was always glad to be in his company, especially as Sir Modava was to be his companion. The first sight they saw in the street was a regiment of Punjab sepoys, a well-drilled body of men, not very different from the soldiers they had seen in other countries.

They wore frock-coats, buttoned tight to the throat, and a sort of turban on the head. Their faces were swarthy, but none of them wore full beards. There were plenty of street sights after the regiment had passed. The different kinds of vehicles attracted their attention first. In a kind of gig drawn by a horse, two men and two women were crowded together. The driver seemed to be seated behind, and one of the women was on the floor in front of the two who were seated. By the side of the man on the seat was a girl of sixteen or eighteen, and she was very pretty.

In a two-wheeled cart drawn by a humped bullock were a couple of Hindu ladies, under a canopy supported by four poles. Then came a camel bearing two bearded men on his back. Two or three palanquins were seen; but they were an old story, and they turned their attention to the architecture of the houses that lined the street. There was an abundance of what we call bay-windows, and ornamented balconies. There was a great deal of variety in the construction of these appendages of the houses; and all of them were occupied by ladies, who wore no veils over their faces, though most of them were doubtless Mohammedans, and the yashmak had evidently gone out of fashion.

"There is the dak-bungalow," said the Hindu gentleman as they passed a building of considerable size.

"What is a dak-bungalow?" asked Louis.

"It is one which answers the purpose of a hotel. I pointed one out to you at Baroda. Sometimes they are free so far as the rooms are concerned; but here the guest pays two rupees a day, or fifty cents of your money, and the food is furnished at a low price."

"But this is not half so much of a place as I expected to find," said Louis, after they had walked an hour, and it was time to return to the hotel.

"It is a place of considerable importance, though there are not so many temples, mosques, tombs, and other fine structures, as in many other cities of India; and I wondered that the commander had placed it in his list of places to be visited. Jeypore and Oodeypore would have been far more interesting to your party," replied Sir Modava. "Yet you will see some of the finest structures in the country before you reach Calcutta."

The company returned to the hotel at an early hour, and all of them were tired enough to retire at once. But they were up at six in the morning, and the four boys went out to explore the city by themselves for a couple of hours. Even at this early hour the ladies, old and young, were in the balconies, and they were much occupied in observing the latter. Though the yashmak, or veil, was not often used to cover the face, it appeared to have been only thrown back upon the head.

After breakfast carriages were at the door to convey the party to the more interesting sights of the city. At the request of Lord Tremlyn, they were driven first to the office of the lieutenant-governor, to whom they were presented. The government buildings are in Lawrence Hall Gardens, where there is also a memorial building in honor of Lord John Lawrence, the first lieutenant-governor, who won his distinction in subduing and ruling over the Punjab.

They were next conveyed to the mosque of Jehanghir, built of red stone, and so much like a score of other mosques that they were not much interested in the building. The mosque of Vazir Khan pleased them more; for it was a beautiful edifice, though crumbling before the ravages of time. But even here they were more pleased on observing the loafers around the entrance and in the court in front of it. An old bald-headed Hindu, with a beard as white as snow, was a study to the boys; and perhaps it was fortunate that the subject of their remarks did not understand English, or there might have been another war in the Punjab.

The cook-shops in the street were instructive to them, and they watched the customers with interest; but, as they had attempted to eat in a Turkish restaurant in Constantinople, they were content with looking on. The minarets of the Vazir Khan pleased all the party, for they were certainly very beautiful. They went to the Golden Temple of Amritsar in the afternoon, and were impressed with the beauty of its surroundings.

Lahore was rather a disappointment to the tourists, though it would not have been if they had not spent some days in Bombay before visiting it. The train in which they had come from Baroda was to be used by them as far as Calcutta, and they were ready to leave that night. The journey was by a different route from that by which they had come, and through a more densely populated region. It was a bright moonlight night when the train passed out of the capital of the Punjab.

They had gathered in what they had come to call the Conference Hall compartment; and as they looked out into the light of the evening they believed they could see some of the peaks of the Himalayas, though Lord Tremlyn doubted it. Possibly they saw some of the peaks, for Mount Nauda Devi was within a hundred miles of the point on the railroad where they would be in the morning; and this is more than twenty-five thousand feet high. Mont Blanc is seen in very clear weather at the distance of a hundred miles, and it is about eight thousand feet less in height.

They were awake very early in the morning, and they certainly saw some high mountains in the distance, but could not identify them by name. At eight o'clock the train rolled into the station at Delhi, perhaps the most wonderful city of India.

CHAPTER XXIX

THE WONDERFUL CITY OF DELHI

The Mohammedans of Bombay whose acquaintance General Noury had made were wealthy and influential men; they had notified their friends in other cities of the coming of the distinguished Moroccan, and he had several invitations to make his home in Delhi with them. Lord Tremlyn and Sir Modava were even more abundantly tendered accommodations from British and Hindu persons of distinction.

Captain Ringgold had no friends, and received no invitations, though the entire company of tourists were included in those of both the general and the distinguished gentlemen who had insisted upon being the hosts of the party. But the commander was a wealthy man himself, and a very independent one. To throw a company of a dozen and a half upon the generous hospitality of private individuals, or even public officials, seemed like an imposition to him.

The viscount and his Hindu companion were equally sensitive on this point; and it was proposed by Sir Modava to divide the guests among those who had not only given the invitations but had pressed them upon the travellers. The others did not like this plan; and, after some consideration, it was decided to go to a hotel; at least it was suggested as the remedy by the commander, who again insisted upon paying the bill. But there was no suitable hotel in the place. The dak-bungalow was the only resort, though a hotel was soon to be opened. Those who were consulted in the party were all for the bungalow, and the problem was finally settled in this manner.

A couple of small omnibuses were taken, and the party proceeded to the dak-bungalow, which was in the centre of the city. Their apartments were not elegant, but they were comfortable; and no one found any fault at the absence of the splendors with which they had been surrounded in the palace of the Guicowar, or even those of Bombay. A good breakfast was obtained, and the forenoon was given up to rest; but after a couple of hours in their chambers the company were assembled in the coffee-room.

"Delhi is a city which figures largely in the history of India," said Lord Tremlyn, seated very informally in an arm-chair. "It existed fifteen or twenty centuries before the time of Christ, and was the capital of the great Aryan empire. It was founded by the invaders of India. The chronology of India is not reliable, but it is claimed that this event dates back to 3101 B.C. Its name was Indrapechta, which it holds to the present time among the learned Hindus, so that the city appears to have existed while Egypt was still in its infancy.

"It became the great Mussulman capital; but one

and another of its princes changed its location, till its ancient sites extend for thirty miles along the river, and its ruins, more extensive than even those of Rome, cover this range of territory. But I shall not go into the details of those migratory periods, but speak only of the city as we find it.

"Delhi is on the Jumna River, which you saw in the early morning. This stream has its entire course in Hindustan, and is the principal tributary of the Ganges. Both of these rivers are sacred with the natives. The Jumna rises in the Himalayas, at a height of nearly eleven thousand feet, and of course it is a mountain torrent at its upper waters. After a run of eight hundred and sixty miles, it falls into the Ganges about three miles below Allahabad. On each side of it is an important canal, both built before railways were in use here.

"Delhi is nine hundred and fifty-four miles northwest of Calcutta. It stands on high ground, is walled on three sides, and has ten gates. A series of buildings formerly composing the grand palace of Shah Jehan have become the fort, overlooking the river, with a fine view of the surrounding country, covered with woods and agricultural grounds. You will see the palaces, mosques, and temples, and I will not describe them. Delhi is the seventh city in population, which is a hundred and ninety-three thousand."

After luncheon half a dozen landaus were at the door of the bungalow, in which the party seated themselves according to their own choice; and the first stop was made at the Jummah Musjid Mosque, which the Mussulmans of India venerate and admire more than any other. It is built on an immense esplanade, which is mounted by three flights of stairs, each in the form of the three sides of a pyramid, and each leading to an immense pointed arch, the entrances to the buildings.

Before the party entered a carriage arrived, from which General Noury and another person alighted. The Moroccan had accepted the invitation of a Delhi Mussulman to be his guest, and this gentleman had begun to show him the sights of the city. The general presented him to the members of the party as Abbas-Meerza. Evidently in honor of his host the Moroccan had put on his Oriental dress, which was certainly a very picturesque costume, though it called up unpleasant memories in the minds of the commander and the Woolridges.

Abbas-Meerza was evidently a Persian, or the son of one; for he was clothed in the full costume of that country. He wore a rich robe, reaching to his ankles, with a broad silk belt around his waist. His cap, of equally costly material, was a tall cylinder, with the top slanting down to the left side, as though it had been cut off. He spoke English as fluently as the general. He invited the party to step to a certain point, and view the mosque as a whole.

The wall of the esplanade was a continued series of pointed arches, with a handsome frieze above it. On the elevated platform was a colonnade of the same arches on each side, with a pillared tower at each corner, interrupted only at the grand entrances. It looked as though one might walk entirely around the vast structure in the shade of this colonnade.

Within the enclosure could be seen three domes, the one in the centre overtopping the other two, two lofty minarets, with small domes at the summit, supported by several columns, and an immense pointed arch leading into the great mosque. The whole edifice is built of red sandstone. The visitors mounted one of the staircases, and entered a court paved with marble tiles. They walked around the esplanade under the arches of the colonnade, or cloisters as some call them, and finally entered the mosque itself. The interior was very simple in its style, but very beautiful. The roof, pavement, pillars, and walls were of white marble, ornamented with carvings in the stone. Slabs of black marble presented sentences to the praise of God, and in memory of Shah Jehan, who was the founder of the mosque.

"Formerly no person not a Mussulman was permitted to enter this mosque," said Sir Modava, while the general and his host were engaged in their devotions; "but for more than thirty years it has been open to all. From the top of one of the minarets a very fine view of the surrounding country can be obtained; but the ascent is by a very narrow flight of circular stairs, two hundred in number. He advised Dr. Hawkes and Uncle Moses not to attempt it."

A venerable mollah was found, who put half a

dozen of the party in the way of going up; and they reported the view as worth the labor and fatigue. The aged priest then proposed to show them the relics of the mosque; and a fee was paid to him, and to the man who unlocked a door for their admission. The mollah produced a small golden box, from which he took a silver case. Muttering the name of Allah very solemnly all the time, he unscrewed the top of the receptacle, and took from it a single hair, about six inches long, red and stiff, and fixed in a silver tube.

"The beard of the holy Prophet!" he announced, with a reverent inclination of his head; and the two Mussulmans of the party followed his example.

"According to the tradition, this hair really came from the beard of Mohammed," said Sir Modava. "I believe it, because I have inquired into its history. It is the glory of this mosque and of Delhi, for only three others exist in the world. You need not believe it is genuine if you prefer not to do so."

They were also permitted to gaze at one of Mohammed's old shoes, a belt, and some of the clothing of the Prophet. A number of dusty ancient manuscripts were exhibited, copies of the Koran, one in fine characters, said to have been dictated by Mohammed himself. The party returned to the carriages, filled with admiration of the magnificent structure they had visited, and were driven to the palace of the emperors, now turned into the fort.

They left the landaus at a point selected by Abbas-

Meerza, from which an excellent view of the ancient structures could be obtained. It was a magnificent building, whose dimensions the Americans could hardly take in. The most prominent features from the point of observation were a couple of octagonal towers, very richly ornamented, with several small domes at the summit, supported on handsome columns.

The party entered at the principal gate, and came to the guard-house, which was filled with British soldiers wearing straw helmets and short white coats. A soldier offered his services as a guide, and they were accepted. He gave the Hindu names of the apartments. The Dewani-Am was the hall of audiences, from which they passed to the Dewani-Khas, the throne-room, both of which recalled the Alhambra, which they had visited a few months before. The pillars, arches, and ornaments were similar, though not the same.

The tourists wandered through the pavilion, the emperor's rooms in the palace, the bath, and numerous apartments. But in transforming this magnificent palace of the emperors into barracks, much of the original beauty had been spoiled; the lapse of years had made great rents in the walls, and the visitor was compelled to exercise his imagination to some extent in filling up what it had been centuries before.

Abbas-Meerza was a very companionable person, and made the acquaintance of every one in the company. He then invited them all to dine with him that day, as he had evidently intended to do in the morning, for the dinner was all ready when they arrived at his palace. He was a magnate of the first order, and his apartments were quite as sumptuous as those of the Guicowar of Baroda. The dinner was somewhat Oriental, but it was as elegant as it was substantial.

The noble host apparently wished to show the Americans what the Mussulmans of India could do, and he crowned his magnificent hospitality by inviting the entire company to install themselves in his mansion, which was large enough for a palace; but for the reasons already set forth, the invitation was gratefully declined. The next morning the travellers visited the Mosque of Pearls, where the ancient emperors came to perform their devotions. The interior is of carved ivory.

From this little gem of a church the company were driven to the Chandi Chowk, which is a boulevard, planted with trees and lined with elegant buildings. The stores of the principal merchants of Delhi were here, and most of them were on the plan of an Oriental bazaar. The little square shops challenged the attention of the party, and most of them alighted to examine the rich goods displayed.

In the course of the ride they passed the Black Mosque, the only building in the city dating farther back than the reign of Shah Jehan. They found the bungalow surrounded and partly filled, on their return, by venders of relics, curiosities, and other wares, anxious to find customers for their goods. But they were not very fortunate in the enterprise, and finally they were all driven away by an officer.

In the afternoon they drove out on the plains of Delhi, among the ruins of palaces, tombs, and temples. They stopped at another black mosque, near which was a handsome pavilion, which had been the library of the emperors.

"One of these emperors was Houmayoun, who recovered the throne after a long banishment. He lost his life in consequence of a fall from the top of a ladder he had mounted to obtain a book," said Sir Moava. "He was the real founder of the Great Mogul dynasty. His mausoleum, to which we will go next, is one of the noblest monuments on this plain;" and the carriages proceeded to it.

It is a mass of white marble and red sandstone. It has a fine dome, around which cluster several smaller structures, such as we should call cupolas in America or England. Under the great dome in the building is a plain tombstone, beneath which are the remains of the first of the Mogul emperors. The mausoleum is placed on an esplanade, like the great mosque in the city. The sides present a vast display of pointed arches, and its shape on the ground is quite irregular.

The party were driven to the tower of Koutub, a Mussulman conqueror, who commemorated his victory by building this triumphal column, which is two hundred and twenty-seven feet high. It consists of five stories, becoming smaller as they ascend. The remains of his mosque were visited, the columns of which look like enlarged jewellery, elaborately worked into fantastic forms. By its side is an iron column with contradictory stories about its origin. The tourists visited other mosques and tombs, which reminded them of the tombs of the Mamelukes.

For two days longer they looked about Delhi; and Lord Tremlyn pointed out to them the scenes of the massacre, which he had described on board of the Guardian-Mother. On the train by which they had come they proceeded to Agra.

CHAPTER XXX

THE MAGNIFICENT MAUSOLEUM OF AGRA

SEVERAL hotels were available on the arrival of the travellers at Agra, and they were domiciled at Lawrie's. The journey was made in an afternoon, and was through a densely populated territory, so that the trip was very enjoyable. After dinner the party assembled in a parlor provided for their use; and Lord Tremlyn gave a talk, for he objected to the formality of a lecture. He seated himself in an easy-chair, and took from his pocket a little book, to which he occasionally referred.

"Agra, on the whole, is the handsomest city of Upper India, though of course there may be some difference of opinion in this matter," he began. "It is eight hundred and forty-one miles north-west of Calcutta, and one hundred and forty south-east of Delhi. Like Delhi, it is on the Jumna, which is here crossed by a floating bridge. One of the most prominent buildings is the fortress of Akbar, and you must know something of this sovereign in order to understand Agra.

"He was known as Akbar the Great, the Mogul emperor of India, and the greatest Asiatic monarch of modern times. He was the son of Houmayoun, whose mausoleum you visited at Delhi. The father was robbed of his throne, and retreated to Persia; and it was on the way there that Akbar was born, in 1542. After an exile of twelve years, Houmayoun recovered his throne, but lost his life within a year after his return. The government was committed to the care of a regent, who became a tyrant; and the young prince took possession of it himself at the age of eighteen.

"At this time only a few provinces were subject to the rule of his father; but in a dozen years Akbar had made himself master of all the country north of the Vindhya Mountains, or of a line drawn from Baroda to Calcutta, though he was not so fortunate in subduing the southern portion of the peninsula. He was a great conqueror; yet, what is not so common with the mighty rulers of the world, past or present, he was a wise and humane monarch, and governed his realm with wisdom and vigor. His reign was the most unparalleled, for his justice, energy, and progressive character, of any in the East. In this manner he made his empire the greatest of the age in which he lived.

"He fostered commerce by the construction of roads, by the establishment of an excellent police system, and introduced a uniform system of weights and measures. He looked after the administration of his viceroys in his numerous provinces, permitted no extortion on the part of his officers, and saw that justice was impartially meted out to all classes. He was a Mohammedan, but he was tolerant of all the prevailing sects in religion.

"He gave the Hindus entire freedom of worship; though far in advance of his successors, he prohibited cruel customs, such as the burning of widows, and other barbarous practices. He founded schools and encouraged literature. He inquired into the various forms of religion, and even sent for Portuguese missionaries at Goa to explain the Christian faith to him. From the various beliefs he made up a kind of eclectic religion; but it was not a success outside of his palace. A history of his reign of fifty years was written by his chief minister. Akbar died in 1605, and was interred in a beautiful mausoleum, near the city.

"With the ordinary sights of India you are already somewhat familiar; and, aside from what you may see in any city here, there is not much to interest you, with the grand exception of the Taj, and some of the mausoleums, of which I will say nothing, as we are now to visit them."

The company retired early, and after breakfast the next morning the carriages were at the door. In the first one were Captain Ringgold, Mrs. Belgrave, and Sir Modava. Lord Tremlyn had more than once manifested a desire to be in the same carriage with Miss Blanche; and he went with her and Louis on this occasion, while Mr. and Mrs. Woolridge invited General Noury to accompany them.

"Akbar made Agra the capital of the Mogul Empire," said Sir Modava, as the carriage started. "He changed its old name to Akbarabad, and the natives call it so to this day."

"The termination of that name seems to be very common in India, as Allahabad, Almedabad, Hyderabad," added the commander.

"In the Hindu, *abad* means a town or a village; and if you cut off that ending you will find the person or place for whom it was named, as Akbar--abad."

"Precisely as it is in our country, where we have Morris-town, Allen-town, Morgan-town, and a thousand others," added the captain.

"After the death of Akbar his successors reigned in Delhi. The Mogul Empire came to an end in 1761; and Agra was sacked by the Jats, and later the Mahrattas completed the destruction they had begun. It was captured from Scindia in 1803 by the English under Lord Lake, and has since remained in their possession. In all these disasters its population, which had been seven hundred thousand, dropped to ten thousand; but under British rule it recovered some of its former prosperity, and it is now about one hundred and seventy thousand.

"If a man wants to build a house here he has only to dig for the material, for not far down he will find the stone and brick of the structures that crumbled into the earth after the death of the great emperor. We are now approaching the fortress, or the citadel as it is oftener called. It is a sort of acropolis, for it contains palaces, mosques, halls of justice, and other buildings."

The carriages stopped at the principal gate, opposite to which is the mosque of Jummah Musjid, or the Cathedral Mosque. About all the great structures here are built of red sandstone, with marble bands on many of them, so that it is hardly necessary to mention the material, unless it varies from the rule. This mosque is a fine one, mounted on a marble esplanade or platform, like most buildings of this description.

Crossing the drawbridge, the visitors came to the Palace of Justice, built by Akbar. It is six hundred feet long, enclosed by a colonnade of arches, like a cloister. It is now used as a military storeroom, divided by brick walls, and filled with cannon and shot. The English have made a sort of museum here; and the superior officer who did the honors to his lordship showed them the throne of Akbar, a long marble seat, inlaid with precious stones, with a graceful canopy of the same material over it; and the boys thought he would have had a more comfortable seat if he had put off the period of his reign to the present time.

The gates of Somnath, twelve feet high, were beautiful pieces of carving. They once guarded the entrance to the temple of Krishna, in Goojerat; but in the tenth century they were carried off by Sultan Mahmoud, of Ghuzni, in Afghanistan. He captured Somnath, and destroyed all the idols. The Brahmins offered him immense bribes if he would spare the statue of Krishna; but he spurned the money, and destroyed the image with his own hands. He found that it was hollow, and filled with jewels of great value.

When the English conquered Afghanistan, Lord Ellenborough sent the gates to Agra; but some think they were not the gates of the temple, but of Mahmoud's tomb, for they were made of a wood that does not grow in India, and they are not of Hindu workmanship. From the museum the party walked to the imperial palace of Akbar, still in an excellent state of preservation. Some of the apartments, especially the bath-room of the monarch, made the visitors think of the Arabian Nights.

The great black marble slab on which Akbar sat to administer justice was pointed out. When one of the Jat chiefs seated himself upon it, the story goes, it cracked, and blood flowed from the fracture. Lord Ellenborough tried the experiment, and the stone broke into two pieces. The Mosque of Pearls is a small building of white marble on a rose-colored platform. It is considered by experts the finest piece of architecture in the fortress. Nothing could be simpler, nothing grander. Bishop Heber visited it and wrote this of it:—

"This spotless sanctuary, showing such a pure spirit of adoration, made me, a Christian, feel humbled, when I considered that no architect of our religion had ever been able to produce anything equal to this temple of Allah."

Following the Jumna, the carriages reached the Taj, the wonder and glory of all India. It was built by the Emperor Shah Jehan, as a mausoleum for the Empress Mumtazi Mahal. She was not only beautiful, but famous for mental endowments; and the emperor had so much love and admiration for her that he determined to erect to her memory the most beautiful monument that had ever been constructed by any prince. It was begun in 1630, and twenty thousand workmen were employed upon it for seventeen years. History says that one hundred and forty thousand cartloads of pink sandstone and marble were brought from the quarries of Rajputana; and every province of the empire furnished precious stones to adorn it. Its cost was from ten to fifteen millions of dollars.

The golden crescent of the Taj is two hundred and seventy feet above the level of the river. The magnificent temple is placed in the centre of a garden nine hundred and sixty feet long by three hundred and thirty in width, filled with avenues flanked with cypress-trees, and planted with flowers, on a terrace of sandstone. In the centre of this garden is a marble platform, two hundred and eighty-five feet on all sides, and fifteen feet high, which may be called the pedestal of the mosque. The principal entrance to the garden is more elaborate and beautiful than the fronts of many noted mosques, for it is adorned with towers crowned with cupolas.

Entering the enclosure, and walking along the

avenue of cypress-trees, one obtains his first view of the great dome of the Taj. It looks like about three-fourths of a globe, capped with a slender spire. From this point, through the trees, may be seen a forest of minarets, cupolas, towers, and inferior domes. The mausoleum is in the form of an irregular octagon, the longest side being one hundred and twenty feet in length. Each façade has a lofty Saracenic arch, in which is an entrance.

The interior surpasses the exterior in magnificence, the ceiling, walls, and tombstones being a mass of mosaics. The resting-place of the empress and Shah Jehan is in the centre of the edifice, enclosed by a marble screen. Some experts who have examined the building thoroughly are unable to find any architectural faults, though perhaps others would be more successful. The party visited several other mosques and mausoleums; but nothing could compare with the Taj. The commander suggested that they ought to have visited it last, as the pie or pudding comes in after the fish or meats at Von Blonk Park.

The members of the party were unable to say enough in praise of the Taj, and no one seems to be in danger of exaggerating its beauty and its wonders. On their return to the hotel, they seated themselves in their parlor, and talked till dinner-time about the mausoleum, for they had many questions to ask of the viscount and the Hindu gentleman.

"There seemed to be two other mosques back of

the mausoleum," said Mrs. Belgrave; "we did not visit them."

"The Mohammedan traditions require that a mosque should be erected in connection with every mortuary temple," replied Sir Modava. "Isa Mohammed, a later emperor, built one at the western end of the terrace. It was a beautiful building with three domes, in keeping with the Taj. But the builder found that it gave a one-sided appearance to the view; and he erected the one on the east end, to balance the other and restore the proportions. Either of them is equal to the finest mosque in Cairo or Constantinople."

"That was an expensive method of making things regular," added the commander. "Some one spoke in Delhi of a durbar in connection with Agra. I think it was Mr. Meerza."

General Noury laughed at this title; for it sounded funny to him, applied to an Oriental, and the captain had forgotten the rest of the name.

"Abbas-Meerza, we call him, without any 'mister,'" he added.

"I will try to remember it," replied the commander. "But what is a durbar? Is it something good to eat?"

"They do not eat it here, and probably it would be indigestible if they could do so," continued Sir Modava. "A durbar is a very important event in India, but is not eatable. It is an occasion at which the native princes acknowledge the sovereignty of the Queen of England. In 1866 the most noted one took place at Agra, a full description of which would require a long time. For the first time after the establishment of the Empire of India, the governor-general, representing the empress, received the homage of twenty-six sovereign princes. It was an act of submission. The ceremonies occupied many days; and kings, maharajahs, rajahs, and other princes bowed to the throne of the sovereign. It was a tremendous occasion; and it was a festival honored by banquets, processions, and royal gatherings. I will get a book for you, Captain Ringgold, when we reach Calcutta, from which you may read a full account of the affair. It grew out of an ancient Indian custom, and many of them on a small scale have occurred."

The tourists spent another day at Agra, and, though they had not exhausted the sights of the place, the commander decided that they could remain no longer, and they left on the following day for Cawnpore.

CHAPTER XXXI

THE TERRIBLE STORY OF CAWNPORE AND LUCKNOW

AGRA is on one of the great railroads from Bombay to Calcutta, though not the most direct one; and it crosses the Jumna at this point, where a vast bridge was in process of construction over its waters, which must now be completed. It was but a five hours' journey to Cawnpore, and the party arrived there in season for luncheon.

"Cawnpore is on the right bank of the Ganges, six hundred and twenty-eight miles from Calcutta," said Lord Tremlyn, when the party were seated in the Conference-Hall carriage, and the train was moving away from Agra. "But, so far as viewing the wonderful buildings of India, you will have a rest at this place; though you need not suppose it is a city of no importance, for it has 188,712 inhabitants, and has a large trade. Here you will obtain your first view of the Ganges, varying in width from a third of a mile to a mile.

"The great river is one of the special objects of interest to the tourist in coming from Bombay, for here he usually gets his first view of it. There are important buildings here, including mosques and temples, but none to compare with those you have already seen. The Indian Mutiny of 1857 attracts many visitors to the place."

"I don't think I care to see any more great buildings," interposed Mrs. Belgrave.

"There are none here to see; and we shall remain here only long enough to see the sites connected with the mutiny."

"I should like to hear the story of the mutiny over again," added the lady.

"I was able to give only a very brief and imperfect account of the rebellion, with so great a subject as India in general on my hands, on board of your ship, and very likely there will be occasion to repeat some portions of it as we point out the various spots connected with it," replied Lord Tremlyn.

The accommodations for the party were ready on their arrival, and even the luncheon was on the table. Before they had disposed of it the landaus were at the door. Three military officers were also in attendance, appointed to render all the assistance to the company they needed. They were introduced to the members of the party, and then they were driven to the fort.

"At the time of the mutiny Cawnpore contained about one thousand English people, one half of whom were women and children," said Captain Chesly, the principal of the officers. "The troops were provided with ill-constructed intrenchments for their defence. I am informed that his lordship has already given you some details of the rebellion, but as I am not aware of the extent to which he has given them I shall probably repeat some of them."

"The party will be glad to have them repeated," added Lord Tremlyn. "I told them who and what Nana Sahib was."

"His first act after taking the lead in the rebellion of the sepoys was to murder one hundred and thirty-six of our people, who were deceived by the sympathy he had formerly manifested for them, and easily fell into his hands. Two hundred and fifty soldiers, with as many women and children, the latter in the military hospital, had taken refuge in the fort. As soon as he had completed his bloody work in the massacre, Nana Sahib besieged the feeble garrison. They defended themselves with the utmost bravery and skill against the vast horde of natives brought against them.

"For three weeks they held out against the overwhelming force that was thirsting for their blood. Their chief had anticipated no such resistance, and he was impatient at the delay in finishing the butchery. He resorted to an infamous stratagem, proposing to General Wheeler, who was in command of the British troops, to grant him all the honors of war if he would surrender, with boats and abundant provisions to enable him and all his people to reach Allahabad.

"The proposition was received with considerable distrust by the besieged; but Nana swore before the general that he would faithfully observe all the terms of the capitulation, and it was finally accepted. The garrison marched out with their arms and baggage, and passed through the hordes of the besiegers to the river. The wounded, with the women and children, were sent to the Ganges on elephants. Now, if you take your seats in the carriages, we will proceed to the scene of the massacre."

The company were conveyed to a Hindu temple on the shore, where the suttee had formerly been performed, and which was provided with a broad staircase leading down to the water. The place had a funereal aspect, to which the terrible tragedy lent an additional melancholy.

"The treacherous commander of the rebels had provided about twenty boats of all sizes, and supplied them with provisions, in order to complete the deception," continued Captain Chesly when the party had alighted. "The boats were cast loose to the current, and the hungry people rushed to the eatables. But the flotilla was hardly clear of the shore before a battery of guns, masked from their view, opened a most destructive fire upon them with grape and solid shot, mostly the former.

"The smaller boats sank, and others were set on fire. The cavalry of the enemy waded into the river, and sabred those who attempted to escape by swimming. In the largest boat was General Wheeler; and, by desperate rowing, it succeeded in getting away from the slaughter. Unhappily it got aground, and all on board of it were captured.

"Nana ordered that not a man should be saved, and all were murdered in cold blood. The various accounts differ considerably; but all the men were killed but four, two captains and two privates, who escaped by swimming down the river, and were protected by a rajah, who was afterwards pensioned for this service.

"After the massacre of all the men, there remained one hundred and twenty-five women and children captured from the boats, who were confined in the town-house of the detested Nana, where they were fed upon the poorest food and subjected to many indignities. They were heroic women, and preferred death to any other fate at the hands of their miscreant captors. They were kept in confinement about three weeks, when it was whispered among them that deliverance was at hand. Sir Henry Havelock was marching from Allahabad to the relief of the garrison, and when he was within two days' march Nana went out to meet him and give battle to him. He was defeated and driven back to Cawnpore.

"Smarting under this defeat, and stimulated to revenge for it, Nana at once ordered the massacre of the helpless prisoners on his return. This order was executed with all the atrocity incident to the character of the savages, and the bodies of the victims were thrown into a well near their prison. Now, if you please, we will drive to the memorials of this dreadful butchery."

A memorial church now indicates the site of General Wheeler's intrenchments, which the party visited first. The scene of the massacre is now a memorial garden, in charge of an old soldier, who was one of the four who escaped. The place of the well into which the bodies of the women and children were thrown is marked by a beautiful marble statue of an angel standing by a lofty cross. It is surrounded by a Gothic fence, with lofty towers in the same style. The party looked upon these mementoes of the terrible events with mournful interest, and had hardly recovered their usual cheerfulness when they reached the hotel. The guides were invited to dine with them, and the evening was more cheerful than the afternoon had been.

Part of the forenoon of the next day was given to a ride along the Ganges, which was crowded with boats of all kinds, from the boat with a cabin covered with a thatched roof to steamboats of considerable size. They found an abundance of temples on the shores of the sacred stream, and a beautiful *ghat* or staircase to the water, which excited their admiration.

"We are now going to Lucknow this afternoon; but it is only forty-five miles," said Sir Modava. "If you prefer to do so, we can return to Cawnpore, and go down the river on one of those fine steamers to Calcutta, a thousand miles from here by the river."

"Or you could go to Benares, our next stopping-place on the river," suggested the viscount.

But it would take too much time, and Captain

Ringgold objected; for he had already marked Allahabad out of the route. Early in the afternoon the tourists were again seated in the conference carriage. The station at Cawnpore excited their attention, for it is five hundred and sixty feet long. A bridge of boats sixteen hundred yards in length was an affair not seen in their own country.

"We are now in the province of Oude, a word of various orthography," said Lord Tremlyn, after they lost sight of the city from which they started.

"Oude!" exclaimed Miss Blanche. "Where did I see that name?"

"In Paris," replied Louis. "We saw the tomb of the Queen of Oude in Père-la-Chaise."

"I will tell you about her presently," continued Lord Tremlyn. "There was a great deal of corruption in the government of the kingdom under the native king. The people were robbed of vast sums in the guise of taxes, the police was miserably inefficient, and it was not a safe region for the traveller. The East India Company drew up a treaty with the king, transferring to the corporation the government, but providing liberally for the ruler and his family.

"The king refused to sign this treaty; the East India Company had been superseded, and the governor-general deposed the king. No compromise could be effected, though many believed the king had been unjustly treated. He removed to Calcutta; but his queen, with her son and brother, went to England, and endeavored to obtain redress for the real or supposed wrongs of the family, but without success. The queen then went to Paris, and died there in 1858.

"The people of Oude never submitted to the new government; and in the Mutiny of 1857, not only the sepoys but the people rebelled. The insurrectionists concentrated at Lucknow, the capital, and captured some of the forts, as has been related to you. This city has now a population of two hundred and seventy-three thousand, which makes it the fifth city in size in India. It is regarded as a very attractive place. The streets are wide, and the buildings are well-constructed, with the wooden balconies you see all over India, and the shops and bazaars may entice the ladies to make purchases. It has a fine park.

"The kings of Oude were ambitious to outshine the glories of Delhi, and, to a considerable extent, they succeeded; but the architecture is fantastic rather than grand and beautiful, and experts are inclined to laugh at it. But our friend Professor Giroud has something to say, and I subside to make room for him.

"I wish to tell the story of a Frenchman, which I think will interest the party," said the professor. "Claude Martine was a Breton soldier who went with his regiment to Pondicherry, the principal French settlement in India, which has been tossed back and forth between the English, Dutch, and French like a shuttlecock, but has been in possession of my country since 1816. He attained the grade of corporal;

but this elevated rank did not satisfy him, and he left for the interior.

"Finally, after a thousand adventures, which he never wrote out, he arrived at the court of Oude, where, by some means, he obtained a captaincy in the royal army, and, what was better, the favor of the king. In 1780 he was commander-in-chief of the native army. But his enterprise did not end here; for he was the king's trusted favorite, and of course he became a millionaire, even though there were no railroad shares in being at that period.

"He brought with him some crude notions of architecture, and he set about reforming that of India. He was not a success in this capacity; and, as my lord says, his work is ridiculed by men of taste. But this appears to have been his only sin; for he used the money he had accumulated in establishing schools, now known under the name of La Martinière, in which thousands of children are educated. As a Frenchman I do not feel at all ashamed of Claude Martine."

"You need not, Professor," added the viscount. "But here we are at the Lucknow station."

As usual, by the kindness of Lord Tremlyn, everything had been provided for the arrival of the company of tourists. There were carriages and servants, and officers as guides, in attendance. Captain Ringgold was very economical of his time; and, as it was still early in the afternoon, he proposed that the party should visit some of the objects of interest before dinner. The baggage was sent to the hotel, and the carriage proceeded to the Residency, which had been occupied by the official of the British government when the province was under the native ruler. It was in ruins, for it was so left as a memorial of the events of the past.

The city was attacked by the rebels; and the little garrison, with the English people of the town, took refuge in this building. It was a three-story brick house, not at all fit to be used as a fort. The cannon-shot of the besiegers wrecked the building, and many of its defenders, including Sir Henry Lawrence, the commander, perished in the fight.

The visitors looked over the house and its surroundings, and then went to the hotel.

CHAPTER XXXII

MORE OF LUCKNOW AND SOMETHING OF BENARES

"I SUPPOSE you recall the events of the Mutiny well enough to understand the situation here in 1857," said Lord Tremlyn the next morning when the company had gathered in the parlor of the hotel. "But there was no massacre here, as in Cawnpore, to impress the facts upon your memory, though many brave men lost their lives in the defence of the place. There were only seven hundred and fifty troops in the town; but Sir Henry Lawrence had done the best he could to fortify the Residency, ill adapted as it was for defensive works.

"An attempt was made to check the advance of the rebels eight miles from the city; but it was a failure, with the small available force, and two days later the enemy attacked the British at the Residency. Three times the brave defenders beat back the assaults of the assailants. These events on the spot you have visited occurred between the last of May and the first of July. It was not till the twenty-second of September that Havelock and Outram arrived, and captured the Alum-Bagh, which we shall visit this morning. It was a terrible summer that the beleaguered people and their brave handful of soldiers passed; and Tennyson has commemorated Lucknow in his immortal verse.

"But the coming of Havelock was not the end; for the rebels besieged the place again, and it was near the middle of November before Sir Colin Campbell arrived, with a considerable force. He captured the Alum-Bagh, and, leaving in it a force of three thousand five hundred men, he escorted the women and children and the civilians to Cawnpore; but returned in March to subdue the rebels. For a week he fought them, drove them from the intrenchments in which they had fortified themselves, and the mutiny was ended, as I related to you on board of your ship."

The carriages were at the door as soon as the party had breakfasted. They were driven to the cemetery, where they saw the grave of Lawrence, whose memorial is that "He tried to do his duty." In the Alum-Bagh, which means the Queen's Garden, was the grave of Havelock. It was here that Outram had his camp and fortifications for the defence of Lucknow during the absence of Campbell.

The Kaiser Bagh, or Cæsar's Garden, contains some of the principal sights of the city, which the viscount pointed out and described. It is a forest of domes and cupolas; and the company halted at the pavilion of Lanka, which a French writer called the least ridiculous of the structures in the enclosure, though the professor insisted that it was quite as bad as the worst. It had an abundance of cupolas with arabesque domes; but the edifice looked like a shell, for the veranda, with lofty columns supporting the roof, appeared to take up the greater portion of the enclosed space.

The most grotesque feature was at the entrance. A flight of broad stairs led to the principal floor, over which was extended what looked like an imitation of the Rialto bridge in Venice, with a small temple under the middle arch and at the head of the stairs. The top of the bridge was on a level with the flat roof, and the two side-arches started from the ground. The building was handsome in some of its details; but the professor said it was an "abomination," and Dr. Hawkes called it "queer." The various edifices are now occupied by the civil and military officials.

"Where does the name of this place come from?" asked Captain Ringgold. "Kaiser Bagh seems to be half German."

"But it is not German," replied Lord Tremlyn. "These buildings were mostly erected no farther back than 1850, by Wajid Ali Shah, the King of Oude, who was deposed by the British government in 1856. He called himself Cæsar, and Kaiser is simply a corruption of that name, with no German allusion in it. He was the husband of the Queen of Oude, whose burial-place you saw in Père-la-Chaise."

The next visit was to the palace of Claude Martine, a conglomeration of all the styles of architecture ever known, and some that were never heard of. At first view it looks like a small palace set on the top of a large one. It is certainly very original and very elaborate. Going to the citadel, they entered by a highly ornamental gateway, which opened to the visitors the view of the vast pile of buildings, in the middle of which is the Imambara. The vastness of the pile presented before them was bewildering, though they had seen so many immense structures that mere size did not now overwhelm them. The Great Imambara is considered the marvel of Lucknow, and should not be confounded with another in the citadel bearing the same general name. To walk around or through this enormous building was simply impossible, and the party contented themselves with a general view from different points. It is located on a lofty terrace; and its long line of walls, crowned with Arabic domes, is very imposing.

"This palace was erected at the close of the last century, by Nawab, with half a yard of other names to fetch up its rear," said Major Shandon, the military officer who was doing the honors of the city, with a pleasant smile. "Like many others of the Indian monarchs, he desired to immortalize his name by erecting a monument in his own honor; and he offered a prize for the competition of all the architects of India, for one that would surpass all others. We think he produced a plan that was worth the money he received; though we don't think he surpassed the Taj, or some other buildings that might be mentioned."

This immense structure is now a vast arsenal. The other building, which sometimes robs this one of its honors, is called the Hoosseinabad Imambara; and perhaps the length of the added name may account, to some extent, for the robbery. It is in the citadel, and in sight of its namesake; but the mausoleum, for it is the tomb of Ali Shah, who died in 1841, stands alone; and it does not fatigue the eyes to look at it. It is a light, ethereal sort of structure, and looks like lacework. It is surmounted by a beautiful dome, and the roof bristles with the points of turrets and towers. It contains, besides the tomb of the monarch, a mosque, a bazaar, and a model of the Taj, which make up a sufficient variety for an edifice erected for a tomb.

This temple completed the list marked out for inspection in Lucknow. The party had not supposed there was much of anything here to be seen except the memorials of the Mutiny; and for these alone they would not have missed seeing the historic locality. The rest of the day was devoted to rides through the streets and suburbs of the city. The avenues were wide, the houses neat and commodious, and the gardens laid out with English taste. The evidences of British thrift were to be seen in many portions of the place.

Lochner's Hotel was their abiding-place, and Major Shandon regaled the party at dinner and in the evening with stories of the place, and proved himself to be a gentleman of "infinite humor." The next morning the company took the train for Benares. They were a very sociable party, and preferred the conference carriage to being confined to the smaller compartments. The route was along the Boomtee River at first, which, some one has said, is the crookedest stream in the world, and the scenery was worth looking at. But as soon as the ladies and gentlemen had satisfied themselves with looking out the windows the commander presented Sir Modava as the "talkist" for the trip of six hours, or as much of the time as he chose to occupy.

"I shall not take more than half an hour for what I have to say, my much-loved friends," the Hindu gentleman began, "though I know you are very patient and long-suffering; and I assure you that I shall not take offence if you look out the windows while I am talking. The Boomtee River is as pretty as it is sinuous. If you write to your friends in the United States about it, you can spell the last syllable t-i, if you prefer; for Indian orthography is not yet controlled by statute, as I hope it will be when we have established an *Académie Indienne*, such as they have in France. But Benares is my subject, and not spelling.

"Where is Benares? It is four hundred and twenty miles by rail from Calcutta, and is on the left bank of the Ganges. I suppose you know which side that is."

"Of course we do," laughed Mrs. Belgrave. "It is on the left-hand side."

"You have put your foot in it, mother," rallied Louis.

"Into the Ganges?" queried the lady. "I did at Cawnpore, but not here."

"Suppose you were coming up the river in a steamer from Calcutta, which would be the left bank?" asked Louis.

"On my left, of course."

"Then Sir Modava will have to oblige you by locating Benares on both sides of the Ganges, and I don't believe it would be convenient for him to do that," said Louis, laughing at the expense of his mother, who blushed, though she did not see what was wrong, when she realized that she had made a blunder of some kind.

"Better not have said anything," whispered Mrs. Blossom in retaliation; for hitherto she had had a monopoly of all the blunders.

"Will you tell me, Sarah, which is the left bank of a river, for it appears that I don't know," added the lady out loud.

"The left bank of the Ganges is the one Benares is on," replied the worthy woman; and she was greeted with a roar of laughter, and a volley of applause started by the live boys who were making their way across India.

"Quite right, madam!" exclaimed Sir Modava, applauding with the others. "It may be a matter of no particular consequence; but you will excuse me for saying that the left bank is the one on your left as you go down the stream, and not at all as you go up."

"I remember now, for I learned that in my geography when I first went to school; and it is strange that I should have forgotten it," added Mrs. Belgrave.

"We know just where Benares is now," Sir Modava proceeded. "It is the largest city in this part of India with the exception of Lucknow, to which it stands next, or sixth among those of the country, having a population of 219,467. It extends along the Ganges for three miles; and the shore is lined continuously with staircases, called *ghats*, which lead up to the temples, palaces, and the vast number of houses on the banks of the river. The stream sweeps around the place like a crescent, presenting one of the finest views you ever saw, with the ornamented fronts of dwellings, public offices, and a forest of towers, pinnacles, and turrets. To the Hindus it is the most sacred city known to them.

"When I was a boy I came here for the first time, brought by my father on account of the religious character of the place, if I may call anything idolatrous by such a name. But the city, when you get into it, will disappoint you. It is like Constantinople, very beautiful to look at from the Bosporus, or the Golden Horn; but its dirty, narrow streets disgust you. I am afraid this will be your experience in Benares. You will be obliged to forego the luxury of carriages in making your tours through the place, for the streets are so narrow and crowded that it is impossible to get along with a vehicle. An elephant is equally impracticable, and even in a palanquin your progress would be so slow that you would lose all your stock of patience."

"The city must be 'done' by walking, must it?" asked the commander.

"Whew!" whistled Dr. Hawkes; and the sibilation was repeated by Uncle Moses, for each of them weighed over two hundred and a quarter.

"If the ship were here I would lend you the barge with eight rowers, to enable you to see the sights from the river," suggested Captain Ringgold.

"A steam-launch shall be provided for all the company, and our obese friends shall be provided with stuffed chairs, for the survey of the river scenes; but carriages can be used in some parts of the city, though what you will desire to see can best be observed from the river; and we can land when you wish to see interiors," added Lord Tremlyn.

This interruption was heartily applauded by the Cupids, as the fat gentlemen had been called in Cairo, assisted by all the others.

"The famous Monkey Temple is just out of the city, and that can be reached by carriages," continued Sir Modava. "There are fourteen hundred and fifty Hindu temples, pagodas, and shrines, and two hundred and seventy-two Mohammedan mosques, so that our good friend, General Noury, need not neglect his devotions."

"The good Mussulman never does that, whether there be a mosque at hand or not, for he says his prayers at the proper time, wherever he may be," replied the general.

"I know that some of your people are better Christians than some who bear the name," replied the Hindu gentleman politely. "Benares is so holy, and the Ganges is so holy, that hundreds of thousands visit it as the Mussulmans visit Mecca. Men of wealth, and those who have the means without being rich, come to this city when they feel that they have been seized with a malady likely to prove fatal; for to die here with the Hindu is a passport to eternal happiness. But I am talking too long, though there is much more that might be said; but perhaps it could be better said on board of that launch my friend mentions, and in sight of the temples, towers, and other objects of interest."

In the middle of the afternoon the train arrived at its destination; and the party proceeded in carriages to the western suburb, the location of the cantonment, or English quarter of the city.

CHAPTER XXXIII

A STEAMER TRIP UP AND DOWN THE GANGES

CLARKE'S HOTEL, at Secrole, received the tourists, and everything was in readiness for them when they arrived. Lord Tremlyn had announced the coming of himself and his large party, and a person of his distinction and influence could command anything he desired. The rest of the day was given to rest, though in the evening Sir Modava talked to the tourists about the city.

Early the next morning the party were conveyed to the river, where they embarked in a steam-yacht which had been provided for their use. It was more than a launch; for its standing-room would seat the whole company, while an awning was spread over a portion of the upper deck, from which a full view of the shore could be obtained. The city is on the north shore of the river, which has an easterly course in this portion of India, and the houses are packed in about as thickly as they can be.

"This is the Dasasvamedh Ghat," said Sir Modava, with a smile. "I thought you might wish to recall it after you get home to America. I think it is rather pleasant to know the names of places one has visited."

"We could not speak the word now without an

hour's practice, and I am sure not one of us will know it when we get to the other side of the Atlantic," said Mrs. Belgrave.

"You can write it down in your diaries."

"We might as well attempt to copy the top of a tea-chest," added Louis.

The ladies were assisted on board of the steamer. The captain was a very gentlemanly Englishman; and he was all devotion to the wants of his passengers, who seated themselves on the promenade deck. The steamer belonged to the government; and she was fitted up in the most comfortable manner, though it was not so gaudy as the craft of a maharajah would have been. The ghat was at the western extremity of the crescent to which Sir Modava had alluded, and from this point the town looked like an amphitheatre.

The river is ordinarily about half a mile wide, but in the season of high water it is double that width. The captain called the attention of the party to the ghat as they receded from it, the broad flight of stairs being a rather wonderful sight to the strangers, though they had seen something of the kind before in Delhi and Cawnpore.

The steps are adorned with small temples with plenty of spires. Near the top of the flight was the Man Munder, the great observatory. Though the building is plain, as a whole, Captain Carlisle pointed out a highly ornamental window, with a profusion of handsome brackets. The stairs on the city side of the river were unlimited as far as the eye could see. Behind them was a forest of spires, domes, and cupolas.

"You ought to have left the ghat before sunrise," said the captain, who was walking up and down the deck, with an eye on the Hindu pilot. "Then you would have been in time to see the sight of the day, for the appearance of the sun is the holy moment for the natives to plunge into the holy river. For miles along the shore the ghats are thronged at the first appearance of the orb of day, and there is a continuous murmur of voices. No matter how cold the water is, they dive in and swim like fishes. You can see a thousand heads in the water along the shore at any moment. Then they support themselves on the surface, and gaze motionless at the sun as it mounts in the sky."

"Are you a sailor, Captain Carlisle?" asked Louis, who thought he was rather poetic for an uneducated man.

"Not as the commander of your ship would understand it, though I was in command of a Thames steamer, and fell into the same business when I came to India," replied the captain, laughing at the question. "My father was a good Baptist; he wanted to make a minister of me, and I was educated far enough to enter the university; but I concluded that I did not like the business, and took to steamboating."

"But aren't the women as religious as the men?" inquired Captain Ringgold.

"More so, if anything. But they come down to the river before sunrise and take their swim. If you had been here this morning you would have seen them coming out of the water just as the men are ready to go in, and you would have observed them in their white garments, dripping like drowned rats. That pagoda you see ahead of us with the bell tower and shining in gilt is the only temple the Buddhists have in Benares."

"We are coming now to the Munikurnika Ghat. It is a five-syllable word, but you can easily pronounce it," said Sir Modava, who thought he would "spell" the captain for a time; and he was quite as familiar with the banks of the Ganges.

"And it is quite musical," added the captain.

"Pronounce u like double o, and the rest of the letters as in English, and you can speak it without choking," said the Hindu gentleman. "But there are some letters in Hindu that have no equivalents in English."

"Moo-ni-koor-ni-ka Ghat," added Louis, pronouncing the word. "But what is it all about?"

"It is the place for burning the dead, such as you saw in Bombay, but on a much larger scale," replied Sir Modava. "You see that it extends a considerable distance. Please keep to the leeward of the smoke, Captain Carlisle."

"That is what I am doing, Sir Modava."

"These funeral pyres are burning all the time, night and day. The people whose bodies are consumed in these fires, and their friends, believe that the souls of the deceased will pass from this spot into paradise, where, if they have not been very great sinners they will be transplanted into the bodies of future Brahmins. Many deceased persons are brought even hundreds of miles to be burned on the Munikurnika by the Ganges, as their sure passport to the realms of bliss."

The obliging captain took the steamer near enough to the ghat to enable the tourists to see the process of burning. An occasional puff of the horribly offensive odor came to the nostrils of the sightseers; but the captain sheered off, and they got very little of it.

"It smells just like assafœdita. It is awful-smelling stuff; and I wonder if they don't make it out of this smoke, for it hits my nose in just the same way," said Mrs. Blossom. "I took care of old Jotham Beeling when he had the apoplexy, and gave the stuff to him. The room smelt then just the same as it does here."

"You are quite right, madam," said Dr. Hawkes, laughing. "It gets part of its name from its bad odor; but it is not made out of smoke. Asa is the gum of a tree that grows here. It has a very offensive odor, which gives it the rest of the name, from *fœditas*, meaning foul, filthy."

The workmen who were operating the burning were nearly naked, begrimed by the sooty smoke, and looked like so many imps. They were stirring up the fires with long iron pokers, and throwing vessels of oil upon them. The boat passed beyond the fumes of the pyres, and came up to the ghat, at the request of Lord Tremlyn. A multitude of hideous-looking cripples, humpbacks, and beggars made an onslaught on the steamer; and the boys and gentlemen pelted them with coppers, with which they had been forewarned to supply themselves. It was fun to them, and the mendicants enjoyed it quite as much.

"There is a procession of pilgrims just arrived," said Captain Carlisle, pointing to the high ground beyond the ghat. "They are coming here all the time. The Hindus under the umbrellas are Brahmins, who collect the fees for bathing from the steps; and they sell certificates of purification, indulgences, and amulets."

The boat continued on her course, and they did not wait to see the bathing, though the heads of the swimmers were soon in view. A staircase is reserved for women, who are watched over by the elders of their sex. But they could be seen in the distance, frolicking in the water; and they were so hilarious that their shouts could be heard on board of the Sylph, as the boat was called.

The steamer next came to a long row of palaces on the high ground, whose fronts were profusely ornamented with staircases that exceeded in extent and beauty anything they had before seen. Every rajah has a residence here, not permanent, but where he comes to celebrate the religious festivals. The king of Nagpore has the finest one, with one hundred stairs of white sandstone reaching down to the water.

"Now we come to a building worth looking at," said Sir Modava, as they passed beyond the assemblage of palaces. "This is the mosque of Aurungzeb. Those two lofty minarets are one hundred and forty-seven feet high. They are very slender, and look like a couple of needles; but, though they are only eight and a quarter feet in diameter on the ground, they have spiral staircases reaching to the top. If you wish to land and go to the cupola you can do so."

"I pray thee have me excused," interposed Uncle Moses; and Dr. Hawkes said "Me too!" And no one cared to ascend to such a height.

"This mosque was built by the Emperor Aurungzeb, on the site of a Hindu temple of Siva, which he caused to be pulled down, to the scandal of the worshippers of that deity, for it marked the spot where Vishnu himself first appeared to man. A flight of one hundred stairs leads to the mosque, which the Hindus formerly ascended on their knees when they went to the worship of Vishnu. But we have gone as far in this direction as we need go."

The Sylph came about, and went back up the river, landing above the funeral pyres. From the ghat, they walked into one of the crowded streets. They were conducted by Sir Modava to a square, which was thronged with natives. In the middle of it was a small round temple, the spire of which was overlaid with plates of gold. At the present day this is the holy of holies of the Hindus. Its principal object of adoration is a plain stone post, which is believed to form a part of the very body of the deity, Siva in this instance.

The narrow streets, through which the party made their way with difficulty were very clean. They were thronged with pilgrims from all parts of India, dressed in their best garments, loaded with gold and silver ornaments. The men were carrying great brass trays, piled up with flowers, as offerings for the various deities. The little stalls, which were the stores, made the thoroughfares look like bazaars. They passed no end of temples; and all of them were small, though they were very pretty, what there were of them.

Emerging from these narrow streets, the company came to a section where the avenues were broad, with handsome houses built upon them. This portion was practicable for carriages, and half a dozen *calèches* were drummed together after some delay; and the ladies were glad to be seated again, for they had had a long and tiresome walk through the narrow and crowded streets. Sir Modava directed the drivers, and when he said Dourga Khound no one knew what he was to see next. The word means the Fountain of Dourga; and when they came to it they agreed that it was one of the most beautiful buildings in Benares, though it was painted all over with red, which made it look rather fantastic.

Sir Modava said nothing about the use of the building, and led the way into the enclosure. The moment they entered the grounds they realized that the Hindu gentleman had worked a surprise upon them; for the yard was filled with monkeys, and the walls were covered with them. The chattering creatures immediately surrounded them, holding out their paws for something. Sir Modava gave the most dignified one a rupee, and Lord Tremlyn made a similar gift to another.

"They can't eat silver," suggested Morris.

"The money is for the Brahmin who has charge here. You see they have gone to give it to him," replied Sir Modava, as he opened a large paper package he had bought at a store, and proceeded to distribute its contents, consisting of nuts and parched corn, to the members of the monkey community.

For half an hour they fed the animals, which were very tame, and made friends with them. The live boys were more pleased with this occupation than in looking at temples and mosques. They all visited the sanctuary of the temple, which was said to date back a thousand years. The party greatly enjoyed the ride back to Secrole, which is the English town of Benares. After dinner Sir Modava told them about the Feast of Ganesa.

"He is one of the most popular deities of India," said the Hindu gentleman. "He is the embodiment of wisdom, prudence, and commerce; his presence wards off all perils. You will find him over the door of places of business; and contracts open with an invocation to Ganesa, sometimes given by a picture of the god. He was the son of Siva and Parvati. His picture is that of a short, fat man, with four arms and an elephant's head.

"Though he was Siva's son, the father was jealous of him, and struck off his head. Siva was sorry for what he had done, and wanted to bring Ganesa back to life; but his head was gone."

"Couldn't he put a head on him?" asked Scott very seriously; and the other boys laughed.

"That was just what he did," replied Sir Modava, wondering what the boys and some of the others were laughing at. "Siva selected a young elephant, cut off his head, and affixed it to his son's shoulders; and that is how he happens to have such a head. This head sometimes takes the place of the whole figure on contracts. His festival is celebrated the last of April, with the greatest magnificence. Effigies of the god are made of terra-cotta, painted and gilded, and borne by processions through the streets. Priests and musicians surround the idol; and young girls, widowed before they are wives, dancing and waving their scarfs in solemn cadence, lead the way.

"When the processions reach the river, they embark in fairy-like boats propelled by sails or oars, forming a grand aquatic spectacle. At sunset the idols are thrown into the river, and the festival terminates with a grand frolic on shore, with fireworks, in which many Europeans take part; and the river is thronged with boats decorated with many-colored lanterns."

The party spent two days more at Benares, and visited temples, mosques, and many places of interest. They were visited by British civil and military officers, who were extremely kind to them, and offered them every facility for seeing the city. After dinner on the last day, Captain Ringgold asked Lord Tremlyn to tell them something about Patna; and he evidently did so with a purpose.

"Patna is the fifteenth city in India in population, one hundred and forty miles from Benares," replied the viscount. "It extends nine miles along the Ganges, and an average of two back from it. The streets are narrow and crooked. The houses are mostly of mean appearance, and there are but very few buildings there of any importance. You laid out your list of cities to be visited yourself, Captain, and generally very judiciously; but if I had made it out I should have omitted Patna. It has a population of about one hundred and sixty-five thousand."

"I asked the question with a view to omit it from the list if there are no sights of importance, and, after what you have said, I shall do so; and to-morrow we will take the train for Calcutta," added the captain.

This decision pleased the party, and at six the next morning the special started with them for the greatest city of India.

CHAPTER XXXIV

ALL OVER THE CITY OF CALCUTTA

"I SHALL be glad to be on board of the Guardian-Mother again," said Scott, after the four live boys had taken a place by themselves in the conference carriage. "I have seen enough of India."

"But you have not seen one-half of India," replied Louis.

"I read a story in an old schoolbook Uncle Moses had used when he didn't weigh as much as I do now, which was called 'The Half is Better than the Whole;' and it proved the proposition with which it started out. That is just what is the matter now."

"But you have been seeing new things all the time, and learning something," added Louis.

"That's very true; but we have seen all the big mosques and things, and enough is as good as a feast," suggested Scott. "I suppose if we stayed here a couple of years more we should not see the whole of the country. We have got a specimen brick of the principal cities; and a dozen specimens of the same thing don't amount to much."

"But you haven't seen Calcutta yet, and that is the biggest toad in the puddle," said Felix. "The ship will be there, and if you are homesick you can go on board of her."

But the call for attention from Captain Ringgold interrupted the conversation, and Sir Modava had seated himself in front of the company to give one of his "talks."

"Our route will be along the Ganges till we come to Luckieserai Junction, where the loop-line falls into the main line," the Hindu gentleman began.

"Is it much of a fall, sir?" asked Felix.

"I don't understand you, Mr. McGavonty," replied the speaker blankly.

"The expression 'falls into the main line' is somewhat different from what we use at home; but the young man ought to have understood you," interposed the commander.

"What would you have said, Captain?"

"The loop-line we call a branch, and we say connects with instead of falls into," replied the captain. "But your meaning was plain enough, and our boys must fall into the methods of expression used here."

"Though you have seen the Ganges several times, not much has been said about it; and I will tell you a little more concerning it before we leave, not to see it again. It rises in Gahrwal, one of the Hill states, north-east of Delhi. It has its source in an ice-cave nearly fourteen thousand feet above the level of the sea. It is not called the Ganges till it has received the flow of two other rivers, a hundred and fifty miles or more from its lofty source. Just below Allahabad it takes in the Jumna, itself a mighty stream.

"As you have learned, it is the holy river of the Hindus; and it deserves their homage, for, aside from the religious character they give to it, three hundred thousand square miles are drained and fertilized by the Ganges and its tributaries. Of its sanctity, that it washes away sin, and that death in its waters or on its shores is the passport to eternal bliss, you have learned. But it renders a more immediate and practical service to the people; for it is navigable for small craft from the point where it enters the lowlands, seventy or eighty miles north of Delhi.

"The river is 1,509 miles long. Though it rises and falls at different seasons, it never fails, even in the hottest summer; and its inundations render, to some extent, the benefit which the Nile does to the soil of Egypt. Like the Mississippi, in your country, it has sometimes changed its course, as proved by the ruins of cities that were once on its banks.

"Now you have a view of the Ganges for quite a distance, and can see the kinds of boats that navigate it. It is one of the most frequented waterways in the world, though the building of railways and canals has somewhat diminished the amount of freight borne on its tide. About £6,000,000 is needed to complete the Ganges canal, which will reach all the cities through which you have passed. There is a very complicated mythology connected with the river, which it would take me all day to relate, and therefore I will not meddle with it."

For a couple of hours the passengers watched the boats and steamers on the river, and the scenes on the other side. While they were thus employed, Lord Tremlyn gave to each person a map of Calcutta, intimating that he should soon tell them something about the city; and they all began to study it, so as to form some idea of the place they were next to visit. Of course they could make out but little from the vast maze of streets, but some of them obtained a very good idea of the situation of the city and many of its important buildings.

"People coming from England or America generally arrive at Calcutta or Bombay, the larger portion at the former. From the sea the metropolis of India is reached by the Hoogly River, the most western outlet of the Ganges," his lordship began. "It is sometimes spelled Hugli. Under this name, the stream is known sixty-four miles above Calcutta and seventeen below. Vessels drawing twenty-six feet of water come up to the city; though the stream, like the Mississippi, is liable to be silted up.

"I see that some of you look at me as though I had used a strange word. Silt is the deposit of mud, sand, or earth of any kind carried up and down streams by the tide or other current. But the river engineers here are constantly removing it; the course is kept open, and the Hoogly pilots are very skilful.

The river has also a bore, though not a great bore, like some people I know.

"We know the book-agent better than this one," said Scott.

"Some of our rivers in England have bores, though not book-agents; so have the Seine, the Amazon, and others with broad estuaries. High tides drive a vast body of water into the wide mouth; and, as the stream is not large enough to take it in, it piles it up into a ridge, which rolls up the river. It forms a wall of water in the Hoogly seven feet high, which is sometimes dangerous to small craft. Enough of the Hoogly.

"Calcutta, by the last census, 1891, had a population of 861,764; but it is not so large as New York, Philadelphia, or Chicago; and London is the only larger city in the United Kingdom. It became a town in 1686. After it had attained considerable importance, in 1756, it was attacked by the Nawab of Bengal, the king or rajah; and after a siege of two days the place yielded. The tragedy of the 'Black Hole' followed."

"I have heard of that, but I don't know what it means," said Mrs. Belgrave.

"You observe the large open enclosure at the right of your map of the city, the esplanade. Within it is Fort William, which has existed nearly two hundred years. It had a military prison, which has since been called the 'Black Hole.' The nawab caused one hundred and forty-six prisoners, all he had taken, to be shut up in a room only eighteen feet square, with only two small windows, both of them obstructed by a veranda. This was but a little more than two square feet on the floor for each person, so that they could not stand up without crowding each other. They spent the night there, pressing together, the heat terrible, enduring the pangs of suffocation. In the morning all were dead but twenty-three.

"The nawab held the fort for seven months, when it was recaptured by Lord Clive. Calcutta extends about five miles on the bank of the river, being about two in breadth. I shall not follow out its history, for you will hear enough of that as you visit the various localities."

"I used to think Calicut and Calcutta were the same city," said Louis.

"Not at all, though the names of the two may have been derived from the same source. The name of the great city is from Kali, a Hindu goddess of whom you heard in Bombay, and cuttah, a temple; and doubtless there was such a building here. Calicut is on the south-west coast of India, and was a very rich and populous city when it was visited by Vasco da Gama, who was the first to double the Cape of Good Hope, in 1498. The cotton cloth, calico, generally called print, gets its name from this city."

Dinner was brought into the carriages; and the tourists slept in the afternoon, arriving at Calcutta in the evening. The Great Eastern, one of the two largest hotels in the city, was prepared to receive them. Here, as in Bombay and elsewhere, every guest is attended by his own servant. Half a dozen of them had been retained, but when the omnibuses set them down at the hotel a hundred more could have been readily procured.

The business of sight-seeing began early the next morning with a visit to the esplanade, which may be called a park, though it contains a variety of buildings besides Fort William, which is half a mile in diameter. The enclosure is a mile and three-quarters in length by about one mile in depth from the river. The Government House occupies a position next to it, and they passed it as they entered.

"Whose statue is that — the Duke of Wellington?" asked Louis, as he walked on one side of Sir Modava, with his mother on the other side.

"Not at all; most of our streets and buildings are named after persons noted in the history of India," replied the Indian gentleman, laughing. "That is the statue of Lord William Cavendish Bentinck, the first governor-general of India; and many important events dated from his time, for he suppressed the suttee and thugging."

"Thugging?" repeated the lady interrogatively.

"You have not been told about it; but I will give you its history when we have time, for here are the Eden Gardens," replied Sir Modava.

"Not the Garden of Eden?" suggested Mrs. Belgrave.

"Only named for it; but it is a very beautiful

garden in English style, though the trees and plants are, of course, different. It has water enough for variety; and there is no difficulty at all in getting it, for the city is hardly above the river at high tide. All there is of the fort you can see from here."

"But what are those things over the other side of the park?"

"They are all tanks; and, of course, they are to hold water. Each of them has its name, generally Indian. Now we will walk across to the Chowringhee Road, where the finest private residences of the city are situated. On our left is the Government House, which we passed when we came in. It is a fine building, and it has a large garden of its own."

"But what is it for?" asked the lady.

"It is the residence of the governor-general, generally called the viceroy; and he has his offices there. Now, if you look beyond Fort William, you will see the race-course."

"I don't care for that," replied Mrs. Belgrave, whose memories of the sport were anything but pleasant.

"Near it is the presidency jail, and there are two hospitals farther along."

The party walked along the road to view the residences of the nabobs, and returned to the hotel, where they seated themselves on the large veranda overlooking the street. The first thing Louis did was to look at a thermometer he discovered on a post.

"How hot is it, Louis?" asked his mother.

"It isn't hot at all; it is only 70°."

"The glass varies here from 52° to 100°; but we don't get the latter figure except in summer," added Sir Modava.

"But you have awful cyclones here, an English lady told me last night," said Mrs. Belgrave.

"We do; but we never have them at this season of the year; they come in May, September, and October, and sometimes in November the belated ones. In 1867 we had one in the latter month which destroyed thirty thousand native houses; but you know they are built of bamboos and such stuff, and it does not take much of a breeze to demolish them. Another in June, 1870, did nearly as much damage."

"I should think the bore would make mischief here," suggested Louis.

"The monsoons here begin in July, and during their time the bore is the most mischievous. The big wave comes up the river at the rate of twenty miles an hour. All boats run for the middle of the river, where the billow does not break against the shore. Ships often part their cables, and knock themselves to pieces against the walls. Sometimes the bore is twelve feet high, though not much more than half that generally."

"What are the prices at a hotel like this one, Lord Tremlyn?" asked Dr. Hawkes.

"Here is the list of prices," replied his lordship, handing him a card taken from the wall.

"Coffee at six in the morning, breakfast *à la fourchette* at nine, tiffin at one, and dinner at seven. Price, Rs. six per day," the doctor read. "I suppose Rs. means rupees; and that makes it about twelve English shillings, or three dollars a day, which is not high."

"There are no extras except for wines, liquors, and beer, which none of your people use," added the viscount. "But you have to pay for your own attendance; and your servant's pay is from eight to ten rupees a month, or about a pound."

"Cheap enough!" exclaimed the surgeon. "I have to pay my waiter at home six pounds a month."

"Now, what is there to be seen in Calcutta?" asked the commander after breakfast.

"If you wish to see mosques, temples, pagodas"— the viscount began.

"We do not," interposed the captain. "At first those were very interesting; but we have seen enough of them."

"I supposed so," added Lord Tremlyn. "I have ordered carriages, and to-day we will take a general view of the city."

This plan was agreeable to the party, and it was carried out. From the hotel they proceeded to the river. There was a crowd of shipping at anchor, and at the landing-stages and jetties. Among them

Louis was the first to discover the Guardian-Mother. She was in the middle of the river, off Fort William. Half a mile below her they saw the Blanche. At the request of the commander, the carriages went down to the fort, where the passengers all alighted, and gathered together on the shore. The gentlemen cheered, and the ladies waved their handkerchiefs.

"I see that Mr. Boulong has painted the ship, and she looks as taut and snug as a man-of-war," said the commander, who was evidently glad to see his vessel.

"They are lowering the boats," added Louis; and in a few minutes the barge and first cutter came up to the shore.

There was a general handshaking with the first offcer, in command, and the boys extended this courtesy to all the crews of the boats, going on board of them for a few minutes. It was a happy meeting; but it could not be long continued, and the carriages drove off again.

As he was about to take his place in the landau, Mr. Boulong informed the commander that he had received a visit from Captain Mazagan. He wanted to see Captain Ringgold, but did not state his business. The first officer could not tell whether the visitor knew the Blanche was in the river, for he had not mentioned her. With the statement that the party would go on board in two or three days, they parted, and the boats returned to the ship. The commander had something to think of now; but he came to the conclusion that the reprobate was not aware of the presence of the Blanche or her owner.

The carriages followed the shore road till they came to the upper end of the city, and then turned into the first of the long streets with several names in different parts, which extends entirely through the town. Near the esplanade they found the finest shops, and the ladies went into some of them to see the goods. Then they struck the Circular Road, and drove entirely around the city.

"This reminds me of Moscow, in some parts, where palaces and shanties are side by side in the same street," said Captain Ringgold. "There does not seem to be any aristocratic section, unless that by the esplanade is such."

They saw plenty of mosques, temples, and churches, some of the latter very fine. They believed they had taken in the whole city. After dinner Lord Tremlyn invited them to an excursion on board of a steam-yacht the next day, the use of which was tendered to him by a high official.

CHAPTER XXXV

A SUCCESSFUL HUNT IN THE SUNDERBUNDS

A BREAKFAST at six o'clock was provided the following morning for the tourists, and they came down from their chambers prepared for the aquatic excursion, which was to include something more than sight-seeing, for the gentlemen and the boys were directed to take their rifles along. Mr. Boulong had called upon the commander the evening before, and he had been invited to join the party; but he had excused himself, and suggested that Mr. Gaskette would enjoy it more than he should, and he was asked to go.

By half-past six the party were on The Strand, as the road in the esplanade bordering the river is called. The second officer of the ship was there; and he was not only a sailor and an artist, but he had the reputation of being a dead shot. The company embarked on the steam-yacht, which was large enough to make voyages to Madras and Ceylon. The excursion was not intended as a mere shooting-party, Lord Tremlyn explained, but to enable the company to obtain a better view of Calcutta than they could get in any other manner.

From the river a full view was obtained of the multitude of columns, belfries, and cupolas, as well as of the Government House, the Town Hall, and the line of magnificent houses beyond the esplanade. Along the shore The Strand, as it is called the whole length of the city, the jetties, and the landing-stages were crowded with men; for, where labor is so cheap, work is not done by small forces of men. There are several lines of steamers running between London, Southampton, and Liverpool to this port; and they were constantly arriving and departing.

"You don't see such a variety of races here as you did in Bombay," said Lord Tremlyn as he was pointing out the sights to be seen. "You observe some Chinamen and Burmese; but most of the laborers are of the low class of natives, Bengalese, and they are very sorry specimens of the Hindus."

"But what are the merchants and shopkeepers?" asked Captain Ringgold.

"They are Baboos, which is a name given to the Bengalese. The better class of them, in contact with the English, realize that education is a power; and they have labored for years to improve their countrymen. They have established schools and colleges, and when young natives applied for government situations the authorities felt obliged to admit them. To-day you will find many natives acting as clerks in the post-office, railway, and telegraph-offices, as well as in the courts in minor capacities.

"In fact, there has been a social revolution in progress here for half a century or more, and its effects may be seen now. The government has modified the lot of woman to some extent, as you have learned. The Hindu law weighed terribly upon her. When a woman lost her husband, custom required that she should be sent back to her own family. Her relatives shaved off her hair, dressed her in the coarsest clothing, and compelled her to do the severest drudgery of the household. She is forbidden to marry again, and is treated as though she was responsible for becoming a widow. The reforming of this evil is in progress; but the people are baked into their prejudices and superstitions of forty centuries, and it is worse than pulling their teeth to interfere with them.

"One of the favorite divinities of the natives here is Kali, the wife of Siva, the goddess of murder. Her worship is odious and disgusting; for her altars were formerly sprinkled with human blood, and the idols were surrounded with dead bodies and skulls. Their great festival is the Churuk-Pooja, which is still celebrated, though the government has forbidden all its brutal features. You have all seen a 'merry-go-round' machine in which children ride in a circle on wooden horses.

"An apparatus like this, but without the wooden steeds, was used by these fanatics. At the end of the four arms hung ropes with sharp hooks at the end, on which were hung up the devotees, as the butcher does his meats in his shop; and the machine was revolved rapidly till the hooks pulled out, and the victim dropped upon the ground, fainting or dead. At the present time the festival is attended by Baboos of the best class; but it amounts simply to an athletic exhibition with music. The government and the reformers have brought about this change of performance."

"Do the English attend such shows?" asked Dr. Hawkes.

"Sometimes, from curiosity. But they are here just about what they are in London, and their habits are much the same," replied the viscount. "The river here is about a mile wide. Formerly we could not have come as far as we have without seeing hundreds of corpses floating on the surface. Natives who were too poor to pay the bill for the funeral pyre threw the bodies of their friends into the river. Of course this was a menace to the health of the city; and the practice was forbidden by the government, which built an immense tower, wherein is kept a fire constantly burning, in which the bodies of the poor are consumed without expense."

"See that big bird on the shore!" exclaimed Mrs. Belgrave. "I saw several of them yesterday, and I meant to ask what it was."

"That is the *arghilah*, generally called the adjutant," replied Sir Modava. "He is the licensed scavenger of Calcutta, for it is forbidden by law to kill or molest him. You see him walking about in a crowd with as much dignity and gravity as though he were a big banker; and he is also seen perched upon the walls and buildings. They have an enormous bill, as you observe. A friend of mine had a tame one; and one day when the table was ready for dinner he took a chicken from the dish and swallowed it whole. He has a searching eye, and discovers a hidden bit of meat, a dead cat or other animal, and bolts it in the twinkling of an eye."

The steamer continued on her course down the river, and in less than four hours arrived at Diamond Harbor. It contained a fort, a signal-station, and a telegraph-office, though there is nothing in the shape of a village. The East India Company's ships made this their port; but the improvement of the navigation of the river enables all the steamers to go up to the city, to which their arrival is telegraphed.

The extensive territory included in the delta of the Ganges is called the Sunderbunds, and is about equal to the State of Massachusetts in size. It is a muddy region, cut up by a network of streams; and it is full of swamps, morasses, and mud-holes. Nearest to the sea is a belt of land, forming a wide extent of jungle, with a dense undergrowth of tropical plants and verdure; for it is in the Torrid Zone, which the tourists entered about forty miles north of Calcutta. This jungle was the objective point of the hunters of the party.

The captain of the steam-yacht took the company on board through a number of the lagoons and cut-offs to enable them to see the wild character of the scenery. Lord Tremlyn, Sir Modava, and Dr. Ferrolan were kept busy explaining the trees, plants, crocodiles, storks, and other animals.

At a pleasant basin, dinner was served on board, and it was quite as good as they would have obtained at the Great Eastern; for just now the party were government guests, and the officials could not do enough for a person of Lord Tremlyn's influence in England. After the meal the hunters prepared themselves for the sport in which they were to engage. Mrs. Belgrave warned her son to be very careful, and Mrs. Blossom did as much for Felix.

The steamer started into a cut-off leading through to the Bay of Bengal, the polite captain explained. It was full of game of all sorts, including the wild buffalo, rhinoceros, tiger, leopard, wild hog, deer, and the trees and bushes were as full of monkeys as they could swarm. It was agreed among the hunters that none of the latter should be shot, for they were harmless animals.

"Captain, dear, are there any schnakes forninst the joongle?" asked the Milesian, who was much exhilarated at the prospect of the sport, and easily slipped into the vernacular of his mother.

"Plinty av thim, Musther McGavonty," replied Captain O'Flaherty, with a broad grin on his honest face. "They air as thidck as broken heads at a Donnybrook fair."

"Faix, ye's air a brither o' moine!" exclaimed Felix, grasping the hand of the captain.

"Air ye's from the County Carhk?"

"Oi'm from the county and parish of Kilkenny; or mi mudther was, thou' she's dead now, long loife to her! Wud I foind ary cobry in here?"

"All you'll want uv 'em; and pythons too."

"What is a poithon?" asked Felix.

"A big schnake; a boa, or loike him."

"Is it the bore that runs up the river to Calcutty?"

"Not the same boa," laughed the captain. "But you speak English, for I have heard you do it; and I have about forgotten my native brogue."

"If the boa is a snake, he is the fellow I want to see," replied Felix.

"There's one of them now!" exclaimed Captain O'Flaherty, pointing to one wreathed around a bush.

The young hunter brought his rifle to his shoulder, and fired before the captain had time to say anything more. The python began to writhe and wriggle in the bush, and Felix fired again. Then he dropped off into the water. The rest of the company had been aft with the ladies, but they all rushed forward at the report of the rifle. The captain stated what the hunter had done, as he rang to stop and back the boat. They saw the bamboo on which the serpent had been, but the game could not be seen. They wondered what had become of him.

The rest of the hunters began to shoot ducks, herons, and other water-fowls. As fast as a bird dropped into the bayou he disappeared, and not one of them could be recovered. Captain Ringgold wondered what became of them, and the Indian gentlemen only laughed at his perplexity.

"But what becomes of them, for they do not sink?" demanded the commander.

"You shall see," replied Sir Modava. "Don't shoot the adjutants; but there is a long-legged heron. I will bring him down, for he waits very patiently to be shot. Now watch the water when he comes down."

The bird dropped the moment he fired, and the instant he touched the water a pair of jaws closed upon him, and drew him under water. The company were astonished, and looked for an explanation.

"I never counted the crocodiles in this river; but I should guess there were at least a million of them, and they steal your game as fast as you bring it down," said Sir Modava.

The ladies were interested; and another bird was shot, to enable them to see the operation of the saurians. The python was about ten feet long, and he must have been a meal for one of them. The cranes, herons, and storks were numerous; but the party decided to kill no more of them, for they held still, as though they were all ready to be shot; and there was no sport in such game.

The boat continued on its course for half an hour longer, and then came up to a sort of stockade, extending out into the water, and near it were a couple of bamboo huts. This wild region is sparsely peopled with Hindus, who are obliged to keep guard over themselves and their families all the time, and are occasionally the victims of the ferocious monsters of the jungle and of the water.

"What is that stockade for?" asked the commander, as soon as the steamer was moored to the shore.

"The Hindus are a cleanly people, as required by their religion," replied Captain O'Flaherty in the hearing of all the party. "That stockade contains a big trough for washing their scanty clothing. It reaches into the water, so that they can fill their washtub without going out of it."

"I don't see why?" asked Mrs. Woolridge.

"If they went to the border of the stream to dip up water the crocodiles would pick them up as fast as they did so," added the captain; and all the ladies shuddered, and wanted to get out of such a horrible place.

"But the hunters are to land here; and they will find all the heavy game they can dispose of, for there have been no hunters here yet this season to scare them off. You will find the biggest tigers of India here, gentlemen."

The hunters went on shore, and as they passed down the gangway they saw a couple of the crocodiles in the water. Louis put a bullet into the eye of one, and Mr. Woolridge served the other in the same way; but all of them thought saurians were mean game. Near the huts they found two men, and Sir Modava had a talk with them, which no one else could understand; but he employed them to guide the party and show them their traps.

"The wife of one of these men was devoured by a crocodile a year ago, and the daughter of the other, a child of six, had been borne off by a tiger," he explained, as they proceeded after the two men.

They soon came to the traps. The tigers were exceedingly numerous on all the islands formed by the cut-offs, and swam without difficulty from one to another. The first trap they saw was a broad trench, the bottom and sides armed with stakes of the hardest wood, sharpened to a wicked point. A roaring sound attracted the visitors to another of the same kind, in which a monstrous tiger was floundering about, trying to escape the points that pierced him. He was suffering fearfully; and Captain Ringgold shot him at once, though the Hindus were delighted by his torture.

Another kind of trap was more ingenious. It was on the plan of the twitch-up snare, common in New England. A young tree, very strong and flexible, is bent down till the upper end touches the ground. To this extremity is attached a stout cord, and fastened to a stake in the ground. A slip-noose is so arranged that the tiger thrusts his head through it in order to reach the meat with which the cord holding the tree is baited. As the animal pulls the cord he casts off the line holding the tree in its bent position. The slip-noose is tightened around his neck, the tree flies up into the air, carrying the tiger with it. Everything about the trap is made very strong,

"Captain Ringgold brought down another." — Page 349.

and there the savage marauder hangs till he chokes to death.

The party moved on, and they had not gone ten rods before a cobra elevated his head. Felix claimed the right to fire first, and he killed him with one ball. A large python was Scott's first prize; and, after a long walk, they came to a nest of tigers, as it seemed, for there were not less than five of them drinking at a brook. It appeared to be the only place in the vicinity where fresh water could be obtained. The first of the tigers was killed by Louis with a single shot, for he put the ball through the eye of the beast.

Captain Ringgold brought down another with three shots from his repeating rifle. Felix did not care for tigers; he was looking for snakes, and they came to the brook to drink. In a couple of hours he had half a dozen of his favorite game. He declared that he was following the blessed example of St. Patrick, and if he did not die too soon he would rid the world of all the snakes in it.

The five tigers lay dead by the brook; and, taking the advice of the coolies, the hunters returned into a thicket, where Felix killed another python. The party could see the brook. A pair of timid deer came next to drink; but they fled at the approach of what seemed to be a family of leopards, for two of them were evidently cubs. They were all shot; but the repeated reports of the rifles had probably scared off others, and no more beasts of any kind came.

"These men say you have killed more tigers and leopards than any party of hunters who ever came here," said Sir Modava, who carried a rifle, but had not fired it once; and Lord Tremlyn's weapon had not been discharged; for both preferred to leave the game for their friends.

It was a great hunt, and the Americans were correspondingly proud of their success. Louis and Felix had been trained in a shooting-gallery, and neither of them missed his aim; but the shooting had all been at short range. With the help of two coolies, all the game was carried to the steamer, where it was exhibited to the rest of the company. The tigers were all skinned by the coolies and the crew of the steamer, as were the leopards; but after Mrs. Blossom and the others had seen the snakes, they were fed out to the crocodiles. The coolies were abundantly rewarded, and seemed to worship their visitors. They presented to them four mango fish, golden-yellow in color, and exquisite in flavor.

The steamer cast off her fasts, and headed for Calcutta; but it was late, and the fish presented, which abound in the markets of the city, were the burden of a fine supper they ate on the way.

CHAPTER XXXVI

THE PARTING FESTIVITIES ON THE HOOGLY

WHILE the hunters were so successfully bagging the big game of the jungle, Captain O'Flaherty had taken the party who had remained on board the steamer on an excursion through some of the waterways of the Sunderbunds, so that they were not wearied by waiting for those more actively employed. The united party had thoroughly enjoyed the day, even into the evening. The skins of the tigers and leopards were sent to an expert, to be prepared for future preservation when the time should admit.

At the hotel the wonderful success of the hunters was the theme of the other guests; but the place was regarded as a dangerous one, though that would not deter Englishmen from visiting it if it were not so difficult of access, for a government steam-yacht was not available for many parties. The next morning the tourists were taken to the Botanical Garden, a short distance above the city, which is said to be the finest as well as the most spacious in the world.

It was not an affair of greenhouses, like most of such places they had seen; for they were superfluous in the Torrid Zone, and all the plants grew in the open air. The ladies and most of the gentlemen were greatly interested in the plants and flowers, and the whole forenoon was agreeably passed in viewing them. Uncle Moses insisted that the baobab and the Indian banyan were literally the "biggest things" there; for the trunk of the former was ten feet in diameter, while the latter covered half a square mile of ground. The latter had been considerably damaged by a cyclone.

At the end of a week in Calcutta, every day of which had been occupied to the pleasure and instruction of the tourists, Captain Ringgold insisted that they must remain no longer. It was the middle of March, and the hot weather was coming on, and the company must return to the Guardian-Mother on the following morning. It was not an unpleasant announcement, as they had all become greatly attached to the steamer, for they had always been exceedingly happy on board of her.

"It is time for me to settle up our accounts, Lord Tremlyn," said the commander, as they were seated on the veranda after the intended departure had been announced.

"That time has not come, Captain Ringgold; and it never will come," replied his lordship very decidedly. "I thought we had disposed of that question once for all at Bombay. You and your party have been our guests from the moment we landed. Sir Modava and I have done our best, in the time allotted to us, to make you acquainted with India, and to make the time pass pleasantly with you. As far as we had influence, we have used it to promote the objects of your visit."

"You have done a hundred times more than we had any right to expect, and certainly we should not have asked for what you have given us; but it seems to be no more than right that we should pay our own expenses, and we shall be just as grateful to you for the vast service you have rendered us."

"What we have done does not extinguish a tithe of our obligations to you and your ship's company. Any money allusion grieves me, and the very thought of being paid almost breaks the heart of Sir Modava. I beg you not to allude to the matter again. Now, my dear Captain Ringgold," continued his lordship, taking what looked like a picture-frame from a table near him, "I ask the privilege of presenting to you this testimonial of the gratitude of the three cabin survivors of the wreck of the Travancore, which I will ask you to hang up in the cabin of the Guardian-Mother."

The commander took the frame, in which was a printed testimonial, containing a full account of the rescue of the survivors of the wreck, with a concluding paragraph, expressive of the obligations of the principal persons rescued, to the captain and his ship's company for their noble and successful exertions in saving them and all the people on board. It had the autographs of Lord Tremlyn, Sir Modava, and Dr. Ferrolan at the foot of the printed statement. It was on parchment, printed in plain, clear type, and the frame was as elegant as money could buy.

"I accept this as the property of the ship, and to me personally nothing could be more valued," replied the commander, extending his thanks at considerable length; but he said nothing more about payment, though he could not help thinking that their elegant and bountiful hospitality had cost the viscount and the Indian gentleman several thousand pounds.

"But we do not separate just yet; and I have another favor to ask of you, Captain Ringgold, which is that you will give us a passage to Colombo," added Lord Tremlyn.

"For myself and my party, we shall all be delighted to have you remain with us indefinitely," replied the commander, taking his lordship's hand. "I extend to you, Sir Modava, and Dr. Ferrolan a cordial invitation to complete with us our voyage around the world; and we will endeavor to be as hospitable to you in the United States as you have been to us in India."

"Nothing would afford me so great a pleasure," replied Lord Tremlyn; "but it would be quite impossible for me to accept the invitation, for I must return to England, and report upon my mission to India."

Sir Modava and Dr. Ferrolan also declined, for reasons given. The company had called upon some of the officials of the government and officers of the army, at the request of his lordship, and most of them made parting calls the next forenoon; and the viceroy sent his private secretary, with the best wishes of his Excellency for a prosperous voyage, to them. After tiffin they all went on board, where their baggage had been sent before, the Italian band playing all the time on Captain O'Flaherty's steamer, which put them on board.

General Noury had sent word to Captain Sharp that he should continue with the party to Colombo, and that he could proceed at once to that port. In fact, he liked the company of the party on board of the Guardian-Mother so well that he was not inclined to part with them at present.

The passengers took possession of their staterooms, and there was still one left for the general, and the band was quartered in the library. The hour for sailing had been fixed at three o'clock; and just before that time the Cherub, Captain O'Flaherty, appeared, having on board a regimental band and the friends of Lord Tremlyn, Sir Modava, and Dr. Ferrolan, who extended to them the compliment of an escort, and, incidentally, to the commander and his passengers.

About half an hour before the time for sailing a shore boat came up to the gangway, and a well-dressed gentleman with a swarthy face ascended the steps. He asked to see Captain Ringgold, and he was called down from the upper deck. It was Mazagan.

"I have called, Captain, to remind you that our

account has not yet been settled," said the villanous Moor. "I have another to add to it, for the destruction of the Fatimé, his Highness the Pacha Ali-Noury's steam-yacht, which he authorizes me to collect."

"Does he, indeed?" replied the captain, laughing; for, having the "weather gauge" of the rascal, he was disposed to treat the matter very lightly.

"I have the account in the handwriting of his Highness," added Mazagan, as he presented a paper written in good English.

"Very well; but I prefer to settle the account with his Highness himself," added the commander, as he touched an electric bell, which brought Sparks to the boudoir into which they had gone. "Ask the general to come here," he said in a low tone to the steward.

"But I do not choose to wait a year or two for a settlement," protested the visitor.

"You need not wait five minutes," added Captain Ringgold.

The Moor began to go over his story again, but it was interrupted by the entrance of General Noury. Mazagan looked at him, and seemed to be unable to believe the evidence of his own eyes. The commander stated the case to him.

"Is this account in your handwriting, General?" he asked.

"Certainly not," replied the Pacha. "We have discussed this matter fully, and I have no claim whatever against you; neither has this man. I settled all my accounts with him; and I have his receipt in full, signed by him, and witnessed by Captain Sharp and his wife. He is a swindler and a villain; and if I ever catch him in Morocco he shall have the bow-string!"

The general denounced him in the severest manner, and then asked the commander to send him out of the ship. Knott was at the gangway, the pirate was turned over to him, and hustled down the steps into his boat. The general expressed his regret that the captain had been annoyed by the villain again, and was confident he would never see or hear from him again; and he never did.

Promptly at the hour set the Guardian-Mother got under way, and the Cherub's band played its liveliest airs. When it stopped to rest, the Italian band played, and thus the music was kept up for three hours, when the steamers were at Diamond Harbor. Here they came alongside each other, and all the company on board the Cherub were invited to a collation on board of the Guardian-Mother, at which Captain Ringgold presided, and many speeches were made by the residents of Calcutta, and by the passengers on board.

The ship's company on each vessel were not left out in the cold; for, while their officers were at the collation, Baldy Bickling, the second cook, regaled them from the abundant stores provided for the occasion, of which notice had been given to Mr. Melanchthon Sage, the chief steward, the day before. At this point adieus were exchanged, the Guardian-Mother went to sea, and the Cherub returned to Calcutta. The passengers were tired out and retired early.

It was an easy run, from Diamond Harbor to Madras in two days and a half, for the Guardian-Mother. The weather was favorable, and the tourists used their time in getting rested. The social occasions, the playing of the band, and the singing in the music-room, made plenty of variety. But the commander did not lose sight of what he regarded as one of the principal objects of the long voyage, the instruction of the young people, and incidentally of the elder ones.

On the forenoon of the second day out the passengers were called together in Conference Hall, and they were glad to assemble there again. The temperature was moderate, the sea was in its most cheerful mood, and, after their long stay on shore, they were glad to be out of sight of land again. Mr. Gaskette had been busy during the vacation the ship's company had obtained at Bombay and Calcutta; had made several new maps, one of which was the shores of the Bay and Sea of Bengal from Calcutta to the southern point of Ceylon; and he had enlarged a small map of Ceylon, to be used when the ship arrived at Colombo, or sooner. It was Sir Modava who mounted the platform for this occasion; and he was received with the heartiest applause, for he had become even more popular than at first.

"I am to tell you something, not much, about Madras, where we shall arrive about this time day after to-morrow," the Hindu gentleman began; and the usual smile which had fascinated all the ladies was on his face. "Madras is the third city in population of India, or next to Bombay, with 452,518 souls, by the census published last year. It is on the Coromandel coast, which is nearly the whole of the Madras Presidency. It is nearly the entire western shore of the Sea of Bengal, including the bay, as the northern part of it is called in modern times. There is scarcely a single safe harbor for large vessels.

"I suppose you have often heard the expression, 'in the Carnatic,' for it is memorable as the scene of the struggle in the last century between England and France for the supremacy of India. Though there is no state with that name, nearly the whole coast region south of the Godavery River retains this name. In fact, there is no little confusion of names in many parts of India. The country near the Arabian Sea still receives the designation of the Deccan, from the Kistna River to the Gulf of Cambay on the north. But this name does not belong to a political division," continued the speaker, pointing out every location and river he named.

"Madras extends along the shore nine miles, and is thus exposed to the fury of the sea for this distance; for it is not on a river, like Calcutta, or a sheltered bay, like Bombay. Formerly, on the approach of a cyclone, vessels lying in the roadstead, as the only harbor it had, which was no harbor, had to put to sea to avoid being driven on the shore. Decidedly it was a very inconvenient place to build a city; but the town formerly consisted of a number of villages, which have been united, after the fashion of some of your American cities.

"An attempt has been in progress the last twenty years to make a harbor in the shape of an enclosure of strong walls, about half a mile square. It was seriously damaged by a cyclone a dozen years ago; but they are still at work upon it, though it is said to be doubtful whether or not it will ever be safe for ships in a violent storm. There is always a heavy surf rolling in on this coast, even in what the commander would call a smooth sea."

"Then how shall we get ashore there?" inquired Mrs. Belgrave.

"The natives construct a boat, which is a sort of raft of planks, tied together with ropes, called a *masulah*, which passes through the surf very well in ordinary weather; but no boat could live in a cyclone in a sea there, for the waves are fourteen feet high."

"I should like to try it with the second cutter, so far as the waves are concerned; but bumping on the bottom might spoil the attempt," said Mr. Gaskette, who was standing by his map.

"It would not be prudent in a cyclone, and I trust you will have no occasion to try the experiment," added Sir Modava. "But cyclones are rare here, except from the last of May and into June, and in October, November, and early in December; so that the port is not liable to more than two storms a year. The average rainfall is forty-nine inches, falling on ninety-five days; but in seventy-four years, ending two years ago, it varied from a foot and a half to seven feet and four inches. It is dry here some years, and rather damp when they get eighty-eight inches.

"Going to Madras in March, the temperature of the place is of no consequence to you, except as a matter of curiosity, being in the Torrid Zone. It will be from 76° to 88° while you are here. The average temperature for the year is 82°; in the hot months it rises to over 100°; the highest in twenty-seven years was 113°, and the lowest 57.6°. A sea-breeze often sets in about noon, lasting till sunset, greatly modifying the heat. I think I need say no more about the city till we get there."

This talk was followed by a concert by the band. The ship sped on her course, though something to instruct and amuse was going on all the time. At the time set Madras was in sight, and a little later the surf was seen rolling in on the shore. The depth is shallow near the land, which causes the water to break. The Guardian-Mother was anchored in the deep water, and Lord Tremlyn invited the party to proceed to the apartments at the Royal Hotel which he had bespoken for them. The commander made no further objections to the matter of expense, and the invitation was promptly accepted. A number of the masulah-boats, not the rafts, were engaged to land them. They were much like any other boat, though they were paddled, and not rowed. They saw the catamarans, constructed as the Hindu gentleman had described, paddled on the waves by a single man, wearing a sugar-loaf hat.

The masulah-boats went to the shore very comfortably, and carriages were in waiting for the party on the beach near where they landed. As they passed through the streets everything seemed to be very much as it was in Calcutta; and they saw similar palanquins, bullock-carts, and elephants. The Malabar Hindu was not very different from those of other sections of the country, though he had some peculiarities of costume.

When they reached the hotel, which was a very comfortable one, in English style, it was two hours to tiffin, and most of the party preferred to pass the time in the parlor. The live boys could not keep still, and they went out for a walk. The sights were not novel enough to hold them; and when a driver of a bullock-cart salaamed to them, and pointed to his vehicle, Felix suggested that they should take a ride. Of course, they could not speak a word of the language; and, however it may have been with other conductors of vehicles, this one did not know a word of English.

"Mavalipoor?" interrogated the driver, when the "Big Four" had seated themselves in the corners of the vehicle, which had a body like an omnibus for four, with a top like the dome of a small temple.

They had no idea what the word or sentence used by the driver had been, but supposed it was something worth seeing in the town. Two palanquins went by them at full tilt, and they saw what was to be seen in the street. They went on several miles, till they appeared to be leaving the city behind them, and they thought it was time to call a halt. They talked vigorously to the cartman, and all of them pointed back to the city, and yelled "Madras!"

"Mavalipoor!" screamed the driver, pointing with equal energy in the direction the cart was headed. But the fellow would not stop, and the lively boys all leaped out of the cart to the ground. He would not go on without them; but fortunately a gentleman in English costume came along on horseback. The quartet touched their hats to him, and he stopped his steed. Louis stated that they wished to go to the Royal Hotel.

"The hotel is not in this direction," replied the horseman with much suavity. But at this moment the driver had something to say, and delivered himself with energy. "He says you engaged him to take you to Mavalipoor," the rider explained. Louis stated their position, that when the cartman said "Mavalipoor" they had assented, without knowing what he meant.

"You can make it all right with the man by giving him a rupee when he leaves you at your hotel," replied the gentleman, laughing heartily at the mistake, and then informed them that there were some Hindu temples at Mavalipoor, more than thirty miles distant, that were visited by strangers. He then ordered the driver to convey his fare to the Royal Hotel, in a very peremptory manner, and the man obeyed. Thanking the gentleman for his kindness, they parted. The cartman was in a hurry now, and he urged his humpbacked bullocks into a lively trot.

At the door the boys gave the driver two rupees, and the fellow salaamed as though he had received a guinea. There are plenty of landaus in Madras at three rupees a day; and the dak, as the cart is called, and palanquins are becoming things of the past. Tiffin was ready; and a line of carriages was at the door waiting for the tourists when they had disposed of the lunch, and they seated themselves for a drive.

"I warn you," said Sir Modava, as the carriages drove off, "that you will find little here to interest you, after visiting, as you have, the principal cities of India."

"We are about tired of sight-seeing," added Mrs. Belgrave rather languidly; and this was about the situation of most of the party.

They passed the People's Park, an inviting enclosure, with ponds and pleasant walks, to the Black Town, which contains the homes of the natives, though there are plenty of shops; and it is crossed by several good avenues. They came to a street like that called The Strand in Calcutta, and they drove the whole length of it. They passed into Fort St. George, which seemed to be a city of itself. Leaving it, they crossed the little river that meanders through the town, and flows into the ocean at this point.

On this shore road were the principal public buildings of the city, and near the end of it was St. Thomas's Cathedral. This is said to be the site where the apostle of this name, "Doubting Thomas," was martyred. Early tradition buried him in Edessa, in Mesopotamia, but a later account sent him to India; but this is something for learned doctors to discuss. At St. George's Cathedral the party entered to see the statue, made by Chantrey, of Bishop Heber, who looks gently and tenderly upon a native convert at his feet.

They rode all over the town, and found several ponds, called tanks; and the great fort is washed on one side by the river. The second day the party were driven into the suburbs. At a rocky point on the river they found a party of half-naked men washing sheets and pillow-cases. The ladies were interested, and the carriages stopped to enable them to see the operation. They had something like washboards, laid on the bank of the stream, which they were hammering with all their might with the sheets, standing in the shallow water as they did so. Mrs. Blossom declared they must tear them all to pieces, and she was quite indignant at the way it was done.

Another day finished Madras; and, though there

was little to see, compared with the places they had visited before, Mrs. Belgrave declared they had had a good time. On the morning following they went on board of the Guardian-Mother, and she sailed for Ceylon.

CHAPTER XXXVII

THE FAREWELL TO CEYLON AND INDIA

If the tourists had been in a safe place they would have been glad to see a cyclone on the shore of Madras, on Napier bridge for instance; and it would have been a grand spectacle to observe the great billows rolling in on the beach, breaking at a distance of a thousand feet from the land. But they had all seen great waves, and they were not anxious to see them here. At her ordinary speed, the Guardian-Mother would arrive at Colombo at one o'clock the next day. The weather was fine, and the passengers assembled in Conference Hall to talk with the three experts on board about the various places they had visited in India.

Lord Tremlyn and Sir Modava were full of information, which they adorned with stories from history and mythology. The good people from Von Blonk Park were sorry they had not seen the Temple and Car of Juggernaut, though they had been fully described to them. They had visited the missions in Bombay, Calcutta, and Madras, as well as wherever they had found them elsewhere. They were much interested in them, and regretted that they had not been able to devote more time to them.

The next forenoon, with the northern shore of Ceylon in sight from the deck, Lord Tremlyn went upon the rostrum, with the map of the island, and a portion of the main shore included, on the frame. Though the ship was in ten degrees of north latitude, the weather was delightful and the sea was smooth. The thermometer stood at 70°, and the ladies declared that the temperature was just right.

"You know the location of the island on the south-east of India, and it takes in about four degrees of latitude and two of longitude, without going into the matter too finely, with an area of twenty-four thousand seven hundred and two square miles; about the size of your State of West Virginia, I find, or as large as three or four of your New England States. Perhaps the most lovely scenery in the whole world is to be found in this island. The Greeks and Romans visited it, and it is mentioned in 'The Arabian Nights,' under the name of Serendib.

"The mountains are near the southern part, and the highest one is Mount Pedrotallagalla, — don't forget the name, my young friends, — eight thousand two hundred and sixty feet high. In your visit to Ceylon you will go to Candy, which will please those with a sweet tooth better than Kandy, as it is often spelled. Many precious stones are found in Ceylon; and the pearl fishery is a very important source of wealth, though its value is variable in different years. In six years only out of the last thirty have the fisheries been productive, and in the other twenty-four they yielded hardly anything. In those six years, the largest yield, in 1881, was not quite sixty thousand pounds, while the smallest noted was ten thousand pounds.

"The fisheries are under government regulation. An official announces when the work is permitted, and then it lasts only from four to six weeks. Thirteen men and ten divers are generally the crew of each boat, five of the latter going down into the water while the other five rest. Each diver has a stone, weighing forty pounds, attached to a line long enough to reach the bottom, with a loop near the weight, into which he puts his foot. The water varies in depth from fifty-four to seventy-eight feet. They work quickly; for a minute is the usual time they remain in the water, though some can stand it twenty seconds longer.

"One would suppose that the sharks, which abound in these waters, would make it dangerous business; but very few accidents occur, for the commotion about the boats seems to scare them away. When the diver gives the signal he is hauled up, with his bag of oysters, as rapidly as possible. But the ladies know more about pearls than I do, and I will say no more about them.

"There are many rivers in Ceylon, rising in the high land, and flowing into the sea; but none of them are as long as the Mississippi. The climate of the island is simply magnificent; the average heat in Colombo on the high lands never exceeds 70°. I shall permit you to describe the flowers after you have seen them; but the vegetation generally of the island is exceedingly luxuriant. In regard to animals, the tiger does not reside in Ceylon. The elephant, generally without any tusks, is the chief ruler in the forests here. The bear and the leopard are found. There is no end of monkeys. There are sixteen kinds of bats here, and all your base-ball clubs could be supplied from the stock; and there is a flying fox, which might amuse you if you could catch one. He is a sort of bat; and the more of them you shoot, the better the farmer will be pleased, for they feed on his fruit. Plenty of birds of all sorts are found in the island. The crocodile is the biggest reptile found in Ceylon."

"But the snakes, your lordship?" suggested Felix.

"There are a few poisonous snakes; and the two worst are the cobra and the ticpolonga, the latter a sort of viper; and the former is an old friend of yours, Mr. McGavonty. The people are called Singhalese, but more generally Cingalese, and are believed to be the descendants of immigrants from the region of the Ganges. There are other races here, as the Malabars. The religion of Ceylon is the Buddhist, and it has a very strong hold upon the natives here as well as in Burma.

"Gautama, the founder of Buddhism, is said to have visited Ceylon three times, and to have preached his doctrines here. His sacred footstep on Adam's Peak, 7,420 feet high, the second highest elevation in the island, is still adored by the people. But the most sacred relic here is the tooth of Gautama, kept in an elegant shrine and carefully guarded at Candy. But it is said to be well known that the Portuguese destroyed the original; and the substitute is a discolored bit of ivory, without the least resemblance to a human tooth. There are many temples, sacred caverns, some of them sculptured like those near Bombay.

"There is something like ancient history in connection with Ceylon, dating back to 543 B.C.; but it would be hardly edifying to follow it. It has also a Portuguese, a Dutch, and a British period; and it was finally annexed to the British crown by the Treaty of Amiens, in 1802.

"Thirty years ago coffee was the principal commercial production of the island; but a kind of fungus attacked the leaves of the trees, and within ten years the planters were obliged to abandon its cultivation to a great extent, though it is still raised. Cacao, which is the name of the chocolate-tree, while cocoa is the name of the product, is cultivated to a considerable extent; so are cinchona, cardamoms, and various spices; though Bishop Heber's lines —

'What though the spicy breezes
Blow soft o'er Ceylon's isle,'

are not applicable to the island as formerly.

"It has become evident in very recent years that Ceylon might become a great tea-growing region, and the planters are now largely engaged in its culture.

A dozen years ago only 3,515 pounds were raised; ten years later over 12,000,000 pounds of tea was the crop; and this year it is still greater. The population in 1891 was 3,008,466. It has a governor, who rules with an executive council of five, of which the officer in command of the troops is one."

"Can your lordship tell me the salary of the governor-general of India?" asked Captain Ringgold.

"I figured it up at one time in your money, and forgot to mention it. If I remember rightly, it was $125,400; and that of the governor of Ceylon is $20,000," replied Lord Tremlyn. "The former gets two and a half times the salary of your President. I have nothing more to say of the island, but after a concert by the band, Sir Modava will tell you something about the principal towns;" and as he retired the audience separated, for it was to be a promenade concert.

"I was asked just now by Mrs. Blossom about missions here in Ceylon," said the Hindu gentleman as he took the stand. "The English Baptists sent missionaries here eighty years ago; the Methodists a year later; the Americans three years later; and the Church of England five years after. A great deal of Christian teaching has been done in Ceylon, though I am not able just now to give you statistically the results of missionary work; but it has included the establishment of schools, female seminaries, and even collegiate institutions, carried on by the missionaries, outside of the government system of education.

"Point de Galle, at the south-western extremity of the island, is a town of forty-seven thousand inhabitants, and has a good harbor in a sheltered bay. It was formerly the principal coaling and shipping station in this part of India; but all this has gone to Colombo. The Orient line of steamers, whose principal business is with Australia, sends some of its ships here; and most steamers of the Peninsular and Oriental line, called the 'P. & O.' for short, touch here. A great deal of freight had to be reshipped at Point de Galle for various ports of India.

"The name was given to the place by the Portuguese, and its meaning is doubtful. *Galles* is the French of Wales, and *La Nouvelle Galles* is New South Wales; without the final *s*, the word means an oak-apple, in French. As I heard one of the 'Big Four' say this morning, 'You pay your money and take your choice,' as to the signification of the word. At any rate, the importance of the place is gone, and Colombo has captured its business and its prominence.

"Colombo is the capital of Ceylon. It is about seventy miles from Point de Galle, on the south-west coast of the island. It has a population of almost 127,000, which has been increased at the expense of Galle, as we generally call it to economize our breath. It is located on a peninsula, with the sea on three sides of it, with a lake and moat on the land side. By the way, Mr. Woolridge, do you happen to remember the Italian name of Christopher Columbus, whose discovery of America you are to celebrate at Chicago this year?"

"Cristoforo Colombo," replied Morris promptly. "I read it on his monument at Genoa last summer."

"Quite right, my young friend; and that is where the capital of Ceylon obtained its name, which the Portuguese gave it, in honor of the great discoverer, only twenty-five years after the great event of his life. The buildings are about the same as you will observe in all British colonial towns, and I need not mention them. You will ride out to Lake Colombo, and visit the cinnamon gardens there. The breakwater, which has been the making of the city, cost £600,000; for it is an entirely safe harbor, with every facility for landing and embarking passengers and goods. I believe nothing is left to you but to see what his lordship and I have described."

Sir Modava retired from the stand; and the band started into an overture, which was hardly finished before the bell for lunch sounded. Before the collation was finished the ship had taken a pilot, and in due time the Guardian-Mother came to anchor at her last port in India proper. As the ship came into the harbor she passed abreast of the Blanche, and was greeted with three cheers, which were promptly and vigorously returned.

Accommodations had been bespoken by Lord Tremlyn, and early in the afternoon the party were quartered in the Elphinstone. Carriages were obtained, and before night they had visited the principal parts of the town, and even the cinnamon gardens, in which they were greatly interested; and some of the ladies told what it was good for, both as a spice and a medicine.

"I suppose you know all about cinnamon, Mrs. Belgrave," said Sir Modava, as they were looking at the trees.

"I only know enough about it to put it in my apple-pies when I make them."

"This island produces the finest article in the world. It is a very old spice, mentioned in the Old Testament, though I forget the name by which it is there called," added the Indian gentleman.

"But I did not suppose it grew on a tree; I had an idea it was a root."

"No; it is the inner bark of the trees before you. They are from twenty to thirty feet high, and are sometimes a foot and a half through. But the cultivated plant is not allowed to grow more than ten feet high. The leaves average five inches long, and taste more like cloves than cinnamon. There are two crops a year in Ceylon, the first in March, the last in November. The bark is taken off with considerable labor and care, and when it dries it curls up as you find your stick cinnamon."

"I used ground cinnamon," added the lady.

"It is the same thing, passed through the mill. Cassia is another species of cinnamon, and its oil is often substituted for the true oil; and very likely you buy it ground for the real thing."

The experts explained some other plants, especially cinchona, one of the most valuable medicinal plants, from which Peruvian bark, quinine, and other drugs are made, in which the three doctors were much interested. The company returned to the hotel; and after dinner the Italian band gave a concert on the veranda, as they had done in every city where the tourists remained overnight, which called forth repeated rounds of applause from the citizens of Colombo.

The next morning the travellers proceeded by railroad to Kandy, which Sir Modava insisted was the right way to spell it. The route was mostly through an elevated region, and when they reached the place at noon they had attained an elevation of 1,665 feet above the sea. They remained at Kandy three days, and were sorry the commander would not allow them to stay longer, for it was the most delightful region they had yet visited. They were in sight of the lofty mountains of the island before mentioned.

They found here the remains of ancient temples from one hundred and fifty to four hundred feet high; and one of them was built to contain the shrine of Gautama's tooth, and another for his collar-bone, both of which the English believe are frauds. Another was the Brazen Palace, nine stories high, and supported on sixteen hundred pillars. But most of the party took no interest in these structures, they had seen so many more that were larger, grander, and finer. They saw here the sacred Bo-tree, of which they had before been informed.

With great regret they left Kandy, and were soon in Colombo again. The Guardian-Mother was announced to sail the next day early in the afternoon. The time for parting with Lord Tremlyn, Sir Modava Rao, and Dr. Ferrolan had nearly arrived. The hosts of the party had provided a grand dinner for the last one. The governor and a number of officials, the American consul, and others had been invited.

Lord Tremlyn presided with Captain Ringgold on his right; and after the fine dinner had been disposed of the commander was the person called upon to respond to the first toast, "The Guardian-Mother and her Passengers." The name announced was received with the most tremendous applause, and "For he's a jolly good fellow!" was sung by Englishmen, assisted by the Americans, including the ladies.

Captain Ringgold began his speech, for which he had prepared himself, and reviewed the incidents which had occurred since the survivors of the Travancore had been taken from their perilous position. He set forth the obligations to which his passengers and himself were under to the distinguished gentlemen who had conducted them through India. He was frequently interrupted by hearty applause, and his speech was as eloquent as it was sensible; and it was worthy a Senator in Congress.

Lord Tremlyn was equally eloquent in the acknowledgment of his obligations, and those of his friends, to the noble commander and his ship's company; and possibly he was a little extravagant in some things that he said, but that was excusable on such an occasion. The next person presented was Mr. Louis Belgrave, who declared that he represented the "Big Four," which puzzled the strangers, though he explained the term and where it came from. The boys had been happy all the time. They admired and loved the noble gentlemen under whose guidance they had had six weeks of the best time in all their lives. When he said what he had to say, he approached the chairman with a large and handsome frame in his hand, containing a testimonial from the passengers, attested by the autographs of all, which he presented to Lord Tremlyn, with the best wishes of all the signers, who had profited so extensively from their kindness, for the health, happiness, and length of days of the trio.

This ceremony, not set down in the programme, brought forth rapturous applause and ringing cheers. The band played, and everybody seemed to be enjoying the happiest moment of his life. All the principal personages at the table made speeches, of which the Indian reporters, if any were present, have not given in their reports. It was a remarkably joyous occasion, and it was two o'clock in the morning when the banquet-hall was cleared.

All the forenoon was spent in exchanging the parting greetings. Both Lord Tremlyn and Sir Modava invited any or all of the party who might be in India or in England to visit them; and the commander and Mrs. Belgrave, as well as the others, extended similar invitations to the three gentlemen. After tiffin, when the party started for the steamer that was to convey them to the two ships, it seemed as though all the citizens of Colombo, with their ladies, had gathered to assist in the parting benedictions. The military band alternated with the Italian, cheers without number rent the air, and the party had all they could do to return the salutes, and answer all the kindly words spoken to them by entire strangers.

The steamer cast off her fasts, and then the din was greater than ever. The guests at the banquet went off to the ships, from the smoke-stacks of which the black smoke was pouring out, as if to emphasize the reality of the departure. All manner of courtesies were exchanged, but finally the passengers were all on board of the Blanche and Guardian-Mother. A salute was fired from the heaviest guns on both vessels, the screws began to turn, the final words were shouted, and the steamers stood to the southward.

It required some time to digest the sights the voyagers had seen in India; but when, a few days later, the Nickobar Islands were reported off the port bow, the "Big Four" began to think and wonder what new and strange climes they were to visit. They were inclined to believe they had seen everything that was worth seeing in the civilized world, and they had some decided views of their own in regard to the future. They were eager to engage for a time in something more stirring than gazing at palaces, churches, temples, and other wonders of the great cities; and they were not diffident in the expression of their wishes when the commander called a meeting in Conference Hall to consider what ports the Guardian-Mother should visit next, as well as to inform the tourists in regard to the islands in the immediate vicinity. Those who are interested in the decision of the company, and in the events which followed in consequence of it, are referred to the next volume of the series: "HALF ROUND THE WORLD; OR, SOME ADVENTURES AMONG THE UNCIVILIZED."